T0323632

UNITING THE TAILORS

UNITING THE TAILORS

Trade Unionism amongst the Tailoring Workers of London and Leeds, 1870–1939

ANNE J. KERSHEN
University of London

Routledge
Taylor & Francis Group

LONDON AND NEW YORK

First published in 1995 in Great Britain by
FRANK CASS & CO. LTD

Published 2023 by Routledge
4 Park Square, Milton Park, Abingdon, Oxon OX14 4RN
605 Third Avenue, New York, NY 10017

Routledge is an imprint of the Taylor & Francis Group, an informa business

British Library Cataloguing in Publication Data

Kershen, Anne J.   Uniting the Tailors: Trade Unionism Amongst
the Tailoring Workers of London and
Leeds, 1870–1939
I. Title
331.881870942

Library of Congress Cataloging-in-Publication Data

Kershen, Anne, J.   Uniting the tailors : trade unionism amongst the tailoring workers of London and Leeds, 1870–1939 / Anne J. Kershen.
      p. cm.
   Includes bibliographical references and index.
   ISBN 0-7146-4596-6 (cloth)   0-7146-4145-6 (paper)
   1. Trade-unions—Tailors—England—London—History. 2. Trade
—unions—Tailors—England—Leeds—History.   I. Title.
HD 6668.C6K47   1995
331.88'187'09421—dc20   94-3697
                                                 CIP

Typeset by Regent Typesetting, London

ISBN 13: 978-0-7146-4596-4 (hbk)
ISBN 13: 978-0-7146-4145-4 (pbk)

*To Martin and the children
and
In memory of my parents
Esther and Harry Rothenberg*

Contents

List of Illustrations   ix
Foreword by Professor W.J. Fishman   xi
Acknowledgements   xiii
Preface   xvii
Abbreviations   xxi

1 Backcloth   1
2 The Leeds Wholesale Clothing Industry:
   Origins and Growth   25
3 Organising the Tailors of Leeds,
   1870–1915   60
4 The Structure of the London Tailoring
   Trade, 1870–1915   97
5 Organising the Tailors of London   126
6 Uniting the Tailors   163

Conclusion   185
Appendix: Tables   192
Bibliography   212
Index   222

List of Illustrations

Between pages 12 and 13
1 Joseph Finn (courtesy Cecily Zimmerman)
2 Lewis Lyons (courtesy Henry Rollin)
3 A typical account from a top tailor, *c.* 1880 (courtesy Henry Poole)
4 A balance sheet of the Amalgamated Society of Tailors, 1889 (Henry Rollin)
5 A balance sheet of the International Tailors' Machinists' and Pressers' Union, 1890
6 The Trades' Union Institute, Leeds (Henry Rollin)
7 In English and Yiddish: a membership card of the Manchester Jewish Machinists' and Pressers' Trade Union (Henry Rollin)

Between pages 102 and 103
8 Morris Cohen (courtesy Clive Moss and the London Museum of Jewish Life)
9 Chart showing Morris Cohen's contribution to the mantle-making trade and the kinship and company connections that developed, 1895–1988 (Maxine Sparrow)
10 Morris Cohen's mantle factory under construction in 1895 (Clive Moss and the London Museum of Jewish Life)
11 Procession to the Great Synagogue of 'Jewish Unemployed and Sweaters' Victims', 1889
12 The Tailors' Strike of 1889
13 Poster advertising the Great Strike of 1889

Between pages 176 and 177
14 Officials of the Tailors' and Garment Workers' Trade Union, 1926: A. Conley, J. Young, M. Sclare and Miss A. Loughlin (*The Garment Worker*)

15 The first Executive Board of the United Garment Workers, 1915 (Henry Rollin)
16 Seventeen years later, the Executive Board of the newly amalgamated Society of Tailors and Tailoresses and the Tailors' and Garment Workers' Union, 1932 (*The Tailor and Garment Worker*)
17 Mick Mindel reliving the ballot of 1938 (London Museum of Jewish Life)
18 A call for stronger Union membership in the Depression years
19 Voting for – or against – the proposed amalgamation of the United Ladies' Tailors with the National Union of Tailors and Garment Workers, 1938

The author and publishers are grateful to the following for permission to reproduce the illustrations listed above: London Museum of Jewish Life; Clive Moss; Henry Poole; Henry Rollin; Maxine Sparrow; *The Tailor and Garment Worker*; Cecily Zimmerman.

Foreword

As the author has indicated, the last three decades have registered a growing list of academic researchers in the field of labour history. Some have directed themselves towards the study of the east European Jewish immigrant settlements in Britain, with emphasis on the political and social ideas and activities that they brought with them, and their individual struggles within the labour movement. In this context, little has been formulated about their relationship with the host trade unions to date. This has certainly been rectified here in Anne Kershen's splendid exploration into the tailoring trade (a majority immigrant occupation) in London and Leeds. She not only chronicles and analyses the changing nature of the trade but also brings to life the characters of the main Union figures – both British and immigrant – who led and influenced the course of union activities, revealing their strengths and weaknesses, imposed from within and without, that helped or hindered inter-ethnic combination. As she rightly suggests, it is 'men and women who make history', until recently a rather unfashionable conjecture.

As for women, her contention that 'the industry grew strong on the backs of an unskilled female work-force' is borne out by the wealth of evidence submitted in the text. Anti-alienism, compounded by male chauvinist attitudes, were major obstacles which had to be overcome before a unitary tailoring union could be achieved. So were the destabilising effects of craft divisions and rivalries accruing from specialisation of functions, and aggravated by the insecurity brought about by 'busy' and 'slack' seasonality in production. The author skilfully weaves her way through the intricacies of her theme to produce a cohesive whole. By scholarly research into a formidable list of primary sources, many hitherto untouched, she has presented us with a remarkable story. (Not least is her perceptive insight into the characters of those men and women who participated at all levels in the fight for better working conditions.)

But the lessons of the past have again to be relearned. The author notes that 'the evil of sweated labour has yet to be eradicated from the [present] immigrant landscape', where 'the conditions of the 1880s and 1890s are replayed one hundred years on'. Quite so! A reading of this book could surely help those immigrant organisers who are facing the problem today.

It must be stressed that this is not only about Jewish immigrants. It embraces the conditions of British factory workers, craft divisions and sweated labour, focusing in on tailors within the clothing trade. The author has filled a vacuum in both British and Jewish social history, and thereby offers us a unique contribution to knowledge. Her scholarship is impeccable and she brings a sympathetic approach to her human characters. It makes for easy reading, a facility aided by keeping statistics well apart at the end. This book is strongly recommended for historians, students and laymen alike.

William J. Fishman
Queen Mary and Westfield College,
London, 1994

Acknowledgements

My interest in tailoring trade unionism began following my gradua-
tion. The original intention was to evaluate the influence of eastern
European refugee intellectuals on the English trade union movement at
the end of the nineteenth century. My search for an answer led to my
becoming a postgraduate student at the University of Warwick, to
completing the dissertation from which this book has been developed
and to receiving help from many people along the way.

I must express my thanks at the very outset to Peggy King who
provided the kick-start for my academic career. I am indebted to the
postgraduates and staff at the Centre for the Study of Social History at
the University of Warwick for providing an intellectual sounding
board and, most particularly, to Professor Royden Harrison, Dr Jim
Obelkevich, Dr Bill Lancaster, Mrs Deidre Hewitt and my supervisor
Dr Tony Mason who ten years on is still ready and eager to discuss
problematics. Early in my research I had the good fortune to be
welcomed into the home of Drs Henry and Maria Rollin and given the
opportunity to research Henry's father Aaron Rollin's superb archive
of trade union and labour history. When I had completed my task Dr
Henry Rollin handed the collection over to the Modern Record Centre
at the University of Warwick and into the capable hands of Richard
Storey the archivist. I must express my thanks to Richard for his care in
preserving and cataloguing the collection and for his continued help
which enables me to economise on my travels up and down that
tortuous M1. I should also like to recognise the help of the librarians
and archive staff at the University of Warwick, the British Library in
Bloomsbury and Colindale, the TUC Library at Congress House, the
Rose Lipman Library in Hackney, the GFTU Library in central
London, Leeds City Archives and Library, University of London
Library and at Tower Hamlets Local History Library, most especially,
librarian Chris Wright. A very special thank you to Eilis Rafferty and

the library staff at Queen Mary and Westfield College and to Anne Cutts for endless cups of tea and coffee while I have been glued to the word processor.

A considerable quantity of primary material was housed at the headquarters of the then National Union of Tailors and Garment Workers in Charles Square, London. I am indebted to the staff of the Information Office who were there during the first half of the 1980s and to the union's last General Secretary Alec Smith who was so generous with his time and knowledge, and, when the union merged with the GMB in 1991, in handing over the union's archives to Queen Mary and Westfield College. I value the opportunities I had to debate and discuss my research with Diane Atkinson, Dr Gerry Black, Rickie Burman, Dr David Cesarani, Dr Brian Cheyette, Professor Todd Endelman, Dr David Feldman, Professor Colin Holmes, Dr Sharman Kadish, Professor Aubrey Newman, Dr Geoffrey Raisman, Monty Richardson, Marlene Schmool, Dr Elaine Smith, Charles Tucker and Bill Williams. I must also express my thanks to Harold Pollin for all his help. In 1988, when Rickie Burman took a year's sabbatical from her position as Curator of The London Museum of Jewish Life, I had the good fortune to take over her role. During that year I was able to further my research into the clothing trade, to mount the exhibition Off-the-Peg and to meet Clive Moss, grandson of Morris Cohen, who provided me with original archive and photographic material which helped put the flesh on the bones of his grandfather's contribution to the mantle-making trade. I am also indebted to the daughters of Lewis Lyons and Joseph Finn for providing insights into their fathers' careers and to the late Ben Bloom, Charlie Bromberg, Maurice Segal and Dayan Dr M. Lew for giving me insights into workshop life.

Any work which involves research into the eastern European immigrant community in England by its very nature demands a basic knowledge of the Yiddish language. When I began my research I was unable to read Yiddish, and had virtually no Hebrew or German, the basic constituents of the language of the Pale. I will be forever indebted to Mrs Esther Held for taking me on as a pupil and responding to my plea to 'teach me Yiddish in six weeks'. After the six weeks I was duly able, with some effort, to read Yiddish sufficiently well to provide the translations that appear in this book. Though Esther oversaw my work I take full responsibility for the quotations that appear and, with their source in mind, for the somewhat quaint language.

Shortly after my term as Museum Curator ended I was offered the opportunity to become Barnet Shine Senior Research Fellow at Queen Mary and Westfield College. In this I was following in the footsteps of the famous East End historian, Professor W.J. Fishman — more of him later. It was a position I was delighted to take up and I must express my thanks to my colleagues in the Department of Political Studies, Dr Diana Coole, Professor James Dunkerley, Dr Raymond Kuhn, Dr Helen Leigh-Pippard and Dr Shamit Saggar. I am most especially grateful to Dr Wayne Parsons for discussing the manuscript with me in the traffic jams between Mile End and Mill Hill and to Debbie Emery for her help with the complexities of printing out the manuscript. I thank Michael Keating for all his work on the NUTGW archives and Professor Ken Young, Vice-Principal of QMW, for his continuing encouragement. I should also like to express my indebtedness to Martin Paisner, both as Trustee of the Barnet Shine and Porges Foundations and personally, for his unfailing support.

I have reserved some very special thanks until last. In the early days of my research I was fortunate to be introduced to the late Mick Mindel, whose whole life was dedicated to tailoring trade unionism. Mick spent endless hours recounting his experiences to me and taking me to workshops and factories in order that I might gain empirical knowledge of clothing production. The time spent with Mick and his wife Sylvia has been one of the bonuses of my academic journey.

The name of W.J. Fishman appears above. In academic terms this work would not have been possible without Bill's guidance, encouragement and 'madness'. Not only is Professor Fishman acknowledged as *the* chronicler of East End history, he is also one of the academic 'givers' of this world, always ready to dig deep into that wealth of knowledge and give of it freely and with such obvious enjoyment. It is with great pride that I stepped into the shoes of the man for whom the Barnet Shine Senior Research Fellowship was created, it is with great delight that I now work with him as a colleague. I thank him for having devoted time to read through the manuscript of this book, for his most helpful comments and criticisms and for agreeing to write the Foreword. It is with great pleasure that I count Bill and his wife Dot among my greatest friends.

The quest for the story behind the growth of trade unionism amongst the tailoring workers of London and Leeds began when my children, Deborah and James, were growing up. They have had to contend with a parent making the transitions from just a mum to undergraduate, postgraduate, museum curator and now academic. They have survived the ordeal remarkably well, and along the way have given me their support whenever needed. Thank you, James, Deborah and son-in-law Paul. My thanks also go to Maxine Sparrow, who produced the chart (No. 9). None of my student or academic work would have been possible without the love, support and patience of my husband Martin. He is my sternest critic and my most ardent fan, always there when needed to correct the syntax and to pull me out of the depths when the gremlins appear. To Martin, as always, my deepest love and thanks.

Anne J. Kershen
Queen Mary and Westfield College,
London, 1994

Preface

Just over a quarter of a century ago labour history began to appear on the agenda of social historians. While the institutions of labour took pride of place, others encouraged by E.P. Thompson's now classic seminal work, *The Making of the English Working Class*, began to examine the ground floors of trade and industry, many of whose occupants fell within Thompson's definition of the 'losers of history'. At the same time students of immigration and ethnicity were starting to explore the Jewish immigrant experience. Increasing attention was paid to the processes of assimilation, Anglicization and acculturation undergone by eastern European immigrants in Britain during the last half of the nineteenth century. Following the appearance of Lloyd Gartner's *The Jewish Immigrant in England*, a number of historians went on to investigate the social, economic and political conditions under which alien communities developed in major cities such as London, Leeds and Manchester. With the exception of Gartner there was general agreement that the evolution and organisation of the Jewish working class in England took place within the wider framework of the English labour movement. In what is otherwise a detailed and scholarly work Gartner omits all reference to the common features of English and Jewish trade union activity during the last decades of the nineteenth century and the first decades of the twentieth. Whether the new arrivals were intent upon a rapid integration process or were determined to live their lives beneath the carapace of ethnicity, at some point interaction was bound to take place. The immigrant experience does not occur in a vacuum, and the debate as to the effect of that interaction on host and immigrant societies is destined to continue until well into the next century.

During the mid-1980s the emphasis moved away from studies of institutions and trade organisations. Instead attention was focused on leisure, culture, religion and the role of women within the working-class home and economy. The gestation period of this book straddled both phases, as my postgraduate research was begun at the University of Warwick's Centre for the Study of Social History in the early 1980s and completed at the end of 1986.

My original intention had been to confine my research to a study of one sector of the immigrant Jewish work-force in London in the years between 1872 and 1914, the period when the trickle of immigration became a flood and when trade unionism in England progressed from 'new model' to 'new'. By the end of the nineteenth century each sector had grudgingly accepted the need to work in concert rather than in opposition. My aim was to define the location of the alien Jewish work-force within the general labour market and to record the responses to that alien presence by English workers and trade unionists. Three things immediately became clear. First, the study could only be of the tailoring community since the clothing trade dominated the Jewish labour movement in the years within the parameters of my research. Second, in order to comprehend the complexities, vagaries, eccentricities and disparities of Jewish tailoring trade unionism it was necessary to travel beyond the boundaries of the capital, specifically to Leeds, where the wholesale manufacture of tailored garments began in the 1850s. The role of the Jewish-operated sub-divisional workshop was central to the burgeoning Yorkshire industry. Initially through recruitment and subsequently by reputation, Leeds became the destination for thousands of Jewish exiles from the Pale of Settlement. Third, and most important, I could not contain my research solely to Jewish clothing workers. Their economic, political and organisational experience was strongly linked to that of their English peers. It was therefore imperative to incorporate the story of the male and female English clothing workers employed in the factories and workshops of London and Leeds: more especially so as, until now, their history has been largely ignored, even though the Leeds clothing workers had constituted the major body of trade unionists who came together in 1915 to create the United Garment Workers' Trade Union.

That amalgamation and the events which preceded it are central to this book. Never before had Jewish and English workers participated jointly and equally in the setting up of a national union which, for the first time, would represent all branches of industry, all levels of skill and both genders. The eastern European immigrant, previously considered unorganisable, was now a member of the same union as the highly skilled English cutter. The assimilation process had developed to a point at which ethnicity was no longer a barrier. The occasion was therefore deserving of more than the three lines devoted to it in the Webbs' *History of British Trade Unions* and the sparse, and in several instances inaccurate, coverage given in the official history of the National Union of Tailors and Garment Workers, *The Needle is Threaded.* Even more recent works have avoided an event which had in fact crossed the bounds of labour history and ethnic relations.

This book is an attempt to redress the balance. For the first time the history of the Leeds male clothing operatives and their union (gleaned from the pages of the *Yorkshire Factory Times*) is revealed, along with the craft snobbery that existed between East End and West End and the extent of the Soho tailoring ghetto. At the same time, the relevance of industrial structure and regional location to trade union survival is debated.

The book is not just about English and Jewish tailoring workers and their industry, however. It is about relationships, the relationships of people who, even though divided by reasons of religion and ethnicity, found themselves united through the iniquities of exploitation. It is about the nexus of community and the divisions that existed within the supposed 'homogeneous' Jewish ghettos of Whitechapel and the Leylands; the bridges that were built by Jewish and English socialists and their influence on the organisation of unskilled labour in the 1880s; the relationship of male and female workers and trade unionists and their response to technological innovation and deskilling; craft and trade union jealousies and fiercely protected organisational territories. There is also an opportunity to move away from the world of labour and look briefly at the role of fashion in society, viewing clothes not only as a barometer of socio-economic status and change but also as a means of earning a living.

The main text concentrates on the years between 1872 and 1915 when the foundations were laid for the creation of the United Garment Workers' Trade Union. No excuse is made for this. We cannot understand the future if we are unaware of the past. However, between 1920 and 1939 three further amalgamations took place so that, by the outbreak of the Second World War, all those who had resisted the sacrifice of autonomy, for reasons of skill and ethnicity, were finally under the umbrella of what was truly the national garment workers' union. Those events are explored briefly in the final chapter.

The following pages put the foundation and development of the wholesale clothing industry in London and Leeds under the microscope. They explore the structure of industry in both cities, the composition of the work-force, divisions of gender and ethnicity and the strengths and weaknesses of trade unionism in order that the factors that combined to determine the form and fate of the tailoring trade unions of London and Leeds between 1872 and 1939 can be understood.

Abbreviations

AJTMP	Amalgamated Jewish Tailors', Machiners' and Pressers' Trade Union
ASE	Amalgamated Society of Engineers
ASL	Anti-Sweating League
AST (AST&T)	Amalgamated Society of Tailors (and Tailoresses)
AUCO	Amalgamated Union of Clothing Operatives
GFTU	General Federation of Trade Unions
GGLU	Gasworkers' and General Labourers' Union
ILP	Independent Labour Party
LT&TTU	London Tailors' and Tailoresses' Trade Union
LCCTU	London Clothiers' Cutters' Trade Union (later L&PCCTU)
LLTTU	London Ladies' Tailors' Trade Union
LRC	Labour Representation Committee
LST&T	London Society of Tailors and Tailoresses
L&PCCTU	London and Provincial Clothiers' Cutters' Trade Union
LWCOU	Leeds Wholesale Clothing Operatives' Union
MTA	Master Tailors' Association
MWGMTU	Manchester Waterproof Garment Makers' Trade Union
NUTGW	National Union of Tailors and Garment Workers
SDF	Social Democratic Federation
SL	Socialist League
SOTTA	Scottish Operative Tailors' and Tailoresses' Association
TGWU	Tailor and Garment Workers' Union
UCWU	United Clothing Workers' Union
UGWTU	United Garment Workers' Trade Union
ULTMMU	United Ladies' Tailors' and Mantle Makers' Union

1 Backcloth

The 1916 Report being the first Annual Report of the United Garment Workers' Trade Union will probably help the members to realise that the U.G.W.T.U. is an accomplished fact and that they are no longer members of their old separate organisations, but all members of one Trade Union.

Moses Sclare, Financial Secretary, UGWTU[1]

The formation of the United Garment Workers' Trade Union (UGWTU) in 1915 fused six independent clothing unions which between them covered the spectrum of tailoring, from the highest quality bespoke to the poorest class of ready-made. The 1915 amalgamation was part of a trend towards federations and general unions which began in the early 1900s, accelerated following the 1917 Amalgamation Act and reached its peak in the early 1920s.[2] The new clothing workers' union, with its inaugural membership of 21,457,[3] made little impact on a trade union world which had seen the creation of the mighty 180,000-strong National Union of Railwaymen two years earlier[4] and which was now preoccupied with the effects of war on British industry and its labour force. Though the UGWTU represented less than nine per cent of the 249,467 employed in the manufacture of clothing in Britain,[5] the amalgamation, which few trade union commentators have considered of consequence,[6] was of undoubted significance. It demonstrated to those both within and outside the industry that workers from disparate backgrounds, of both genders and with different levels of skill, could merge into one representative body. Furthermore, it proved that Jewish sub-divisional tailors and tailoresses, Gentile craftsmen and factory operatives could overcome industrial differences and ethnic and religious divides in order to work towards a common goal.

The six participants in the amalgamation of 1915 were:

1

Unions	Membership
The Amalgamated Union of Clothing Operatives	12,000
The Amalgamated Jewish Tailors', Machiners' and Pressers' Trade Union	4,500
The London Society of Tailors and Tailoresses	1,600
The London Jewish Tailors' and Tailoresses' Trade Union	1,800
The London and Provincial Clothiers' Cutters' Trade Union	400
The Manchester Waterproof Garment Makers' Trade Union	700

Note: (The membership figures given above are based on those that appeared in the 'Result of Ballot Vote re-Amalgamation' statement issued by the Scottish operative Tailors' and Tailoresses Association in September 1914.[7] The difference between the 1914 total and that issued at the time of the 1915 amalgamation is accounted for by the expansion of industry and work-force due to the demands of war.

The Amalgamated Union of Clothing Operatives (AUCO) originated in Leeds as the all-male Leeds Wholesale Clothing Operatives' Union (LWCOU) in the climactic year of 1889. At the time of the amalgamation its membership was composed of male and female clothing operatives employed in factories throughout the country. Jewish male and female tailors employed in workshops in Leeds and other major provincial cities were represented by the Amalgamated Jewish Tailors', Machiners' and Pressers' Trade Union (AJTMP), founded in Leeds in 1893 after previous Jewish tailoring unions in the city had failed. The London Society of Tailors and Tailoresses (LST&T), essentially a craft union, was created after the West End branch of the Amalgamated Society of Tailors and Tailoresses (AST&T, originally the Amalgamated Society of Tailors – AST – until the admission of women in 1900) broke away from its parent body in 1905. The élite of the industry, the skilled cutters, were represented by the London Clothiers' Cutters' Trade Union (LCCTU) while over 30 per cent[8] of the organised Jewish tailoring workers employed in the capital's tailoring workshops were represented by the London Jewish Tailors' and Tailoresses' Trade Union (LJT&TTU), founded in 1908. The Manchester Waterproof Garment Makers' Trade Union, founded in 1889, was the only one of the six unions whose headquarters was in neither London nor Leeds. At the time of the amalgamation the union

2

had a predominantly, though not totally, Jewish membership, but although 50 per cent of its 700 affiliates voted in favour of fusion, the union seceded shortly after the amalgamation took place.[9]

None of the above unions existed prior to what Professor Clegg has termed the 'phenomenon of new unionism'.[10] But this is not to suggest that there were no links with the past. As will be illustrated below, while in some instances it took the arrival of new unions such as those of the match-girls and dockers, combined with the efforts of members of the Social Democratic Federation (SDF) and the Socialist League (SL), to persuade the disgruntled labour force of the benefits of combination, other tailoring workers had been involved with trade societies, in one form or another, since shortly after the emergence of a market-based economy.

The wholesale production of tailored garments in London and Leeds was begun at different times and under different conditions. In each case the composition of the labour force was fashioned by the pattern of development. In London's East and West Ends the sale of clothes, both new and second-hand, could be traced back to the fifteenth century.[11] In Leeds, with the exception of the presence of a small number of bespoke tailors,[12] the birth of the clothing industry was very much a part of the second phase of industrialisation and the golden decade of the 1850s.

London, as the centre of finance, government and the Court provided a natural market for high-class bespoke tailored garments.[13] Custom came from the affluent members of the resident population and from wealthy visitors from the provinces and overseas who wanted their 'best clothes made in London', if possible in Savile Row, the area in the heart of Mayfair renowned for exclusive craft tailoring. During the first half of the nineteenth century the market expanded to encompass consumers who, even if unable to afford the more expensive tailoring establishments, still wanted newly made garments. As a result shops selling lower quality bespoke clothes opened around the periphery of Savile Row. Production methods varied. Some orders were made up on shop premises by craft tailors while others were produced by outworkers employed in the workshops of nearby Soho. A small percentage was sent to the East End where levels of skill and quality of garment produced varied even within individual workshops.

The area along the eastern perimeter of the City of London had an association with second-hand clothing that dated back to Tudor times. During the first half of the nineteenth century second-hand gave way to new slop and shoddy garments. In 1830 H. Hyam opened a shop in the East End to sell slop clothes in large quantities. The feasibility of the mass production of garments which were of poor quality and rough material resulted from three main factors, (a) the earlier industrial revolution in textile production which had increased supplies and reduced costs, (b) by the early 1830s, the availability of shoddy[14] and (c) the increased use of sub-divisional labour. Several years later E. Moses opened his 'humble warehouse' at 154 Minories. By 1846 the warehouse had been transformed into a vast emporium 'to which custom came from all over the metropolis' to purchase clothes which ranged in price from 8s. 6d. for a ready-made suit to as much as three or four guineas for a bespoke garment suitable for those members of the aristocracy unable to afford Savile Row prices.[15] With the exception of the unemployed and the unemployable and those caught in the poverty trap of casual, seasonal and exploited labour, the second half of the nineteenth century was a period in which the working population enjoyed an improving standard of living. For the first time there was surplus money to spend on clothing, food, the home and leisure.[16] A new category of consumer was emerging. In order to accommodate its needs the cheaper sector of the tailoring industry developed. It catered for white-collar workers, artisans and that part of the emergent working class wishing to be seen dressed in newly made clothes, however poor and shoddy.

The Leeds wholesale clothing industry owed its origins to Surrey-born John Barran. In 1856 Barran linked business acumen with technical ability and brought the industrial revolution to the tailoring trade. Having invented a bandknife which could cut up to one hundred thicknesses of cloth at one time, Barran then combined factory production and the use of sub-contracted, sub-divisional labour. In 1856 he opened his first factory in Leeds. Using drapers' shops as retail outlets, Barran began to supply off-the-peg suits for both men and juveniles on a wholesale basis, that is, in quantity to the retailer in anticipation of consumer demand.

By the 1870s in London and Leeds the tailoring industry was firmly established and expanding, spurred on by the increased purchasing power of consumers at home and abroad. The tailoring work-force that served the industry in both cities could be divided into the following groups, skilled or semi-skilled and unskilled; English or alien (that is, eastern European Jewish immigrant); male or female; factory worker or workshop hand and homeworker. Though the last twenty years of the nineteenth century were the most expansionary in the tailoring industry until the post-First World War era, by 1870 the demographic dividing lines had been laid down, if not always clearly separated. English females worked in both factory and workshop, while Jewish females rarely, if ever, entered factories prior to the first decade of the twentieth century. English workers were both highly skilled and semi-skilled; aliens almost never found employment at the highest levels of bespoke production. Some tailors followed hundreds of years of tradition whereas the clothing operatives were part of a system that was as new as the factories and machinery around them.

The heritage of the English craft journeyman tailor can be traced back to the first appearance of merchant tailors' shops in the mid-seventeenth century. During the eighteenth century demand increased for tailored garments, made up in bespoke tailors'shops or by travelling journeymen tailors who took up domestic residence and stayed until the master of the household and his family were newly clothed, a practice that continued until the end of the nineteenth century.[17] Gradually tailors' clubs and societies sprang up all over the country, many taking on the form of labour exchanges. Based in inns or public houses they became known as 'Houses of Call'.[18] Lists of unemployed journeymen were left at the Houses for perusal by tailoring masters looking for labour. Workers were selected in strict rotation, often in gangs of three or four. By the mid-nineteenth century lists of those wanting jobs had been replaced by the presence of the unemployed themselves, forced to hang around 'on call' for prospective employers. The social investigator and journalist Henry Mayhew described how, as a result of this practice, 'the day is passed in drinking and habits of intemperance are produced which it is almost impossible to withstand'. In fact it was Mayhew's investigation into the plight of the tailors of London which convinced him that, contrary to prevailing mid-Victorian belief, it was poverty which led to drunkenness, not the reverse. As he so graphically explained in his pamphlet *Labour and the Poor*, published in 1850, 'father is made drunk with the liquor he is forced to swallow to get work'.[19]

Surviving reports suggest that the main role of the tailoring societies during the eighteenth century was to petition against low wages and long hours.[20] Membership of the journeymen tailors' societies was restricted to skilled workmen who paid a substantial entrance fee and had a high earning capacity. At the beginning of the nineteenth century the average weekly wage of an employed craft tailor was £1. 7s. 0d.

with the possibility of this rising to as much as £2. 14s. 0d. at times of Court mourning when an excessive number of garments would be required at very short notice.[21] The affluence of the journeymen was cited by master tailor and radical political activist, Francis Place, as the reason for their failure to protest against, or demand a repeal of, the Combination Laws in the 1820s.

From the 1830s onwards the craft sector of the tailoring trade, in which garments were made by 'honourable' tailors who earned their title by virtue of the fact that they could make a garment 'right through', was gradually overtaken by the cheaper bespoke and ready-made branches of the industry. The stability of the bespoke trade was further undermined by the economic depression of the 1840s. London suffered worst of all. Charles Kingsley's Parson Lot revealed that the capital's journeymen tailors were leaving the trade at the rate of 150 a year, many entering the sub-divisional sector.[22] In December 1849 Henry Mayhew reported in the *Morning Chronicle* that of the 454 tailoring masters in the West End only one-sixth now ran 'honourable' shops.[23]

During the 1850s and 1860s the tailoring trade was revitalised. Industrial expansion and economic growth at home and overseas renewed optimism amongst the craft tailors, even though the sub-divisional sector of the industry was now accepted as a permanent feature. The skilled tailor raised craft standards still higher and London's high-class tailors became increasingly selective in their choice of employee. Few would take on journeymen under the age of 18, although in rural areas and the provinces lads of nine and ten could be seen at work even though the usual age of admission to the trade was 13.[24] In the West End indentured apprenticeship had virtually disappeared by 1865 and apprentices were taken on only if their fathers were valued employees. It was outside London that many a skilled journeyman learnt his craft and it became accepted that 'West End journeymen are made in the country'.[25] Conditions for all but the most aristocratic tailors were tough, most especially for the young apprentices who were frequently obliged to sleep and work in their master's workshop in unheated and unventilated rooms with no wage other than food and board. At the beginning of the second half of the nineteenth century the divide between highly skilled craft tailoring and the lower branches of the industry, classed as sub-divisional and ready-made,[26] was far more than just a difference of style, cloth and workmanship. Mayhew suggests it was a gulf between civilisation and savagery: 'In passing from the skilled operative ... to the unskilled workman ... the moral and intellectual change is so great it seems as if we were in a new land and among another race.'[27]

The emerging sub-divisional and ready-made sectors of the industry provided employment for semi-skilled and unskilled tailors and tailoresses in workshops, at home or in the few wholesale clothing factories in operation at the time. Contrary to popular belief the system of sub-divisional tailoring preceded both the arrival of the mechanical sewing machine in 1851 and the mass 'alien invasion' of Jews from eastern Europe after 1881. The system had been developed much earlier, in the late 1820s, by journeymen tailors who initially employed their wives and daughters at home to assist in the production of clothes by making buttonholes and sewing on buttons. The economic viability of the system rapidly became apparent and soon spread beyond the nexus of the family, mushrooming into a complex and sophisticated method of production embracing a diversity of processes and creating its own skilled hierarchy.

The early sub-divisional tailoring work-force was composed of English tailors, who lacked the ability of the highly skilled craftsman, Irish and rural migrant workers plus a growing number of eastern European immigrants. By the 1860s the Irish element was diminishing. The availability and ease of steamboat and rail travel encouraged Irish workers to travel to the greener pastures of the New World. The resultant scarcity of Irish tailors was of sufficient significance to be noted in the 1865 *Report of the Children's Employment Commission*. However, reinforcements soon arrived in the form of eastern European immigrants, and these were eagerly exploited by earlier arrivals who, having ascended the socio-economic ladder to become 'sweaters',[28] manifested little concern for those who came after.

English tailors employed in the sub-divisional sector of the trade reflected both upward and downward economic mobility. Some were men forced to leave the higher levels of tailoring due to age, infirmity or lack of job availability. Others had worked their way up from clobbering[29] second-hand clothes for sale to those unable to afford new. From the 1830s onwards, as the number of sub-divisional workshops grew in response to the demand for low-priced, newly tailored clothes, employment opportunities increased. Those working in the sub-divisional workshops of London's East and West Ends were given the pejorative title of 'dishonourables' by craft tailors, who said that the production of 'cheap and nasty' bespoke and ready-made clothes brought the tailoring trade into disrepute, the underlying fear being that the craft sector would diminish as a result.

Sub-divisional workshops entered the industrial structure of the capital's tailoring trade during the early 1830s. Almost thirty years later they became a feature of the Leeds wholesale clothing industry when, in 1860, Herman Friend, a German-Jewish tailor, adopted the system in order to supply John Barran's newly opened factory with coats and jackets.[30] And it was to the sub-divisional tailoring workshops of London and Leeds that the newly arrived eastern European immigrants looked for work.

Tailoring has been called a 'Jewish occupation' and described as 'unhealthy work, carried on in cramped quarters and in cramped positions'.[31] In his book *A History of Jewish Crafts and Guilds*, Professor Wischnitzer traces the Jewish association with commercial tailoring as far back as five hundred years BC when Jewish tailors first made up garments to sell in the markets of New Jerusalem. One explanation for the proliferation of Jewish tailors in the diaspora is to be found in the biblical law which lays down that no Jew may wear 'a garment mingled of linen and woollen'.[32] In order to be assured that his garments conformed with the tenets of the Torah a religious Jew always frequented a co-religionist tailor, a practice continued today amongst the strictly Orthodox. A second explanation is to be found in the fact that tailoring and shoemaking, the second most popular Jewish trade, were cheap and easy to establish as they required little space and few tools. For a people accustomed to dispersal, occupations which were adaptable to any society at any time would always survive.

During the period from the thirteenth to the seventeenth century restrictions imposed on Jewish business activities varied from country to country and from city to city. In some places a Jew was limited to dealings with his fellow Jews, elsewhere opportunities were far wider. In southern France, in the Middle Ages, Jewish tailors produced clothes for the open markets while in seventeenth- and eighteenth-century Poland, in addition to being involved in a healthy export trade, they were retained by the military to make army uniforms.[33]

From the thirteenth to the seventeenth century, the religious persecution of, and the increasing economic limitations imposed upon, the Jews in Western Europe and the Near East forced a move eastwards and in 1772, at the time of the partition of Poland, the Jewish population of what became Russia-Poland was 900,000,[34] one-tenth of the national total. The Jews were confined in what was, by 1835, explicitly defined as the Pale of Settlement – an area of some 362,000 square miles which included the Ukraine, Belorussia-Lithuania, Polish territories added after the Napoleonic wars and parts of the Baltic provinces.[35] By this time the economic role of the Jewish middleman was diminishing. As a result of the emancipation of the serfs many were forced to leave the villages where they had been active intermediaries between landlord and peasant to find some form of artisan employment in towns and cities industrially unprepared for immigrants. The process of pauperisation and urbanisation of the Jewish population of the Russian Empire increased under the so-called liberal policies of Alexander II. For the small minority of Jewish bourgeoisie, life improved when they were given the opportunity to leave the Pale and use their commercial expertise to the Empire's advantage in the major cities and towns of inner Russia. For the remainder, conditions continued to deteriorate.

The number of Jews in the cities of the Pale grew dramatically while opportunities for employment decreased. Tailoring proved to be the most saturated occupation. Statistics reveal that 25 per cent of Jewish artisans were engaged in the production of clothes.[36] As the historiography of the English journeyman tailor develops into an account of the increasing dichotomy between the highly skilled and the semi-skilled and unskilled so does that of the Jewish tailor. Industry in the Pale was small-scale. A master usually employed one journeyman and an apprentice. The latter was treated very much as a servant and had little opportunity to learn the intricacies of the trade. This goes some way towards accounting for the lack of skill displayed by many young immigrants. Some masters maintained a benign and benevolent relationship with their hands, but in general it was soured by a considerable degree of exploitation which at times exploded into physical violence. In the Pale of Settlement craft differences and class struggles prevailed. A few skilled craftsmen were to be found but the majority of Jewish tailors were semi-skilled and produced garments of inferior quality. Jewish work rapidly became synonymous with bad work. Despite this, the characteristic of determined economic self-advancement, a feature of the Jewish immigrant economy so frequently the subject of discussion by English commentators, was evident even within the inhibited surroundings of the Pale. It was said of the young exploited worker that he had a 'dream of independence and at the first opportunity would leave his master and open his own shop or become a journeyman'.[37] As a result of economic pressures roles were reversed with regularity, the employer of one year becoming employee the next, a cycle which would become a familiar feature of life in the London and Leeds sub-divisional tailoring trades.

Saturation of the labour market created even longer periods of seasonal unemployment and by the 1870s Jewish workers in cities such as Minsk and Kovno were reported as living in 'semi-darkness in cellars or similar hovels'.[38] Conditions for Jews in the urban ghettoes steadily deteriorated as the population increased. Between 1820 and 1880 the number of Jews in Russia and Russia-Poland rose from 1,600,000 to about 4,000,000, an increase of 150 per cent.[39] This factor, allied to the increasing downward mobility of the Jewish working class created conditions of extreme poverty; 40 per cent of the Jewish population existed without any regular form of income, dependent on the benevolence of their co-religionists.[40]

In 1863, after the abortive revolt of Congress Poland against the Russian Tsardom, the plight of the Jews grew worse. Economic deprivation was now accompanied by political and social persecution. For those who could make it, the only hope for material independence and self-improvement lay westward; for the majority to the *Goldene Medineh* (America); for a minority, some 150,000, to Britain. The previously small number of eastern European immigrants in Britain gradually increased and by 1871 there were a reported 9,974 Russians and Russian-Poles resident in the country, the majority to be found in London, Leeds and Manchester.[41] It should be noted that although the influx of eastern European Jewry is commonly taken to be a pheno-menon of the last twenty years of the nineteenth century, the great migration was under way before that period.[42]

Not surprisingly, the newly arrived eastern European immigrants sought employment in tailoring and second-hand clothes dealing. But how much influence did they have on the subsequent growth and development of the sub-divisional system of production? In her book, *Breakaway Unions and the Small Trade Unions*, Shirley Lerner ex-pressed the view that the intensification of the system was a direct result of the influence of the immigrant, 'trained in Talmudic logic which gave him an eye for minute detail'.[43] But how does this theory correlate with the period of eastern European immigration before Russian industrialisation? There are certain inconsistencies. First, as noted above, the system of sub-division was put in place by English journeymen in the 1830s and was well established before the mass migration from the Pale. Second, the majority of children in the Pale had minimal education. Religious training was combined with the basics of writing and arithmetic, taught in poor conditions by poor teachers. Only the gifted minority went on to the Yeshivah for 'intensive Talmudic study'.[44] The semi-skilled and unskilled immigrants, unlike the craft tailors of the Pale who were acknowledged Talmudic scholars,[45] were taught only the rudiments of biblical and Judaic knowledge. Some were unable to read or write even Yiddish, the Hebrew-Germanic language of eastern European Jews. This lack of education, manifested by immigrants in London and Leeds, was seen as a stumbling-block to assimilation and labour organisation by Jewish refugee intellectuals in the 1870s and 1880s. In both cities trade unionists set out to educate the alien work-force. In 1879 a newly formed Jewish Workers' Union in London established an educational programme, setting up a library and providing facilities so that members could be taught to read and write in English and Yiddish. However, within a few months, 'they (the members) had tired of reading all the books ... and paying dues' and the union collapsed.[46] Five years later the newly founded Jewish East End branch of the English craft tailoring society, the AST, announced that its secretary, Mr Stone, and Mr Lewis Lyons were giving lessons in English and Yiddish speech and accounting.[47] The Jewish socialist and trade unionist, Joseph Finn, writing about Jewish workers in Leeds in 1884, complained that 'few can read an English newspaper, they know no English nor do they want to learn to read or write in Yiddish.'[48] The problem of illiteracy survived into the next century. Moses Sclare, who became full-time salaried secretary of the Leeds AJTMP in 1906, giving evidence to the Truck Committee in the same year, revealed that not only were the 'majority of members (of the AJTMP) unable to read'[49] but 'many of the masters were illiterate'.[50] Clearly, the majority of eastern European immigrants were not scholars. Doubtless there were exceptions, some early arrivals, men such as David Lubelski of Leeds, and they may well have organised the extension of the sub-divisional system to the extremes that became part of the city's industrial infrastructure. The increase in immigration acted as a catalyst; a growing labour pool composed of the barely skilled and unskilled was ideally suited to the sub-divisional system. Trained in just one productive operation a hand was easy to replace and unable to demand a craftsman's wage, ripe fodder for exploitation by co-religionist employers.

In addition to alien sub-divisional workers and craft journeymen, the introduction of the factory production of tailored garments created a third group of male tailoring workers, factory operatives. As we shall see later, for economic reasons their numbers were kept to a minimum. Within the factory there was a strict hierarchy as well as gender segregation. The cutter was the aristocrat. Cutting was the only sector of the wholesale ready-made industry to maintain an apprenticeship system. Although the job was made less arduous by the introduction of mechanised equipment, in terms of time and economy, cutting was a vital facet of production. The cutter was responsible for maintaining the flow of 'bundles',[51] cut as economically as possible from the bales of material provided, ensuring the minimum amount of wastage. Initially factory cutters were recruited from the bespoke branch of the industry but, as the wholesale sector expanded, learners were trained specifically for factory work. In the factory, as in the workshop, pressing ranked below machining on the scale of skills. The presser could, with skill and dexterity, turn a disaster into a success. Male operatives also worked as foremen, stock keepers and layers out. A small number of skilled tailors were employed to act as overseers.

In 1871, in London and Leeds, tailoresses represented a minority of the work-force. In London, with its tradition of bespoke and ready-to-wear tailoring, their number had risen by 75 per cent between 1851 and 1871, from 8,294 to 14,780. In Leeds the percentage increase over that same twenty-year period was, although quantitatively smaller, far more reflective of the impact John Barran had made on the city's industrial structure. The number of tailoresses in Leeds increased by 1,500 per cent, from 29 in 1851 to 483 in 1871.[52] The female tailoring work-force of Leeds was spread between factory and workshop. There was not the same complex system of homework as had developed in London during the earlier part of the century. Even by 1887, when the industry was well established, homeworkers represented no more than one-eighth of the total female clothing labour force.[53] The large-scale nature of the Leeds clothing industry and the dominance of the factory resulted in far less reliance on casual female labour.

Females working in the Leeds clothing industry represented varying degrees of financial need, from young girls eager to earn pin money for personal luxuries, to single girls helping out at home and/or saving for a dowry, through to wives and mothers supplementing the household budget. A clear distinction was made between females employed in the factories and those working in the sub-divisional sweatshops. Jewish tailoring masters in Leeds differed from their London counterparts in

1 Joseph Finn (courtesy Cecily Zimmerman)

2 Lewis Lyons (courtesy Henry Rollin)

3 A typical account from a top tailor, *c.* 1880 (courtesy Henry Poole)

AMALGAMATED SOCIETY OF TAILORS
(Jewish Branch).
BALANCE SHEET
of the Branch for the Twelve months from January 1st. to
December 31st. 1889 inclusive.

Income.	£	s.	d.	Expenditure.	£	s.	d.
To Balance in hand January 1st. 1889	21	10	9	By Sick Benefit	6	18	0
Contributions, etc.	91	6	1	Secretary	9	2	3
Bank Interest	0	9	1	President	1	8	0
				Steward & Sick Visitors	2	6	6
Total £113		5	4	Treasurer	1	3	0
				Trustees going to Bank	0	10	0
				Auditors	0	16	0
				Rent of Clubroom	2	0	0
				Committee Meetings	0	10	6
				Deputations	2	8	0
				Stationery & Postage	1	16	4
				New Box	0	18	0
				Equalization to Omagh Branch	7	0	0
				Call to Permanent fund	1	13	0
				New Stamp	0	10	6
				Organisation & Printing	7	18	0
				Strike Pay	3	0	0
				Commission collecting Contributions	1	6	0
				Collecting sweating evidence	1	0	0
				Grant to Furriers strike	2	0	0
				Total expenses £53		19	1
				Total Balance held by Branch Dec. 31st. 1889.	59	6	3
				£113		5	4

Auditors:
Morris Rosenthal,
Solomon P. Berlyn.

President:
Jacob Tofler.

Treasurer:
Woolf Esenberg.

Secretary:
Lewis Lyons,

Cash in Treasurers hands 7 17 6
Cash in Post Office Savings Bank 44 8 11
Cash in late Treasurers hands 6 19 10
£59 6 3

4   A balance sheet of the Amalgamated Society of Tailors, 1889 (Henry Rollin)

אמאלגאמייטעד שניידער סאסייטע.

(אידישע בראנש)

רעכנונג פון די בראנש

אויף צי מאנאטען, פון יאנואר דען 1 טען ביז דעצעמבער דען 31 טען 1889.

אויסגאבען	£	s.	d.		איינקונפט	£	s.	d.
צו קראנקען בענעפיט	6	18	0		צו			
סעקרעטער	9	2	3		צוזאמען געלד אין העגד ביי			
פרעזידענט	1	8	0		דען 1 טען יאנואר 1889	121	10	2
סטואַרד און קראנקען בעזוכער	2	6	6		וואוכער געלד א. ו. ו.	91	6	1
מעדישורער	1	3	0		פראצענט פון געלד	0	9	1
טראמסטיק פיר געהען אין באנק	0	10	0					
נאבצערהערס	0	16	0		זוזאמען	118	5	4
רורה געלד פיר דאם קלוב	2	0	0					
קאמיטע מיטינגס	0	10	6					
רעפרעזאדזיאן	2	3	0					
שרייב געצייג און פאסט געלד	1	16	4					
א גיוען קאסטען	0	18	0					
געשיקט צו אמער בראנש	7	0	0					
געשיקט נאך מאנשעסטער	1	13	0					
א נייע חתימה	0	10	6					
ארגאניזאציאן און דרוקערייא	7	18	0					
פטריק געצאהלם	3	0	0					
קאמפיטשקן פון צוואמען קלייבען וואוכערם	1	6	0					
צוואמען קלייבען סועטינג אויסטאנונגען	1	0	0					
געגענבען צו ריא ריא פערי... סטרייק	2	0	0					
זוזאמען אויסגאבען	£53	19	1					
זוזאמען איו געבליבען געלד רוא בראנש ביו דעצעמבער דען 31 טען 1889	59	6	3					
	118	5	4					
געלד ביים טרעזשורער	7	17	6					
געלד אין פאסט אפפיס באנק	44	8	11					
ביים פאריגען טרעזשורער געלד	0	10	10					
	£59	6	3					

נאכזעהערם:
מאררים ראזענטהאל,
סאלאמאן פ. בערליין.

פרעזידענט:
דזשעקאב מאפלער,

טרעזשורער:
וואלף אייזענבערג.

סעקרעטער:
לואים לייאנם,
43 בעדפארד סטריט, קאמאשיקעל ראד.

BALANCE SHEET

OF THE

International Tailors' Machinists & Pressers' Union,

REGISTERED.

From July 7th. to September 29th. 1890.

INCOME.	£	s.	d.
Balance in Bank last Quarter,			
Tailors and Pressers	51	18	8
" " Clothing Machinist	29	10	4
In hand of Treasurer			
Mr. Levkovitz	0	4	1
" " " Mr. Emanuel	2	8	10½
In hand of late Treasurer			
Mr. Cohen	0	14	7½
" " " Mr. Finelight	0	9	11½
Deposit on Gas	3	0	0
" " Rent	5	0	0
Contributions & Entrance Fees,			
July	18	7	9
" " August	24	10	3
" " September	9	13	0
Security from Treasurer	10	0	0
	£155	**17**	**6¼**

Audited and found correct by

Salomon Abrahamson,
Abraham Samuels, *Auditors.*

Lewis Levkovitz, *Treasurer.*

EXPENDITURE.	£	s.	d.
By Rents, Booth St & Sugar Loaf	18	7	0
" Hall Keeper	9	15	0
" Secretary's Salary & Expenses	3	9	6
Registration Fees	1	5	0
Auditors	0	2	0
Loan to Mr. Isaacs	1	10	0
Postage, Stationary, Telegrams			
and Newspapers	1	10	0½
Printing	4	13	9
New Stool	0	2	0
Grant to Amalgamated Society			
of Lasters	3	0	0
" " Cabinet Makers	3	0	0
Bill Posting	0	15	0
New Bell	0	2	6
Bottle & Glasses	0	1	4
Gas Repairs	0	1	0
Band re Dockers Demonstration	3	12	6
Wages & Fees, Trade Union Congress			
	12	11	0
Banner Painting	0	10	0
Banner Bearers	0	4	0
New Stamp	0	1	0
Gas Bill	2	14	5
Fee to Parlimentary Committee	0	5	0
Wages to Lazarus Goldstein	0	11	8½
Lock out pay	1	0	0
Grant to Australian Strike	10	10	0
Total	£78	13	4
Balance in hand	£77	4	2¼
Total	£155	17	6¼
In Bank	58	11	3
Deposit on Gas and Rent	8	0	0
In hand of late Treasurer M. Cohen			
	0	14	7½
" " Mr. Finelight	0	9	11½
In hand of Present Treasurer			
Mr. Levkovitz	9	8	4½
	£77	**4**	**2¼**

LIABILITIES.	£	s	d.	ASSETS.	£	s.	d.
Printing Penny & Hull	1	15	0	Deposit on Gas	3	0	0
Security to Treasurer	10	0	0	" on Rent	5	0	0
	£11	**15**	**0**		**£8**	**0**	**0**

5 A balance sheet of the International Tailors' Machinists' and Pressers' Union, 1890

בעלענס שיט.

פון דיא
אינטערנאציאנאלע
שניידערס, מאשינערס אונד פרעסערס יוניאן
רעדושיסטערעד.

פון יולי דען 7 מען ביז סעפטעמבער דען 29 מען 1890.

			אויסגאבען.	איינקונפט.			
£	s.	d.			£	s.	d.
0	7		מר חזקי' גינעלד מר בוט סמיטס און שטוער לאאן	געבליבען אין דיא בענק מאריגען קוואיטער פון דיא	8	18	51
0	15		,, ראהל קעסער	שניידערס, מאשינערס און פרעסערס			
8	2		,, סעקרעטער'ס נעהאלט און אויסנאבען	געבליבען אין דיא בענק מאריגען קוואיטער פון דיא	4	10	29
7	5		רעגישטרער'דען בעצאלט	קלאמהינ'ג מאכערס			
0	2		אירישארעס	ביים פרעזידענט מיסטער לעפקאוויץ	1	4	0
0	10		לאאן פר מיסטער אייזיק	,, ,, עמעזיל	10½	8	2
0½	10		מאססם, סטעטשענער, שעלענדראסס און סישונען	ביים מאריגען טרעזשורער מיסטער כדן	7½	14	0
9	13		ר'ונטעריא	,, ,, מרינלים	11½	9	0
0	0		ניו שואל	האנד געלט נעם ארף נעם	0	3	0
0	0		גינענען צו דיא אמאלגאמייטעד לאבשערס קאמיטע	,, ,, רענעם			
0	15		כלם ארישקלעבנען	קאנטרבישענס און אירגעריב געלם זיל	9	7	18
6	2		א. מאשינלאוק	,, ,, ארנאסם	8	10	24
4	1		אין גאושעל און גלמוער	,, ,, סעפטעמבער	0	18	9
0	1		נעג מ'עררבמען	מעקארריף מאן סעקרעטער	0	0	10
6	2		מוזיק צו דיא ראקערס רענבאנספרעטשען				
0	1		וועדושעס בעצאלם פון מרער יוניאן קאנגרעס				
0	4		רעם מאהן ארבער מאהדנען				
0	1		מאהן פרענער				
5	1		א ניו קעטעסם				
0	5		נעו בילל				
8½	1		בעצאלם צו דיא מאלאמעענט קאמטע				
0			וערושעס צו לאאורס גאללדעשטן				
			לאק אאום בעצאלט				
			גינענען צו דיא אירטפראלע סמריקעלס				
4			,, ,, ס"ה				
2½			נעבליבען אין דער				
6½			,, ,, ס"ה				
				6½	17	155

נאכגעזעהען און געפונען ריכמיג ביי

סאלאמאן עברעהמסאן און עברעהם סעטיעלם, אודימארס,
לואם לעפקאוויץ, פרעזודעטטע.

		8	אין בענק				
		0	האנד געלם ארף נעם גען און רענם				
7	כדן	0	אין דער האנד ארף דען מאריגען טרעזשורער מר.				
11½	מרינלים	,,	,, ,, ,,				
4½			אין דער האנד פון יענעסטען טרעזשורער מר. לעפקאוויץ				
2½							

שמעהרעגדע געלטער.

£	s.	d.
0	0	8	האנד געלם ארף נעם גען
0	0	5	,, ,, ,, רענם
0	0	8

לויבילטס.

£	s.	d.
0	15	1	דרק מנני און דיאל
0	0	10	סעקרעדיש מאן שרענ
0	15	11

Trades' Union Institute, Leeds.

6 The Trades' Union Institute, Leeds (courtesy Henry Rollin)
7 In English and Yiddish: a membership card of the Manchester Jewish Machinists' and Pressers' Trade Union (Henry Rollin)

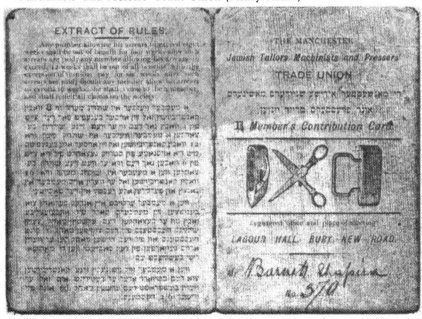

being far readier to employ Gentile females. According to a report published in the *Lancet* in 1888, English girls working in the Leeds sub-divisional workshops came from a lower stratum of society than their factory counterparts and were prepared to work for lower wages and perform the more menial tasks such as felling and finishing.[54] Women employed in the Leeds wholesale clothing factories fell into three main categories, (a) those with previous industrial experience, (b) those with non-industrial experience and (c) those with no previous work experience. Group (a) evolved from the city's earlier use of semi-skilled female labour in the flax and linen industry. In the early 1830s the use of power looms created a demand for female workers with above average ability.[55] The flax, linen and textile industries in the West Riding created a precedent for female factory employment at fair rates of pay. The gradual decline of the flax and linen industry resulted in a nucleus of female workers seeking alternative employment. Groups (b) and (c) were attracted to the clothing factories by reason of the economic benefit to be derived from employment there and the lack of stigma attached to such employment. Conditions were modern and hygienic. Factories run by Leeds wholesale clothiers such as Barran earned a reputation for employing a 'better type of girl'. This was contrary to the image of factory girls in London whom contemporary observers, such as Clara Collet, considered 'low types'.[56] John Barran ensured that his female workers came from what he considered suitable backgrounds, and frequently they were the daughters or sisters of senior male employees such as managers, clerical workers or foremen,[57] an early example of the industrial kinship network.[58] Although female operatives were usually single, very few females under 16 were employed in the clothing factories where the use of machinery required a mature hand. Women aged over 25 in need of a job and with lower levels of skill were rarely taken on by wholesale clothiers. They had little option but to look for work in the insanitary sweatshops.

The sewing machine, although not the reason for the expansion of the cheap bespoke and ready-made tailoring industry, was responsible for bringing 'the greatest change in recent years' to female employ-ment.[59] The *Second Report of the Children's Employment Commis-sion*, published in 1864, stressed that very few young girls or youths were employed in the manufacture of wearing apparel as few had, at an early age, the deftness of hand necessary in the production of tailored garments. The arrival of the sewing machine emphasised the necessity for those using it to be 'young persons rather than children',[60] with a demonstrable level of manual dexterity; though increased dexterity should not be confused with skill.[61] Further evidence is to be found in the Census returns for 1861. The total number of females occupied in the manufacture of covered millinery, dress, shirts, boots, tailored garments and gloves in England and Wales was 27,386, of which only 863 were under the age of 15.[62]

In London semi-skilled and unskilled females were employed in the tailoring trade in the eighteenth century when, during the Napoleonic Wars, they produced soldiers' coats for as little as 5d. a day.[63] There are also records of a very small number of craft tailoresses at work in the fifteenth century.[64] But it was the extension of the sub-divisional system, and the accompanying deskilling of the tailoring trade, that increased job opportunities for semi-skilled and unskilled females in the capital. Women were employed to do simple operations such as felling, buttonholing, sewing on buttons and putting in pockets and linings. In the industry's nascent years women worked at home but, as the sub-divisional sector expanded, they found employment in the tailoring workshops of London's East and West Ends.

London tailoresses came from multifarious backgrounds. Some were of the lower middle classes and had seen better days, 'the daughters of poor clergymen, non-conformist ministers, half-pay officers or tradesmen who had suffered reverses'.[65] Others were widows with insufficient means or the wives (legal or common law) of casual workers; women prepared to take on any form of seasonal work. When the tailoring trade was slack they were forced to look elsewhere, frequently to prostitution. Contemporary investigators reported that this age-old profession was often the exploited female's sole means of survival. The survey carried out by Henry Mayhew and Bracebridge Hemyng in the 1850s revealed that there were at least 80,000 prostitutes in London, many 'milliners, dress-makers ... slop women or those who work for cheap tailors ...' found in the 'numerous brothels London can boast of possessing'.[66] Thirty years later, little had changed. The socialist trade unionist Lewis Lyons[67] revealed in the *East London Observer* that, as the sweatshop masters paid the girls starvation wages, they had 'no alternative but to prostitute their bodies'.[68] At times of economic depression, when the numbers of men employed in the seasonal and casual trades fell, it was left to the women to provide for partner and family. The east London female labour pool expanded accordingly. The 1851 decennial return, taken just before the upturn in the economy, showed the ratio of female to male tailoring workers in

Stepney as 3:1, an exact reversal of the position in the capital as a whole.[69]

The first half of the 1860s was a period of transition for the London tailoring trade and its female work-force. Women slop-workers operating treadle machines in the East End could earn up to three times as much a week as hand workers[70] – speed, not skill, being the order of the day. But though the sewing machine was acclaimed for adding to the nation's wealth and being less harmful to the operative's health, workshop conditions did not improve. The 1864 Children's Commission further revealed that workshops were 'filthy with foul atmosphere and neglected occupants'.[71] Female workshop hands in London's West and East Ends were exploited both materially and physically; subdivisional work paid the lowest and created the worst conditions. Homeworkers fared no better. In 1887 women who made waistcoats at home averaged a daily wage of 9*d*. At best they could expect to earn a maximum of 2*s*. 0*d*. a day.[72]

The number of Jewish females recorded as employed in the workshops of London and Leeds was small. In both cities Jewesses working at the tailor's bench were either the wives of workshop masters or single females – Jewish women in Leeds did not consider factory work until the end of the first decade of the twentieth century. It was only in times of extreme economic necessity that Jewish married women worked outside the home,[73] or so it was believed. The image was that of wife and mother tending the physical needs of the family, managing the household budget and maintaining the domestic tenets of the religion so that, particularly in an alien society where men were frequently required to ignore the demands of Orthodoxy in order to keep their jobs, Judaic observance and family life would not become polluted. The reality was different, 'home' and 'work' were not mutually exclusive and the married Jewish woman was often forced to carry out a variety of money-making occupations within her own or in another's home. These activities extended to the running of shops, the breeding of hens and the provision of credit to neighbours, as well as dressmaking and market trading.[74] The Jewish male, in common with his English counterpart, ever the chauvinist, was not prepared to lose face by admitting, even to himself, that his wife had to work, even though her earnings were more than welcome. A Jewish wife's economic activities were rarely acknowledged as 'work', and would not have found their way on to the decennial census forms.[75]

Although not falling within the category of exploited workers, middlemen and masters cannot be excluded from any examination of the demographic structure of the tailoring industry. The two are frequently referred to as though their roles were interchangeable. This was not always the case, although both were held responsbile for the plight of the exploited workers. Blame was very rarely laid as high up the chain of production as the manufacturer, warehouse owner or foreman, all of whom were culpable, in imposing constant pressure for the lowest production prices. However, the small-scale employer frequently forced to sweat his hands so that his own family might eat elicited some sympathy. The 'romantic revolutionary', William Morris,[76] a founder member of the Socialist League, wrote with compassion of the plight of the small masters: 'They are of the same blood as the men ... It is their position therefore which turns good fellows into tyrants and cheats, in fact forces them to be so.'[77]

It was the middleman who was the parasite of the trade. An entrepreneur, rarely a practical tailor, he took orders for garments from warehouses and tailors' shops and gave these out to be made up in his own, or other, small workshops. The middleman promised the lowest production prices, thus reinforcing the sweating system. It was the middleman who, according to Jewish anarchists and socialists, epitomised the evils of the capitalist system. It was the middleman who, said the first Yiddish newspaper published in England, the socialist *Poilishe Yidel*, 'had food while the workers went hungry ... was strong while the workers were sick'.[78] Some middlemen made substantial profits from their activities, Henry Mayhew wrote of one, a 'Jew from Petticoat Lane' who earned a reported £60 per week.[79]

Before 1870 the diverse craft, geographic and cultural backgrounds of the tailoring communities of Leeds and London were almost matched by the unevenness of their links with earlier forms of labour organisation. The first recorded 'effective' combination of London wage-earning journeymen appears in 1720.[80] F.W. Galton suggests that tailoring societies in the capital and other major centres including Edinburgh, Cambridge and Dublin rose and fell throughout the latter part of the eighteenth and the early years of the nineteenth centuries.[81] In the 1820s fissures began to appear in those craft tailoring societies which had survived but the repeal of the Combination Laws in 1825 and the upturn in the economy, which began in 1829, resulted in a surge of trade union activity which culminated in the formation of the First Lodge of the Grand National Union of Tailors in November 1833.[82] The practice of restrictive association was temporarily forsaken. The new *general* union was composed of unskilled and semi-skilled tailors and a small number of tailoresses. This was in line with the movement towards general trade unionism pioneered by the ill-fated Grand National Consolidated Trade Union. An unsuccessful strike called by London tailors in 1834,[83] and the collapse of the Grand National Consolidated in August that same year, led to the disintegration of the tailors' union and it was not until the next century that the movement towards general unions was renewed. The depression of the 1840s did little to encourage organisation amongst craft tailors and though some attempts were made to reconstitute tailors' societies, as always during periods of economic decline, the employers held the upper hand.

By contrast, the decade of the 1850s was one of a buoyant economy and increased trade union activity. The formation of the Amalgamated Society of Engineers (ASE) in 1851 and its successful stand against the lock-out of the following year put it in the forefront of the 'new model unions' which filled the arena of trade unionism for the next thirty-seven years. Renewed confidence amongst craft tailors led to a reappearance of the House of Call, a strengthening of those trade societies still in existence and the formation of new societies. By the middle of the decade four craft tailoring societies were operating in the capital as well as a number in provincial cities, including one in Leeds.[84]

In 1866, at the suggestion of Peter Shorrocks, the secretary of the Manchester Tailors' Society, a number of provincial tailoring societies fused to form the craft-based Amalgamated Society of Tailors. The Society fitted perfectly into the category 'new model union'. Its code was a virtual copy of that of the ASE.[85] The bespoke tailors of Leeds were among the AST's 7,272 inaugural members[86] and by 1870 membership of the Leeds branch was 200.[87] This figure represented 13 per cent of the tailors in Leeds but, as records are not available to indicate how many of the city's 1,523 tailors[88] were employed in the bespoke sector, and how many worked in the sub-divisional workshops which served the wholesale ready-made industry (the AST did not offer membership to those working in the factories of the wholesale ready-made branch of the industry until the 1890s), an accurate assessment of the Society's local support is not possible.

The London tailoring society voted against participating in the provincial amalgamation. The London Tailors' Protection Association, founded in 1865 after the merging of the four smaller societies, argued that the difference in structure of the London and provincial

17

tailoring industries was such that the capital's unions could not be successfully run by a society with headquarters several hundred miles away. It was a belief that enervated tailoring trade unionism in England for the next sixty years. The London Tailors' Protection Association collapsed in 1867 following a disastrous strike which was supported by 10,000 London journeymen, few of whom were members of trade unions or societies.[89] Attempts to resurrect the Association failed and the journeymen tailors of London remained unorganised until 1870 when the AST entered the capital and opened two branches, one in the West End and one in the City. A membership of 199,[90] out of a total male tailoring work-force of 23,516,[91] highlights the weakness of organisation amongst those employed in the small-scale industries of the capital.

Until 1889 English men and women employed in the production of wholesale clothing in Leeds neither sought nor formed representative trade unions. Theirs was a new industry which boasted no links with medieval guilds or seventeenth- and eighteenth-century craft societies. It was not until pressures inside the factories and the first 'forward march of labour' outside,[92] forced the issue that, with the guidance and leadership of members of the Leeds branch of the Socialist League, the male and female wholesale clothing operatives of Leeds accepted the ethic of combination and formed separate trade unions. As ever, male chauvinism prevailed. It took a further eleven years for women to be admitted to AUCO.

In both London and Leeds the organisation of workers in the tailoring trade highlighted divisions of race and ethnicity. In both cities English and Irish sub-divisional tailors could, if they chose, join a branch of the AST, but until 1883 that Society's doors were firmly closed to eastern European semi-skilled and unskilled workers. A very small number of English-born Jewish skilled journeymen tailors were admitted to the Society though there is no exact record of their number. In Leeds and London during the 1870s eastern European working tailors wishing to join a trade union had no option but to turn to those founded and run by co-religionists. The newly arrived immigrant tailors had no previous experience of labour organisation. In eastern Europe trade unions for the semi-skilled and unskilled were in embryonic form as late as the 1880s and early 1890s,[93] though Ezra Mendelsohn, in his study of Jewish labour in the Pale of Settlement, suggests that the operation of benefit schemes by Jewish trade unions in England may have been a carry-over of the guild tradition of eastern

Europe.[94] In most instances it was left to the refugee intellectuals from eastern and central Europe to attempt to organise, with varying degrees of success, the Jewish sub-divisional tailors, machiners and pressers.

Throughout the years 1872 to 1915 the organisation of female sub-divisional workers proved as much of a problem as the organisation of women employed in the clothing factories. Writing in 1918 G. D. H. Cole expressed the view that 'Women do not enter industry with a view to remaining in it permanently ... and are therefore less interested in attempts to improve their industrial position.'[95] This lack of enthusiasm for combination resulted from a number of factors including: low rates of pay, irregular employment and the prospect of marriage leading to an inability and/or unwillingness to pay union dues; an inherent apathy towards trade unionism which, in the first three-quarters of the century, manifested little concern for the well-being of the female worker; discouragement by male contemporaries in the workplace who perceived organised females as a threat to male bargaining power; discouragement by husbands, fathers and brothers in the home and a blanket refusal by some employers to employ unionised female labour.[96] Antipathy towards organised female labour was apparent in 1834 when the tailoresses' branch of the First Lodge of the Grand National Union of Tailors was founded and in 1867 when, during the London tailors' strike, the tailors' association only opened a tailoresses' branch when it proved the sole means of ensuring female support for industrial action.[97] The failure of the 1867 tailors' strike brought down the tailoresses' branch and acted as a disincentive against further attempts at organisation. During the 1870s and 1880s Emma Paterson and other members of the Women's Protective and Provident League[98] tried hard to stimulate enthusiasm for trade unionism amongst tailoresses in London and Leeds but with little success.

With backgrounds as varied as those of the workers employed in the manufacture of tailored garments in London and Leeds and with systems of production ranging from small-scale to large, the task of creating a single, all-embracing union was not an easy one. The level of labour organisation in the years before the arrival of new unionism may be summarised by saying that in areas where large-scale industry was king, close to sources of raw material and power and with a limited labour pool, organisation was strong; where industry was small-scale and seasonal with a well-stocked and expanding pool of labour, combination was at its weakest.

Between 1851 and 1863, when the new model unions were in their nascent stages, most trade union activity took place in the capital. By the mid-1860s the strength of cotton and coal had pushed the centre of activity to the industrial north.[99] In the last two-thirds of the nineteenth century Leeds exemplified industrial growth and prosperity. It was located in that area north of the Humber and Mersey in which, according to the Webbs' statistics for 1892, were to be found one-half of all trade unionists.[100] During the 1860s the city of Leeds was a centre of organisation. Edward Baines, the Liberal Member of Parliament for Leeds and son of the founder of the *Leeds Mercury*, reported that 'scarcely any trade in Leeds is without its union ... for regulating the management of their trade in various ways'.[101] At the end of the decade investigators A. J. Gales and S. Brighty found 28 trade unions in Leeds, representing between them some 3,500 members.[102]

In the mid-1880s trade unionism in Leeds entered a radical phase. This lasted until the early 1890s when the primacy of organisation of the unskilled and semi-skilled became secondary to the commitment to the foundation and development of an active independent labour party. After 1894 trade unionism, as exemplified by the AUCO and even the AJTMP, followed a moderate course. As E. P. Thompson has written, from that time on Leeds provided 'a remarkable example of arrested development'.[103] Yorkshire after 1892, though 'the centre of agitation for independent labour representation',[104] experienced a diminution of organisational fervour.

Labour historians agree with the Webbs that from the late 1860s the strength of trade unionism in England lay in the industrial north.[105] There is also little disagreement about the weakness of organisation in the capital, for while Leeds was situated in an area where the characteristics of large-scale industry encouraged and facilitated organisation – by 1911 over 20 per cent of the city's employed male population worked in the two industries – [106] the dominant small-scale nature of London industry acted as a disincentive. By the beginning of the 1870s most heavy industry had left the capital, migrating north to more industrialised areas.[107] The remnants of heavy industry that remained were concerned only with repairs. As early as 1871 the area which was to become the largest centre of tailoring production, East London, was, according to Eric Hobsbawm, 'a trade union desert'.[108] Even though the craft tailors of London's West End demonstrated some degree of support for trade unionism the 'area which curved from Camden Town to Stepney and the river was poorly organised'.[109] Until the arrival of new unionism in 1889 the strength of organisation lay in South London among the carpenters and engineers of Southwark and Lambeth.[110] Even after the First World War, combination among the semi-skilled and unskilled workers of London remained weak. By comparison, craft societies such as those formed by bookbinders, cigar makers and craft tailors survived.

Thus the two cities fall into specific organisational categories. London in the south-east was the commercial, financial and political centre of the country, housing a work-force principally engaged in finishing trades, light and service industries; a city sub-divided into numerous districts exemplifying neither industrial nor social homogeneity. Leeds, in the north-east of England, though not exactly a stronghold of trade unionism,[111] was located in a region of organisational strength, manifested in heavy industry and mining. And it is to Leeds that we turn first.

NOTES

1. *United Garment Workers' Trade Union: First Annual Report: June 8th 1915–December 31st 1916*, Rollin Collection, Ms 242, Modern Records Centre, University of Warwick.
2. S. and B. Webb, *History of Trade Unionism* (1920 edn), p.552 and A. Flanders and H. Clegg (eds), *The System of Industrial Relations in Great Britain* (1956), p.22
3. *United Garment Workers Trade Union, First Annual Report*, op. cit.
4. The history of the union is told in *The Railwaymen*, published by the NUR in 1986. In 1911 the total recorded number of employed railwaymen was 400,000. Thus the NUR's initial membership represented approximately 45 per cent of the total work-force.
5. *Decennial Census*, pp.1913, LXXVIII.
6. Webbs, op. cit., p.551, while Clegg, Pelling and others make no reference to the union until it became the Tailor and Garment Workers' Union in 1921. Prof. K. Laybourn in his comprehensive new book, *A History of British Trade Unionism 1770–1990* (1992), makes no mention of any of the amalgamations or fusions of tailoring trade unions in the years between 1915 and 1939.
7. Rollin Collection, loc. cit.
8. A. J. Kershen, 'Trade Unionism Amongst the Tailoring Workers of London and Leeds', in D. Cesarani (ed.), *The Making of Modern Anglo-Jewry* (1990), p.36.
9. As explained in the Preface, the organisation of Jewish workers in Manchester falls beyond the ambit of this book. The origins of Jewish tailoring trade unions in the city are dealt with by Bill Williams in his essay, 'Beginnings of Jewish Trade Unionism in Manchester' in K. Lunn (ed.), *Hosts, Immigrants and Minorities* (1980), pp.263–308.
10. H. Clegg, *History of British Trade Unionism* (1964), p.55.
11. Webbs, op. cit., p.3.
12. Every large city housed a small number of bespoke tailors and outworkers, some of whom were Jews. In the latter years of the nineteenth century the main foreign-

born Jewish tailoring centres were London, Leeds, Manchester, Sheffield and Glasgow. H. Pollins, *Economic History of the Jews In England* (1982), p. 178.

13. Bespoke garments were made directly to the orders of the customer who chose the style, colour and cloth before any work was carried out.

14. Shoddy was produced by adding a small amount of new wool to a quantity of shredded rags. This resulted in a cloth of a very cheap and inferior quality.

15. E. Moses, *The Past, The Present and The Future* (1846).

16. For the history of the growth of consumerism between 1850 and 1914 *see* W. Hamish Fraser, *The Coming of the Mass Market 1850–1914* (1981).

17. S.R. Dobbs, *The Clothing Workers of England* (1928), p. 2.

18. For details of the system *see* C. Dobson, *Masters and Journeymen*, (1980).

19. A.J. Kershen, 'Henry Mayhew and Charles Booth', in G. Alderman and C. Holmes (eds), *Outsiders and Outcasts* (1993), pp. 97–98.

20. F.W. Galton, *Selected Documents: The Tailoring Trade* (1896), p. XXXIII.

21. Ibid., p. LX.

22. C. Kingsley, *Alton Locke* (1881 ed.), p. LXV. In her biography of Mayhew, *Travels into the Poor Man's Country* (1977), Anne Humphreys suggests that Charles Kingsley leant very heavily on Mayhew's articles in the *Morning Chronicle* published in December 1849, for his information on the London tailoring trade.

23. *Morning Chronicle*, 18 Dec. 1849.

24. *Children's Employment Commission, 4th Report*, PP 1865, XX, p. XXXV.

25. Ibid.

26. Sub-divisional tailoring was the system by which the making-up of a garment was divided into a number of different operations. These were performed by workers adept at only one task, e.g. basting, pressing, machining or lining. In some instances the system became so extended that a garment passed through as many as thirty hands before completion. In some Leeds workshops it became economically viable to employ someone, usually a young female, solely to sew on buttons.

27. *Morning Chronicle*, 14 and 18 Dec. 1849.

28. Those who owned and ran the 'sweatshops' in which workers were employed for the longest hours, in the worst conditions for the lowest wages.

29. Clobbering was the method by which the wearable parts of old clothes were roughly repaired and put together to form one saleable garment.

30. J. Thomas, 'A History of the Leeds Clothing Industry', *Yorkshire Bulletin of Economic Social Research* (Jan. 1955), p. 10.

31. W.J. Cohnman, in 'Introduction' to M. Wischnitzer, *A History of Jewish Crafts and Guilds* (1965), p. XXII.

32. *Leviticus* 19:19 and *Deuteronomy* 22. To mingle wool and linen is to commit 'shaatnes', and to disturb the natural order of things by fusing the product of an animal with that of a plant.

33. Wischnitzer, op. cit., pp. 86 and 225.

34. Ibid., op. cit., p. 223.

35. E. Mendelsohn, *Class Struggle in The Pale* (1970), p. 3.

36. Ibid., p. 6.

37. Ibid., p. 9.

38. Ibid.

39. L. Kochan, 'East European Jewry Since 1770', in D. Englander (ed.), *The Jewish Enigma* (1992), p. 119.

40. W.J. Fishman, *East End Jewish Radicals* (1975), p. 22.

41. Thomas, op. cit., p. 17.

42. For the relevance of this debate to Manchester Jewry *see* B. Williams, 'East and

West in Manchester Jewry 1850–1914', in D. Cesarani, op. cit., pp. 16–17.

43. S. Lerner, *Breakaway Unions and the Small Trade Unions* (1961), pp. 86–7.
44. L. Gartner, *The Jewish Immigrant in England* (1961), p. 221.
45. Mendelsohn, op. cit., p. 8.
46. *Poilishe Yidel* [Polish Jew], 29 Aug. 1884.
47. Ibid., 17 Oct. 1884.
48. Ibid., 1 Aug. 1884.
49. *Report of the Truck Committee*, PP 1908, LIX, qq 5936.
50. Ibid., qq 5906.
51. Bundles consisted of different sections of a garment which had been cut out, bundled and tied up ready to be collected by workshop masters or middlemen who would give them to their hands for completion. The completed garment would then be returned to the factory, or warehouse ready for distribution to the customers. A similar system operated in London where the cutting was done by those who ran the wholesale houses.
52. *Decennial Census 1851*, PP 1852–1853, LXXVIII and *Decennial Census 1871*, PP 1873, LXXII.
53. *Yorkshire Post*, 23 Feb. 1887.
54. *Lancet*, 6 June 1888.
55. C. Collet, 'Women's Work in Leeds', *Economic Journal*, Vol. 1 (1891), p. 462.
56. C. Booth, *London Life and Labour*, Vol. IV, p. 313.
57. John Barran & Co., *Staff Selection Book, 1873–1895*, Leeds City Archives.
58. M. Young and P. Willmott, *Family and Kinship in East London* (1972 edn), pp. 73–80.
59. *Children's Employment Commission, 2nd Report*, PP 1864, XXII.
60. Ibid.
61. H. Braverman, *Labour and Monopoly Capital* (New York: Monthly Review Press 1974), p. 444.
62. *Decennial Census 1861*, PP 1863, LIII.
63. M. Dorothy George, *London Life in the Eighteenth Century* (1930), p. 269.
64. B. Hutchins, *Women in Modern Industry* (1915), p. 3.
65. Lord Ashley, 1861, quoted by P. G. Hall in *The Industries of London Since 1861* (1962), p. 61.
66. H. Mayhew, *London Labour and the London Poor*, Vol. IV (1988 edn) pp. 213 and 217.
67. For a detailed account of Lewis Lyons's activities as a trade union organiser *see* Ch. 5.
68. *East London Observer*, 16 June 1888. *See also* W. J. Fishman, *East End 1888* (1988), pp. 70, 122–24 and J. Walkowitz, *Prostitution and Victorian Society*, (1991 edn), pp. 11–47.
69. A. Munby, *Industry and Planning In Stepney* (1951), p. 54.
70. *Children's Employment Commission, 2nd Report*, op. cit., p. 67.
71. Ibid.
72. *Annual Report of H.M. Chief Inspector of Factories and Workshops*, PP 1887 C. 5328.
73. L. Selitrenny, 'The Jewish Working Woman in the East End', *The Social Democrat*, Vol. 11 (1896).
74. For a discussion of the economic dimensions of working-class married life in London *see* Ellen Ross, 'Fierce questions and taunts', in D. Feldman and G. S. Jones (eds), *Metropolis London* (1989), pp. 219–44 and Lewis, op. cit., pp. 59–70.
75. For the economic role of the Jewish immigrant female *see* R. Burman, 'Jewish

Women and the Household Economy in Manchester, *c.* 1880–1920' in Cesarani, op. cit. pp. 55–76 and R. Burman, 'The Jewish Woman as Breadwinner' *Journal of Oral History Society*, Vol. 10, No. 2 (1982), pp. 27–39.

76. *See* E.P. Thompson, *William Morris* (1970).
77. Ibid., p. 323.
78. *Poilishe Yidel*, 15 Aug. 1884.
79. *Morning Chronicle*, 18 Dec. 1849.
80. Webbs, op. cit., p. 31.
81. Galton, op. cit., pp. XIII–XCVIII.
82. Ibid., p. LXXXIII.
83. *The Times*, 12 May 1834.
84. Galton, op. cit., p. XCV.
85. Webbs, op. cit., p. 224.
86. *Journal of the Amalgamated Society of Tailors and Tailoresses*, (Jan. 1909).
87. *AST Annual Report*, (1870).
88. *Decennial Census 1871*, op. cit.
89. *Journal of the Amalgamated Society of Tailors and Tailoresses*, (Jan. 1909).
90. *AST Annual Report*, (1870).
91. *Decennial Census 1871*, op. cit.
92. *See* E.J. Hobsbawm, *Labouring Men* (1979) and *Worlds of Labour* (1984), for discussions about the years 1888–9 and 1910–11.
93. For details of the growth of trade unionism among the Jewish workers of eastern Europe *see* Mendelsohn, op. cit., Chs. 4 and 5.
94. Mendelsohn, op. cit., p. 44.
95. G.D.H. Cole, *An Introduction to Trade Unionism* (1918), p. 71.
96. *See* J. Lewis, *Women In England 1850–1950* (1984), Ch. 5.
97. M. Stewart and L. Hunter, *The Needle is Threaded* (1964), p. 142.
98. The Women's Protective and Provident League was founded in 1874 and became the Women's Trade Union League in 1889.
99. Webbs, op. cit., p. 302.
100. Ibid., Appendix V.
101. E.D. Steele, 'Leeds and Victorian Politics', *University of Leeds Review* Vol. 17, No. 2, (1974).
102. D. Fraser (ed.), *A History of Modern Leeds* (1980), p. 357. Of that 3,500, 1,274 were members of the local branch of the Amalgamated Society of Engineers (*ASE Annual Report 1868*, Modern Records Centre, University of Warwick). How the remaining 2,226 trade unionists were distributed over the 27 other trade unions referred to is not recorded. The average is 82 members per union.
103. E.P. Thompson, 'Homage to Tom Maguire', in A. Briggs and J. Saville (eds), *Essays in Labour History* (1966), p. 302.
104. Clegg, op. cit., p. 184.
105. *See* Clegg, op. cit.; E. Hunt, *British Labour History 1815–1914* (1981); Cole, op. cit.; Stedman Jones, op. cit., and P. Thompson, *Socialists, Liberals and Labour* (1967).
106. *Decennial Census 1911*, op. cit.
107. Stedman Jones, op. cit., Chs. 1 and 2.
108. Hobsbawm, *Worlds of Labour* (1984), p. 142.
109. Ibid.
110. Thompson, op. cit., p. 46.
111. T. Woodhouse, 'The Working Class' in Fraser, op. cit.

2 The Leeds Wholesale Clothing Industry: Origins and Growth

> A navigable river, canals accommodating vessels of 120 tons, and communicating with the Mersey at Liverpool, the Ouse at Goole and thence with the Humber ... railways branching off in every direction ... These advantages give every possible facility for bringing raw materials, sending away manufactured goods, and for the access of men of business.[1]

The above quotation, written in 1858, highlights the advantages Leeds offered as a centre of manufacturing industry. Assets which, by the mid-nineteenth century, had enabled engineering and textiles to become the city's dominant industries. Fifty years later wholesale clothing was second on the list of major employers,[2] though it was not until after the First World War, and the opening of Montague Burton's mammoth factory,[3] that it took first place. How did an industry which began in the 1850s, in a small factory which employed 26 hands, achieve such prominence? In this chapter we explore the origins of that industry and the way in which it was fuelled by new factories using innovatory technology and unhygienic, overcrowded sweatshops. We examine the divisions that existed between factory and workshop and, in addition, those which segmented the Jewish community of the Leylands district of Leeds. Finally we consider the demographic and economic structure of the wholesale clothing industry in order to establish why different groups of workers, at different times, took up the mantle of trade unionism.

ENGLISH FACTORIES

In 1856 a tailor and outfitter opened the first wholesale clothing factory in Leeds. That shopowner was John Barran and the opening of his factory in Alfred Street, though small in comparison with the 'massive palaces' built by wholesale clothiers in the 1880s, marked a watershed in the history of the tailoring industry and a landmark in the industrial development of the city. Barran by no means pioneered the wholesale manufacture of tailored clothes. Some ten years before Moses and Hyam introduced the sale of cheap and shoddy ready-to-wear tailored garments in London, F.W. Harmer combined the 'production of woollens and clothes' in Norwich.[4] In 1854 the ready-to-wear clothing company of Holloway Brothers, founded the previous year in Stroud, introduced steam-driven sewing machines operated by male and female operatives, for the making-up of men's trousers.[5] But neither in Norwich nor in Stroud, nor even in the metropolis of London, was manufacture organised to facilitate the expansion of industry on the scale that developed in Leeds. In 1881 Kelly's *Leeds Directory* recorded the presence of 21 wholesale clothiers in the city,[6] and thirty years later their number had risen to 145.[7]

What encouraged the 21-year-old Surrey-born Barran to leave the security of home and the family gun-making business and pick Leeds as the base for his financial future? More than whim drew him to the town that was reputedly the 'commercial centre' of the West Riding. Leeds in the 1840s was a vibrant city. It had withstood the vicissitudes of economic depressions, natural disasters and the upheavals of Chartism due to the diversity of industries which had blossomed there during the first forty years of the century. By 1842, the year of Barran's arrival, there were 200 factories operating in the city,[8] engaged in industries ranging from flax manufacture and leather tanning to engineering and chemical production. In addition Leeds served as a finishing and marketing centre for the regional textile industry. If one industry failed another replaced it, the new arrival taking advantage of existing labour and plant. The nascent years of the wholesale clothing industry provides a perfect example of this pattern. New and expanding companies took over disused woollen mills and warehouses, recruiting female labour from amongst those who had previously found employment in local flax and woollen factories.

Industrial optimism acted as a beacon for those eager to work in the factories and in the growing number of tertiary and service industries. Population growth was impressive. In the fifty years between 1801 and 1851 it increased from 50,000 to 172,000.[9] At the beginning of the third quarter of the nineteenth century over 500 different trades and

26

occupations were carried on in the city. The burgeoning population of Leeds provided both the core of Barran's factory work-force and the essence of his custom.

Artisans, white-collar workers and factory employees were eager to display outward signs of their new-found respectability and affluence by the purchase and wearing of newly made clothes for themselves and their sons.[10] They were, as the *Leeds Mercury* reported, 'eager and able to afford to act as guinea pigs for new ranges and styles'.[11]

Leeds was ideally located for the development of an industry dependent on the importation of raw materials and the exportation of finished garments to customers at home and overseas. The cloth-producing towns were close by: Hebden Bridge for cotton cord, Huddersfield for tweeds, Batley for heavy cloth and Dewsbury for prints. The modern road, rail and canal systems ensured speedy, cheap and efficient delivery. Barran soon weighed up these assets and, within a few months, had left the pawnbroker's and outfitters, where he had served a short apprenticeship, to set up on his own as a tailor and outfitter. The purchase of a shop at No. 1 Briggate in 1845 was a stepping-stone in the transition from shopowner to wholesale clothing manufacturer. Business prospered,[12] benefiting from the increased spending power of a significant slice of the population. Barran now had the incentive to look beyond his own retail outlet. He began producing men's and boys' tailored garments, the latter becoming known as 'Little Lord Fauntleroy Suits', for sale to other drapers' shops and stores. He used market forces to the full in order to sustain and encourage demand; where they existed they had to be maintained and extended, where trade did not exist it had to be created. Leeds industry had a tradition of marketing at home and overseas. John Barran emulated the system initiated by cloth salesmen earlier in the century. His representatives travelled from John O' Groats to Land's End and, within a short while, were sailing overseas to Europe and the Colonies. At first the range of sizes was wide but the choice of styles limited. However, within fifteen years the company was able to offer a choice of over sixty juvenile styles.[13]

Once the Alfred Street factory was in operation, staffed by six cutters and twenty female hands and equipped with three sewing machines, the young and ambitious Barran explored ways to improve production methods.[14] His invention of the bandknife, next to that of the sewing machine,[15] perhaps the most important technological innovation in the industry, resulted from a visit to a timber and furniture exhibition in

1858.[16] Having seen a bandsaw in operation, cutting out layers of veneer in one movement, he conceived the idea of replacing the saw with a knife and employing the same principle for cutting out layers of cloth. Running a factory in a city renowned for its engineering industry proved its worth. Greenwood and Batley, a local engineering company, turned the brainchild into reality. Having suffered from the recession that followed the Crimean War they were eager to participate in an industry which, though in its nascent stages, had clear potential. At the end of 1858 a working model of the bandknife was in operation in Barran's factory. Subsequent models were sold to the Royal Army Clothing Factory and other wholesale clothiers.[17]

By the early 1860s improved production techniques and increased demand were stretching the productive capacity of Alfred Street to its limits. The cutting process had been intensified by the introduction of the bandknife and it became increasingly difficult for factory operatives to keep pace with demand. Barran reviewed production methods. Investment in additional plant and machinery at such an early stage of the industry's development would mean tying up capital which could be better invested in stock awaiting distribution. The alternative was to utilise labour and machinery indirectly, by means of sub-contracting. In this way money was expended only when goods were produced and not unnecessarily during periods of low demand and seasonal slackness. He first approached a group of local English journeymen tailors to see if they would make up coats and jackets for his company on an 'outdoor' basis, that is, to sub-contract and carry out production in their own premises. The craft tailors refused,[18] explaining that to co-operate would mean sacrificing their image as the aristocrats of the trade. Unspoken was their concern that they would be developing a new and threatening branch of the clothing industry. The fear was not without foundation; in 1870 there were 300[19] craft tailors in Leeds, but by 1903 their number had reduced to under 250. Barran then turned to one of the city's small number of Jewish tailors. He asked German-born Herman Friend, who ran a small workshop employing eight hands in nearby Templar Street, if he would agree to sub-contract the making-up of coats and jackets in his workshop using sub-divisional methods of production. Friend agreed and a system of separation yet interdependence was inaugurated. Females in the factory manufactured the trousers and vests (waistcoats)[20] whilst Friend and his workshop hands produced the majority of coats and jackets. Rowland Barran, John's grandson, explained to the Truck Committee some years later that the making of coats and jackets was 'too heavy for women'.[21] John Barran's concern was as much with the economics of manufacture as with the welfare of the female clothing operative. His method of reducing overheads by synthesising 'indoor' and 'outdoor' production reinforced sexual separation and racial division. It was a system that would be emulated by nearly all the wholesale clothiers in Leeds. By the end of the 1880s only two companies did not employ the services of Jewish sub-contractors[22] and although the volatility and unreliability of the Jewish worker was a continuing source of frustration the system survived.[23]

The wholesale clothiers maintained a preference for variable, as opposed to fixed, capital until after the First World War. For example, in 1884 James Rhodes and Co. carried 30,000 suits as stock awaiting distribution,[24] while in 1911 the variable assets of Barran, at £83,000, represented one-third more than the company's buildings and machinery, valued that year at £65,000.[25]

It was, however, the emergence of new markets for outerwear for motorists, motor-cyclists and golfers, in the early twentieth century,[26] that heralded a change in production methods. Worried about the reduction in the labour pool, following the passing of the Aliens Act in 1905 and the departure of a number of clothing workers for the richer pickings of America and Canada, Barran opened indoor departments for the manufacture of new ranges,[27] though it was not until 1921, when Montague Burton opened, 'The largest clothing manufacturing concern in the world'[28] in Leeds, that any drastic changes were made in the structure of production.

The dynamics of the Leeds wholesale clothing industry were set in motion during the 1860s as consumer markets at home and overseas expanded and units of production multiplied. In the years between 1861 and 1871 the tailoring work-force in the city increased by almost 100 per cent, from 1,038 to 2,006. The numbers of tailors rose by 52 per cent from 935 to 1,523 and tailoresses by 450 per cent, from 87 to 483.[29] During that period a number of 'practical' tailors,[30] including James Rhodes and Joseph Hepworth, previously partners, made the transition to wholesale clothiers. It was not only the Jewish worker who exhibited upward economic mobility; in 1867 William Blackburn, employed by John Barran until the age of 20, opened his own small factory for the manufacture of men's and boys' outer garments. Within thirteen years he had built up a chain of 23 retail shops for which he manufactured stock using factory and workshop labour.[31]

If the 1860s were the nascent years of the wholesale clothing industry then the 1870s were definitely the formative years. It was in these years that clothiers such as Rhodes, Hepworth and Barran accumulated the reserves necessary to finance the building and purchase of factories which so impressed press and public alike. In 1879 John Barran, by now a Liberal Member of Parliament,[32] exhibited his paternalism and economic pragmatism when he moved his company and his 1,000 workers to 'new and extensive' premises in Park Row. Reporting the factory's opening the *Leeds Mercury* stressed the 'magnificence and modernity' of the building, its innovatory technology and light, airy and sanitary working conditions. The Barran family's technological ingenuity was again in evidence, this time through Barran Junior's invention of goose-shaped irons which were heated internally by 100 gas jets controlled by a foot pedal. The factory provided dining, kitchen and toilet facilities and air-filtered workrooms.[33] In order to attract females from what he considered the right social and educational backgrounds John Barran had built the most modern and hygienic factory that was economically viable.

The depression which clouded the British economy from the second half of the 1870s to the late 1880s appears to have had little effect on the Leeds wholesale clothing industry. It displayed all the signs that it could become one of the city's major industries, as indeed it was to do. The widespread availability of credit from the 1850s onwards enabled those in regular work to fill their shopping baskets and furnish their homes. Tallymen and the 'ticket' system put items previously undreamt of within the reach of the working class whilst hire purchase made it possible to buy sewing machines and musical instruments.[34] The purchase and wearing of ready-made clothes was now an intrinsic part of everyday life. The Leeds wholesale clothing industry was supported by a purchasing public impressed and excited by the fact that they could walk into a draper's or tailor's shop and buy new clothes 'off the peg' at prices they could afford. New tailored clothes were now within the reach of every man (women's ready-to-wear tailored garments arrived on the scene later) or so the *Leeds Mercury* wished its readership to believe: 'In every part of England ... the ready made clothes shop is now a recognised feature of social life ... ready made clothes are now purchased by those who a few years ago would not have dreamed of buying a ready made garment.'[35] John Barran and his disciples had indeed spread the gospel of new clothes.

The decade of the 1880s proved to be the most expansive in the history of the Leeds wholesale clothing industry. The number of manufacturing companies increased by 200 per cent, from 21 to 65. Parallel expansion was taking place north of the border, in Glasgow. One of Scotland's most successful wholesale clothing companies was that founded by James Arthur in 1858. By 1878 it had a paid-up capital of one million pounds.[36] James Arthur, together with a number of other Glaswegian companies including Mann Byers, Stuart & MacDonald and Hunter Burr, recognised that if they wanted to get on the band-wagon of a rapidly expanding industry they needed a centralised base. Leeds was the obvious choice. In 1880 Arthur & Co. became the first Scottish company to open a clothing factory south of the border. Within a very short time a number of other companies followed suit.

The sites chosen by wholesale clothiers in the 1880s had the advantage of either inexpensive land for factory building or disused woollen and flax mills suitable for conversion. The close-knit geography of production proved beneficial as the proximity of factories, sub-divisional workshops and engineering companies, all within walking distance of each other, allowed for a continuation of the pattern of separation yet interdependence, established by Barran and Friend when they were based in Briggate and Templar Street; one which proved so influential in the developing structure of what was rapidly becoming one of Leeds' major industries.

Expanding markets at home and strong export links with South Africa and Australia supported a steadily growing work-force. By 1888 a total of 1,000 female operatives and 500 male workers were employed in John Barran's newly opened five-storey factory which extended over an area of 54,000 feet in Hanover Lane. Five hundred female machinists produced juvenile suits, which were lighter to handle and easier to make up than a full-sized adult's, and men's trousers in a machine room which measured an impressive 180 feet by 60 feet. To keep pace with technology, electric lighting was installed and two 80-horsepower steam engines puffed away in the basement, running 'the most up-to-date equipment'.[37] In an era when the public conscience was awakening to the realisation that poverty was the cause, not the result, of drunkenness and gambling, and when the iniquities of sweated labour, overcrowding and insanitary working conditions were seen to be the result of a market-based economy and the extremes of *laissez-faire* philosophy, the city's press used every opportunity to publicise the new factories that were appearing on the skyline. Barran's new factory made good headline material, serving to emphasise the gulf between the Jewish sub-divisional sweatshops and the modern clothing factories.

As early as 1864 John Barran had pronounced the economic benefits of a healthy working environment. In his evidence to the Children's Employment Commission he stressed that exploited workers in poor conditions did not produce high quality work.[38] It was a philosophy few Jewish workshop masters were prepared to acknowledge. However, other factory owners did. In 1884 Joseph Hepworth moved to what had previously been a woollen warehouse in which his 500 operatives worked in 'clean and healthy conditions using sophisticated machinery'.[39] According to *Mercantile Age*, 'remarkably healthy females' operated Singer sewing machines which produced 2,000 stitches per minute in order to keep up with the demands of a circular steel cutting knife, which cut 100 suits at a time, 'at great speed'.[40] Four years later Hepworth's 2,000 operatives were producing garments for the company's 107 retail outlets.[41] Arthur & Co.'s move south proved highly successful. Within ten years the company was producing half a million suits a year and providing employment for 1,500 indoor workers and 400 outdoor workers in sub-divisional workshops.[42] The buoyant market encouraged long-established Leeds companies to change direction. The Co-operative Wholesale Society opened its own clothing production unit in 1888 and, in the same year, capmakers W. Buckley changed over to the manufacture of tailored garments. By the decade's close the eight largest wholesale clothing companies in Leeds employed between them 9,840 clothing workers; Hepworth and Stuart & MacDonald employing over 2,000 each, Barran and Arthur approximately 1,500 each.[43] However, until 1888 clothing operatives showed little interest in labour organisation. As we shall see, within a year, all this changed.

An air of confidence surrounded the wholesale clothing industry. The *Yorkshire Factory Times*, founded by Joseph Burgess in July 1889 with the intention of 'ranking itself by the side of workmen ... as a voice for the workman in the court of public opinion'[44] reported in its third issue that, 'No sooner does a new firm come into town and commence business than they find after a short space of time their premises too small ... failures are conspicuous by their absence.'[45] After the excitement of the 1880s the Leeds wholesale clothiers settled into a pattern of steady growth. The Boer War put a brake on many businesses, but the Leeds clothiers continued to prosper, taking advantage of the demand for uniforms. Some manufacturers even produced garments for both sides in the conflict.[46] Export to South Africa accounted for a large percentage of the wholesale clothing trade,[47] which in the ten years between 1893 and 1903, increased by 18 per cent,[48] encouraging Hepworth to open retail shops in Johannesburg. The entry of Germany and North America into the export market early in the twentieth century reduced the level of trade with the Antipodes[49] but this was compensated for by trade with South Africa exceeding expectations. In 1913 the Board of Trade revealed that the value of 'non-waterproofed apparel of wool or of wool mixed with other materials' exported to South Africa amounted to £3,280,114. The value of garments sent to other colonial territories was as follows: Australia £989,957; New Zealand £710,809; Canada £679,607 and British India £314,359.[50]

As the nineteenth century drew to its close changes crept into the system of production. Fluctuations in wages and the depressed economy forced bespoke tailors in London and some major provincial cities to make surreptitious use of the Leeds factories. A London tailor defended the practice of sending garments to Leeds for making-up whilst the unsuspecting customer believed orders were 'made through' in their tailor's shop,[51] by saying that 'the finest work is up in Leeds'.[52] It may not have been 'the finest' but it did save time and money. A number of Leeds wholesale clothiers, of whom David Little claimed to be the first,[53] recognised the potential in developing what came to be known as the 'special measure' or 'special orders' department. For while the working man had adopted the habit of buying a ready-made 'lounge suit' for Sunday best, thus increasing demand in that sector of the wholesale clothing industry, certain members of the middle class, hit by the depression at the end of the nineteenth century, sought an alternative to the high-class bespoke tailor with his equally high prices. The new 'specials' departments were the answer. Drapers and tailors kept patterns of cloth from which their more discerning clientele could choose the style and material of garments which would then be made up in the factories and workshops of Barran, Arthur & Co., Little and other wholesale clothing companies. It was a forerunner of the system that Montague Burton developed to such an extreme of size and sub-division in the 1920s.

The new branch of the industry was an immediate success. Special order departments grew to enormous proportions, feeding markets all over the world.[54] Separate cutting departments were designated and provisions were made for specialised and skilled workers to be kept on even when times were quiet. This was a far cry from the evils of the lower end of the trade where seasonal workers so often led lives of penury during the 'slack'. The new departure was not without its cost. In the early years of the twentieth century, with the economy once again in recession, John Barran stipulated that his company would not offer the special order service unless retailers 'did a good ready-made trade'.[55]

In spite of the economic peaks and troughs of the first decade of the twentieth century the major clothing companies in Leeds continued to expand. New factories were opened and a balance was found between ready-made and special order. The years ahead were anticipated with excitement and enthusiasm. Hopes were quashed by the outbreak of hostilities in August 1914. The declaration of war resulted in an immediate halt in production. However, this was short-lived, relieved by government orders for more than 100,000 uniforms.

The fifty-nine years between the opening of Barran's Alfred Street factory and the outbreak of the First World War represent a period of impressive growth in the history of the Leeds wholesale clothing industry. In the early 1850s the purchase of newly made tailored outer garments was a privilege reserved for the middle class and the upper stratum of the working class. The building of large factories and the introduction of modern technology, coupled with the use of sub-divisional workshops, enabled wholesale clothiers to increase output, lower levels of skill and satisfy a variety of consumers ranging from labouring men who could afford no more than 15s. 0d. for an overcoat, to artisans, shopkeepers and white-collar workers who bought special order suits which cost as much as £3.15s.0d.[56]

JEWISH WORKSHOPS

Whether the rapid growth of the Leeds wholesale clothing industry would have been possible without the parallel development of the Jewish sub-divisional workshops remains a subject for conjecture. What we do know is that it was the refusal of the English journeymen tailors to sacrifice their craft status that forced John Barran, and successive wholesale clothiers, to turn to the alien alternative. Jewish tailors did not invent sub-divisional tailoring but they did develop and extend the concept; in Leeds to the extreme. Once it was incorporated into the structure of wholesale clothing manufacture it became virtually impossible to dispense with what has to be acknowledged as far more than the peripheral, or subsidiary, group of workers that some commentators have suggested were solely engaged in production generated by factory 'backlogs'.[57] The collaboration between John Barran and Herman Friend created a new industrial structure in Leeds and sowed the seeds for the immigration of Jews from eastern Europe. The development of the Leeds wholesale clothing industry precipitated an 'alien invasion' which changed the face of what had been, until the 1860s, a small artisan and business-class Jewish community.

There had been a Jewish presence in Leeds since the third quarter of the eighteenth century.[58] Chroniclers of provincial Jewry record that in the 1820s there were a Jewish optician, jeweller, silversmith and wool importer as well as professional and business men.[59] The remark made during the 1832 Reform election campaign that the Tory candidate was 'out to capture the Jewish vote',[60] suggests that the small community was mostly English-born, or naturalised, and of good economic standing. The settlement of the early eastern European immigrants followed the traditional urban pattern; the latest arrivals moving into an area vacated by an earlier group. In the case of the Leylands, the alien Jews followed the Irish settlers who had arrived in the first half of the nineteenth century. By 1861 the Irish community which numbered some 15,000 had begun to move away from the triangular area to the north-east of Leeds bounded by North Street, East Street and Briggate, to be replaced by Jews from eastern Europe. The proximity of the two groups and their common occupation of tailoring encouraged a degree of interaction, even though the Irish tailors worked in the bespoke sector of the trade and the Jews found employment in the sub-divisonal workshops. It was from amongst the early arrivals that Friend recruited the workshop hands who enabled him to service Barran's Alfred Street factory. Among them were future master tailors including David Lubelski, Jacob Frais and Solomon Camrass; men whose success would identify them as the stereotypical Jewish economic man, independently successful and upwardly mobile – the Leeds Jewish 'alrightniks'[61]; they were part of a fortunate, if not ruthless, minority. The later arrivals, who formed the army of the Leeds Jewish tailoring work-force, suffered the hardship of a trade which fulfilled the true meaning of 'sweating', long hours, low pay and poor conditions.

But what encouraged the immigrants of the late 1860s and early 1870s to choose Leeds as their destination? They arrived at the ports of London and Hull without skills, jobs or, in most instances, families.

They understood little or no English and apart from their pathetic few belongings carried with them just one vital document, a piece of paper upon which was written the legend LEEDS. It was not by chance that they sought work in the Jewish sub-divisional tailoring workshops of the Leylands. Their presence was a direct result of recruitment by a Leeds-based eastern European master tailor, Moyshe (Morris) Goodman. Goodman, later to prove himself a successful and colourful entrepreneur, arrived in Leeds from Kovno in 1866, conscious of the economic potential the West Riding city's wholesale clothing industry offered. As the industry grew, and with it the need for more sub-divisional workers, Goodman made a number of journeys back and forth to Poland, recruiting tailors from in and around Kovno and Warsaw to work in Leeds.[62] It would not have taken much to persuade the young men of Kovno province that a golden future awaited them in Leeds. The best they could expect as a journeyman tailor in Russia-Poland was an average annual wage of between 100 and 300 roubles for working in conditions which were overcrowded and insanitary[63] in a country where political, religious and social persecution was the order of the day.

It was inevitable that, as the originally small Jewish population of the Leylands expanded and prospered, divisions would develop between the 'Aenglishers' and the more recent 'Grinner' (Greener) arrivals.[64] In 1850 the Jewish population of the city was 100 souls,[65] while by 1878 there were over 500 families. Religious needs were served by two main synagogues plus several small *chevras* (small houses of worship).[66] The increased size and wealth of the Leylands Aenglisher community enabled them to rebuild their synagogue, which was first consecrated in 1860.[67] The new synagogue in Belgrave Street, which was modelled on Leeds Parish Church, had seating capacity for over one thousand.[68] It was a lavish edifice which celebrated the affluence of its congregation. Whilst the Aenglishers worshipped in the Victorian splendour of Belgrave Street the Grinners attended their own, simply designed and furnished synagogue in St Albans Street, founded in 1869 by, amongst others, Moyshe Goodman.[69] Here, too, socio-economic differences prevailed, as one member recalled: the poorer congregants sat apart from their more affluent brothers in a lower 'cellar like' area.[70] Not even death narrowed the division. The wealthier departed were interred in the higher, better drained ground of the Gildersome cemetery, separated by a low wall from their poorer brothers buried downhill. Socio-economic divisions did not always override communal ties.

Within the synagogue,[71] in the Leylands and even in the workshop, bonds of religion and kin at times held fast. The working Jewish tailor, machiner, presser or slipper-maker adopted a role in keeping with the occasion; exploited hand, consoling mourner or even employee inviting his employer to celebrate a son's bar mitzvah[72] or daughter's wedding. Class divisions were sometimes blurred by the nexus of community, a factor not to be ignored when considering the lifespan of small-scale trade unions.

It was not until the 1870s that the leaders of Leeds Jewry, who according to one Leeds historian, were 'a little pompous',[73] reacted to the increasing presence of pauper aliens in the city. Even so, the provisions made were not comparable to those set in place in the capital by the Cousinhood,[74] the London élite of the Anglo-Jewish establishment. Through their network of communal activities, which included schools, such as the Jewish Free School, opened in 1817, a number of religious, charitable and housing organisations, boys' clubs and, as we shall see below, benign trade unions,[75] they operated covert controls, attempting at the same time to accelerate the Anglicisation process. Neither can an analogy be made with Manchester where the established Jewish community dated back to the mid-eighteenth century and which, by the first quarter of the nineteenth century, 'had been transformed into a large and respected body of well-to-do shopkeepers, export merchants and professional men, an integral part of the bourgeoisie'.[76] By the middle of the nineteenth century Manchester Anglo-Jewry was manifesting anxiety about the growing numbers of aliens. This precipitated a response strongly reminiscent of that which was manifest in the capital.[77] There was no such establishment network in Leeds and it was not until 1878 that the Leeds Jewish Board of Guardians was founded. Its founders, the élite of the Belgrave Street Synagogue, evidently subscribed to the Anglo-Jewish philosophy, 'if you have poor and needy in your midst, do not let them become a charge on the Gentile Community. Look after them yourselves.'[78] In common with their London and Manchester cousins the alrightniks of Leeds Jewry were eager to be accepted by the host society. In 1888 the reporter from the *Lancet* commented on the fact that many of the Jews of the Leylands considered themselves to be 'Yorkshiremen who practised the Jewish religion'.[79]

The Jewish tailoring work-force of the Leylands was not as self-contained as that in Whitechapel and interaction with the indigenous community took place on two levels. The demands of trade necessitated the purchase of trimmings and workshop tools from Gentile tradesmen whilst the Jewish addiction to gambling had Jewish workers rushing to the pub to place their bets. On one occasion, when a workshop master refused his hands a small cash advance so that they could put the money on a 'hot tip', the disgruntled tailors called an instant strike. Gambling was a vice which the socialist trade unionist, Joseph Finn, writing in the first edition of the *Poilishe Yidel* in July 1884, believed resulted in 'everyone's miserable wage being squandered away'.[80] The Anglo-Jewish establishment believed that, in keeping with the ethos of self-help, in the same way that the English worker was poor because he drank, the Jewish worker was poor because he gambled. Morris Winchevsky,[81] the Jewish socialist writer, took a more sympathetic and realistic approach, blaming the capitalist mode of production and the iniquitous distribution of profit for the immigrant's propensity for gambling. As he described in his heart-rending Yiddish pamphlet, *Zi Aur* (Let There Be Light), the worker was driven to drink and to gamble out of desperation at the plight of his family, 'When there is no work and a child at home is sick from lack of food ... and the other children cry "father, bread" ... a man can be forgiven for drinking whisky and gambling'.[82]

There are no available records which chart the success and failure of the Jewish workshop hands but it can be safely assumed that only a minority made a successful and lasting transition from hand to master. The journey to independence was hard, requiring tenacity and physical and mental strength and ability. As Professor Fishman stressed, writing of the immigrant in London's East End at the end of the nineteenth century, 'only the ruthless few made it'.[83] In the very early years of the wholesale clothing industry perhaps not all those who made the transition were ruthless. Some were craft journeymen from large cities such as Warsaw, not unskilled peasants and untrained youths from ghetto towns and villages. In other words, they were members of that small minority who benefited from Talmudic training. One such was David Lubelski who arrived in Leeds from Warsaw in 1866.[84] His first job was as a hand in Herman Friend's workshop. In 1873 he set up on his own and by 1887 employed between 60 and 70 hands. In 1889 he opened a factory at Park Cross Street and entered the ranks of wholesale clothiers.[85] Lubelski was a radical believer in the rights of the working man and in the beneficial role of the trade union. He made no secret of this and during the 1888 Leeds Jewish tailors' strike shared platforms with trade union leaders and members of the Socialist

League. A furious Jewish Master Tailors' Association served him with a notice of censure which he promptly tore up.[86] A man of wealth and standing within the community, he was appointed Honorary Treasurer of New Hebrew Congregation ('Greener' Synagogue) in 1881[87] and President of the Jewish Young Men's Association in 1896. In 1904 his son Jack became the first Jew to be elected to the Leeds City Council.[88] Lubelski and the other early workshop masters reinforced the wholesale clothing industry in Leeds, providing the indirect plant, machinery and labour which facilitated its expansion.

By the late 1870s things were changing. There was no longer a need to actively recruit labour from the Pale of Settlement. The ever-widening pool of hungry immigrants now provided a source of cheap fuel for the furnaces of the wholesale clothing industry. Ruthless masters exploited their newly arrived co-religionists to the full, sowing the seeds of labour discontent which would colour the next half century.

The increase in the number and size of the Leeds Jewish tailoring workshops was concurrent with that of the clothing factories. As masters extended their existing workshops and enlarged their work-force, hands took the plunge and set up on their own, taking advantage of cheap sewing machine rental and low rents. The result was a number of large-scale workshops, a plethora of medium to small workshops and intensified competition over price and delivery times. In the final analysis, as the years went by, it became only that 'ruthless few' that made it. Joseph Finn found the growing Jewish proletariat of sufficient significance to make it the subject of a graphic report in the first edition of the *Poilishe Yidel* issued in July 1884:

> There are many Jewish workers (in Leeds). Almost all of them belong to the tailoring trade. Many are machiners, under-machiners, pressers, under-pressers, second (or plain) tailors and tailors who work with needle and thread. I do not know the exact number of workers. I can only say there are a lot ... Most of the workers have not been in England long. Some less than a year, some several years. Mostly greeners learning a part of the tailoring trade. Each worker has a learner living with him. Templar Street in Leeds is a ghetto as existed in the old days in Rome, Prague and Frankfurt on Main.[89]

The decade of the 1880s was one of intellectual and social ferment. New thought currents were flowing through the minds of those concerned with the aim, direction and morality of society. The publication of Henry George's 'aggressive and optimistic' *Progress and Poverty* led to the socialist philosophy becoming more than just a topic for middle class drawing-room discussion. The plight of the unemployed and the residuum, with the accompanying problems of poverty and the sweated industries, were highlighted by works such as Mearns's *Bitter Cry of Outcast London*, the revelations of Sims and Stead and the findings of Charles Booth. The problems of poverty, unemployment and alien immigration could no longer be ignored by a government made uneasy by the restlessness of the poor and fearful of the, albeit unrealistic, threat of revolution. A variety of commissions and surveys were established, one of the most important being that which was launched to investigate the sweating system. Although London was at the heart of the inquiry the major industrial cities were also placed under the microscope. Leeds was drawn into the net following an outbreak of smallpox in and around the Leylands district during 1888. Between 1888 and 1891 a reporter for the *Lancet*, John Burnett on behalf of the government and Clara Collet for the *Economic Journal*, all visited Leeds to report on the sweating system in the city. There was a certain amount of confusion as to the severity of conditions. Miss Collet actually denied the existence of a sweating system in Leeds,[90] a conclusion inconsistent with the majority of reports. Writing some years later, Joseph Finn recalled that the workers suffered fiendish conditions.[91] David Lubelski, in his evidence to the House of Lords Select Committee on Sweating in 1889, confirmed that hands were forced to live and work in 'wretched conditions',[92] whilst bootmaker James Sweeney, one-time secretary of the Jewish tailors' society and a founder member of the Socialist League, giving evidence on behalf of the Jewish tailors' society,[93] described in graphic terms the long hours, low pay and filthy workshops that were the lot of the eastern European sub-divisional tailor.[94] There was also debate over the sanitary state of the workshops. Burnett concluded that the Leeds workshops were 'cleaner, larger and better ventilated than those in London',[95] whilst the reporter from the *Lancet* revealed that even in the largest workshops there was constant danger from infection, 'floors were rarely if ever cleaned ... the revolting state of the water closets resulted in an appalling stench'. There was little consolation in the fact that he found the state of some of the high-class English tailoring workshops to be no better.[96] The Leeds Jewish Master Tailors' Association attempted to minimise the findings but there is little doubt that, irrespective of size, there was sufficient evidence[97] to prove that all but a small number of the Jewish tailoring workshops were as insanitary as their counterparts in London's East End.[98] In the 1890s attempts were made to introduce improvements but, not unexpectedly, employers displayed a general reluctance to undertake any which required financial outlay. In an effort to overcome the language problem a Yiddish-speaking Inspector of Nuisances with special responsiblity for Jewish workshops was appointed in 1889. But in 1910 Inspector Raskin was still criticising the low level of sanitary conditions in the alien workshops of Leeds.[99] One of the worst aspects was the use of domestic or 'bedroom' workshops. Their usage increased during the first decade of the twentieth century as the combined pressures of a depressed economy and increased competition demanded lower production costs. The health hazard became a major issue. Working in the unhealthy conditions of the master's bedroom all night, having done a full day's work elsewhere,[100] was unacceptable. In 1912, the secretary of the AJTMP, Moses Sclare, laid down a resolution at the annual Trades Union Congress Conference requesting the legal prohibition of bedroom workshops, citing examples where soldiers' uniforms were made up in employers' bedrooms. Conditions such as these threatened worker and public alike. The former suffered from overwork and an unhealthy working environment, the latter were subjected to diseases, such as smallpox and scarlet fever, incubated in garments which, during the making-up process, had been used as covering by the exhausted, cold and frequently sick occupants of the bedroom workshops. Sclare's resolution was passed by a majority of 133,000, but legislation, which would have ended the practice, was delayed by the outbreak of war in 1914 and workshop masters continued to hide bedroom workers in cupboards and water closets when inspectors, trade unionists and reporters were rumoured to be nearby.

Further confusion surfaced over the actual number of Jewish sub-contracting workshops in Leeds. The *Lancet* reporter, who spent a week in the city, discovered workshops in which 40, 70 and 80 hands were at work. He also found an old mill which had been converted into five workshops with space for up to 400 workers. From his *one-day* visit John Burnett concluded that, as a result of the structure of the Leeds clothing industry, 'Jewish sweaters needed to [operate], and operated on, a much bigger scale than London' and that large work-shops held in excess of 40 machines and up to 80 hands.[101] Obviously it was much easier to investigate the large to medium workshops than to spend time unearthing those that were small and hidden away in back alleys, attics, living rooms and bedrooms. The *Lancet* reporter found only one small workshop in which ten hands were at work![102] Whilst there was general agreement that the average workshop provided jobs for 25–35 employees and that what was considered large in London, that is, a workshop in which 8–12 hands were at work, was small in Leeds,[103] there was no consensus over numbers. In 1888 when research for the House of Lords Commission on the Sweating System was being carried out, estimates varied from 51 to 101,[104] in 1894 the *Board of Trade Report on the Volume and Effects of Recent Immigration from Eastern Europe into the United Kingdom* stated that there were 98 Jewish tailoring workshops in Leeds,[105] whilst in 1903 the Leeds Medical Officer for Health recorded 180 Jewish tailoring workshops in the city.[106] In each instance the numbers accounted only for those establishments that were 'discovered'. What we can say is that as the years went by the numbers and sizes of the sub-divisional workshops increased. Factory-like workshops, several storeys high, containing over a hundred workers[107] were now a part of the structure of the Leeds wholesale clothing industry. In all but legal definition they were factories.[108]

Gradually a number of eastern Europeans tailors joined the ranks of wholesale clothiers listed in Kelly's *Directory for Leeds* as they made the transition from hand- or foot-operated machinery to power. Market forces meant that not everyone stayed on the higher rungs of the ladder, some being forced to revert back to the role of workshop master or, even worse, tailoring hand. The outbreak of the First World War resulted in an increase in the numbers of Jewish factories and workshops. Masters manufacturing army uniforms were forced to adopt the use of power in order to operate machines that could meet the demands of the heavy materials of which uniforms were made; they now joined the ranks of wholesale clothiers.[109] Numbers were further swollen by the arrival of entrepreneurs and profiteers eager to take advantage of the demand for military uniforms and the accompanying relaxation in stringent conditions of production. In spite of the expansion, Moses Sclare was proud to announce in 1915 that 'not less than 25 per cent of the male membership (of the AJTMP) have enlisted in the various army units and several members have joined the navy.'[110]

As illustrated above, the Leeds wholesale clothing industry developed from small beginnings to become, by the outbreak of the

First World War, one of the city's dominant industries. In the sixty years between 1851 and 1911 its work-force increased by 2,350 per cent.[111] Throughout the period the system of separation yet interdependence survived, as Harry Witney, Leeds Branch Secretary of AUCO, explained: 'all wholesale clothiers in Leeds employ Jewish outworkers for the making of coats and jackets. The waistcoats and trousers are made in the factory workshops.'[112]

WORKERS AND WAGES

Until the early years of the twentieth century when the clothing industry's seemingly never-ending supply of tailors and tailoresses began to slow down,[113] the availability of a constant and regenerating pool of labour was a major factor in the expansion and success of the Leeds wholesale clothing industry. For different reasons and different rates of pay, men and women entered factories and workshops. Some were eager to become part of one of the city's major areas of industrial expansion while others were prepared to accept sweated conditions and low wages in order just to survive. Whatever the motivation there is no doubt as to the growth of the labour force and the change of dominant gender. In 1851 the decennial census recorded the presence in Leeds of 1,935 males and just 29 females[114] engaged in the production of tailored garments. Sixty years later the ratio had reversed; of the recorded total of 23,542 clothing workers in the city 7,625 were male and 15,917 female,[115] three tailoresses to every tailor.

Women

John Barran's invention of the bandknife revolutionised the wholesale clothing industry and catapulted it into the modern industrialising world. He was highly conscious of the growth of new consumer markets and the desire of the working class female to acquire a level of economic independence. By dividing manufacture between factory and workshop and using females as the bulk of his indoor work-force he was able to take advantage of a reservoir of female labour which was ideally suited to that branch of the industry's low skill requirement and the correspondingly lower wage. For though factory girls received a 'decent' wage,[116] before fines, they were still far cheaper to employ, and for the most part far less demanding, than their male counterparts. The developing structure of the wholesale clothing industry in Leeds provides us with an example of Braverman's theory of the secondary role of female labour and the way in which new technology created a labour shift in favour of women,[117] whose expectations were less than those of their male counterparts and who were schooled from birth to accept their subordinate role. Neither must we ignore the way in which the semi-skilled and unskilled immigrants, desperate for work, aided and abetted that movement.

The increase in the number of tailoresses is one of the more striking facets of the growth of the wholesale clothing industry in Leeds. But whilst the female labour force was expanding it was, at the same time, becoming increasingly sub-divided, the divisions those of class as well as those of skill. There is no doubt that the largest and most prestigious companies, with their airy working conditions and reasonable rates of pay, were able to pick the cream of the female labour pool. At the other end of the scale, according to the reporter from the *Lancet*, the lower class, older English females found employment in Jewish workshops where they were paid lower wages to perform the more menial tasks.[118] Jewish tailoring masters disagreed. They told Clara Collet that the English girls in their employ were superior workers to those in the factories.[119] Was this due to age or the extra strength and skill required to work on coats and jackets?

The Leeds tailoresses showed a marked preference for 'indoor' factory work though factory life was not without its pressures, which in 1889 exploded into industrial action. There is no accurate record of the numbers of women employed in the clothing factories. But in 1892 the Royal Commission on Labour distributed a questionnaire to employers in an attempt to collate contemporary statistics. Few of the Leeds wholesale clothiers replied, but from those that did we learn that, of John Barran's 1,440 clothing operatives, 1,120 were female,[120] a ratio of over 3:1. The only other Leeds wholesale clothier to provide information for the Commission was Gaunt and Murson. The company employed a total factory labour force of 500 of which 450 were women, a ratio of 9:1.[121] From the reports of the Leeds tailoresses' strike in 1889 we learn more about the gender balance of Arthur & Co.'s labour force. Fifteen hundred operatives worked in the factory, of which at least 900 were female, as that was the number of tailoresses who went on strike in 1889; thus there was a female to male ratio of 3:1.[122] With only these few statistics available it is impossible to gauge accurately the number of women employed in the Leeds clothing factories in the last years of the nineteenth century. The indefatigable Miss Collet, following her week's stay in the city, reported that 8,000 out of the 10,000 women employed in the industry worked in the factories.[123] The decennial census for the same year as Miss Collet's visit, 1891, put the total figure of tailoresses in factory and workshop at 10,919, whilst the *Yorkshire Factory Times* considered the number closer to 25,000.[124] The actual figure lay somewhere between 16,000 and 18,000.

The information made available to the 1892 Royal Commission shows that those employed in the modern clothing factories of Leeds enjoyed regular and tolerable working hours. John Barran operated a fifty-two and one-half-hour week, from 8 a.m. to 6.30 p.m. Monday to Friday, with one hour allowed for dinner, and a half day, 8 a.m.–1 p.m. on Saturdays (excluding overtime). Employees were permitted ten days' unpaid holiday per year and up to three weeks' sick leave.[125] In 1906, following successful negotiations by AUCO, the working week in fourteen of the major clothing factories in Leeds was reduced to one of between forty-nine and one-half and forty-eight and one-half hours (excluding overtime), with no reduction in wages.[126] If the hours were acceptable, were the rates of pay? On the surface, taking account of what appeared as 'gross' pay, the answer at first sight might appear to be yes.

It was speed of production that determined take-home pay for the female clothing operative. The girls were paid piece rates, or as Clara Collet, whose researches provided the figures quoted below, explained, 'according to how much a worker did in a day'.[127] Therefore the girl who took home the most money at the end of the week was not necessarily the most skilled, just the most dextrous. For example, according to Collet's findings, binders and buttonholers received as much as £1. 10s. and £1. 5s., respectively, for a full fifty-two-and-one-half hour week's work. But it was the machinists, whose top rate of pay was only 18s. 0d. per week, who were considered the most skilled of the female operatives. What Collet's statistics did not make clear was whether the wages quoted were gross or net. For there were undisclosed deductions. One of the industry's more unpleasant practices was the imposition of the fine and truck system to which nearly all the wholesale clothiers subscribed. Fines were imposed for lateness and for work poorly made or damaged. Take-home pay was further reduced by charges for the use of power, thread and kitchen facilities. The *Yorkshire Factory Times* described the system as one which could 'reduce an operative's pay from a living wage to a sum which should induce females in the clothing factories to combine'.[128] The article was published in August 1889 after a young operative told a reporter that she earned only 7*d*. for making a pair of trousers that sold for 13*s*. 0*d*. Not surprisingly, given the explosive climate of that long hot summer and autumn, the Leeds tailoresses went on strike in the October. All the filtered air and dining facilities in the world could not compensate for a wage that fell below the poverty line. The fine system was not peculiar to the clothing industry. It had proved the catalyst for the East End match-girls' strike of 1888. The match-girls, led by that flamboyant Fabian, Annie Besant, had demanded an end to fines imposed for dropping matches, answering back, dirty feet or for leaving spent matches on a bench.[129] Other female workers suffered equally: as late as 1907 shop assistants were being fined for incorrectly addressing a customer as Miss rather than Madam, for uneconomic use of paper and string or for misplacing an invoice.[130]

Although the Leeds tailoresses' strike of 1889 went some way towards removing certain of the iniquities, the women enjoyed little real financial advancement. As the new century dawned money wages slowed almost to a standstill and real wages actually fell. In 1906 the average full-time wage for female operatives was 13*s*. 8*d*.,[131] whilst those on the lower rungs of the ladder earned as little as 7*s*. 0*d*. per week.[132] Whether it was the continued imposition of the fine and truck system in the factory, as suggested by the *Yorkshire Factory Times* in 1910,[133] or redundancies which followed a fall in demand, the decade between 1901 and 1911 saw a rise of only 11 per cent in the female clothing work-force, the lowest in sixty years. Then, as the economy improved and demand increased, there was a sudden flurry of concern over the shortage of female operatives[134] as a number of girls had taken up the offers of free passage and good wages made by Canadian clothing factories.[135]

Although some older English females sought employment in the Jewish tailoring workshops, Clara Collet discovered that the ratio of Jewish to non-Jewish women working in the sub-divisional sector was almost 2:1. In the 75 workshops she investigated in 1894, a total of 900 females were employed, of whom 308 were Gentile.[136] The problems of language and religion meant that Jewesses in search of work had no alternative but the sweatshop, where they were exploited along with their male co-workers. By the second decade of the twentieth century the processes of acculturation and assimilation had reached a point at which ethnicity was no longer a barrier to employment, and consequently some Jewish tailoresses made the transition to factory work.

Females employed in the Jewish workshops worked at least ten and one-half hours a day. Frequently they toiled for fourteen hours or more per day in a working week which varied in length according to season and demand. Workshop masters were adept at condensing production into as short a time as possible, particularly when payment was based on a daily rate; methods of payment varied between piece and daily rates. John Burnett's *Report on the Sweating System*, published in 1888, showed that machinists, working a full three-day week, with a rapid output, could earn betwen 15s. 0d. and 18s. 0d. per week, equal to their counterparts in the factory, an example of dexterity and level of skill determining income and status. Other rates fell below factory level: a feller could expect to take home no more than between 7s. 0d. and 9s. 0d. a week, whilst a buttonholer earned 5d. for every twelve buttonholes she completed.[137] Although technology in the wholesale clothing industry opened the door for the use of female labour and the rhythm of deskilling, at the same time new, if lesser, skills were created which brought with them a hierarchy as well as workshop segregation.

Both John Burnett and Clara Collet remarked on the demarcation lines operating in the Jewish sub-divisional workshops. Machining was the most clearly segregated job. Burnett found that 113 out of the 114 machinists[138] he interviewed were non-Jewish. He quoted the words of one master who stated that 'machinists are mostly English as Jewesses are unable to spare the time to learn machining',[139] though Clara Collet thought it was 'due to their youth that Jewesses are less skilled than their English co-workers'. Jewish girls employed in the sweatshops were either buttonholers or fellers whilst English girls not employed as machinists found work as finishers.[140]

One of the chief indicators of a growth industry in the second half of the nineteenth century was the number of employed single females, as almost all females employed in factories were unmarried. A report in the decennial census for 1901 confirmed that an area in which the number of single female workers outnumbered those who were married or widowed was invariably one of industrial production. Jane Lewis has suggested that, at a national level, the employment of married women was low. According to her study, between 1901 and 1911 the ratio of single working women to married working women was 78 per cent to 13 per cent, the remainder split between widowed, divorced, deserted or separated females.[141] Women who left the work-force only rejoined it if financial circumstances demanded. English and Jewish females employed in the wholesale clothing factories and sub-divisional workshops were almost always unmarried. The 1901 Census Report highlighted the spinster status of female clothing opera-tives: of the 14,021 female clothing workers recorded as employed in Leeds, 11,740 were single.[142] Three-quarters of John Barran's female workers were aged between 18 and 22,[143] and as 'most women under 25 employed in the tailoring, clothing and outfitting trades are un-married',[144] they too were no doubt single. The marital status of the female tailoring work-force and the low numbers of married workers goes some way towards explaining the apathetic support for organisa-tion. Marriage was always in view and thus monies spent on union dues, unless there was a strike in progress and benefits were being paid, were considered an unnecessary outlay. It was not until the introduc-tion of health insurance in 1911 that female trade union membership increased; then tailoresses lost no time in claiming benefits.[145] During her visits to the sub-divisional workshops Clara Collet interviewed 224 English women, of whom 48 were either married or widowed, and 307 Jewish women, of whom only 17 were married or widowed. In line with mid-Victorian thinking, Miss Collet believed that Jewish women rarely if ever worked after marriage, 'a Jewish wife living with her husband makes no attempt to be a wage earner',[146] though wives and daughters would often lend a hand in the family workshop when the occasion demanded. Thus, the Jewish wife may not have been a *wage* earner, but, when times were hard, as research has shown, she 'earned' money from a variety of different sources.

Men

The successful mass production of men's tailored clothes was the result of the introduction of modern technology and the growth of new markets. Working-class and lower-middle-class consumers were less discerning than their more affluent brothers, prepared to buy new garments even if they were not hand stitched or made through by one craftsman. As the deskilling process accelerated the dividing line between the highest quality bespoke and the mass-produced garment became increasingly well defined. This is not to suggest that skill was eradicated or that there were no craftsmen to be found in the factory. On the contrary, the wholesale clothing industry created its own hierarchy at the head of which was the cutter, the aristocrat of the factory. Style, cut and, particularly in mass production, economy, were dependent on his prudent use of the bandknife, shears or whatever cutting technique was favoured. With the exception of the bespoke tailoring shops, cutting in Leeds was carried out in the factories. The measure or pattern cutter prepared the general pattern while the stock cutter positioned patterns so as to cut the cloth as economically as possible. Bundles of freshly cut garments were then passed on to the factory operatives or Jewish sub-contractors and middlemen for making-up. According to the Report of the Royal Commission on Labour, John Barran's factory employed 100 men and boys in the cutting room 'whilst all of the company's 64 apprentices were learning the art of cutting'.[147]

Cutting was a jealously guarded skill. The Leeds wholesale cutters were concerned to protect their craft and did so by restricting apprentice entry. As befitted their status, cutters ranked at the top of the wages scale. Understandably, the highest rate was paid to those working in the bespoke sector where, in the early years of the twentieth century, a craftsman could earn an average of £2. 15s. 0d. for a full week's work. Cutters in the wholesale sector commanded the highest wages. The average weekly income for a cutter in Leeds, in the 1880s, was between £1 and £2,[148] dependent on level of skill, volume of demand and, of course, the time of year. The *Board of Trade Report into Earnings and Hours*, published in 1906, shows that rates increased by 25 per cent over a twenty-year period. The same report reveals that factory machiners earned on average £1. 10s. 0d. per week and pressers £1. 7s. 0d.[149] Although far fewer in number than their female counterparts, there being, by 1911 only an estimated 3,500 to 4,000 male operatives employed in the Leeds clothing factories,[150] it was the male clothing operatives that made up the hard core of AUCO, the major participant in the amalgamation of 1915.

The bulk of the male tailoring work force of Leeds was employed in the sub-divisional sweatshops of the Leylands. Little changed until the 1930s when the practice of sub-contracting was modified and a number of Jewish workers made the move from workshop to factory.[151] The transient nature of the Jewish immigrant population before the First World War makes it difficult to establish the exact size of the Jewish male tailoring labour force in Leeds. Decennial figures suggest that the number rose from 1,588 in 1881[152] to some 7,000 in 1911.[153] Throughout that period the eastern European segment of the city's tailoring work-force was approximately 25 per cent of the total. Of the three-quarters of a million aliens estimated to have passed through England in the years between 1881 and 1911 only between 105,000 to 120,000 took up permanent residence,[154] the majority being on their way to the *Goldene Medineh*. This was confirmed by a Board of Trade investigator in 1894, who found that 'The great majority of Aliens who arrive from Continental ports are reported to be on the way to America and it is considered desirable to enter this fact'.[155] It is one that should be borne in mind when analysing statistics on the domicile or employment of aliens.

The newly arrived greener was ideally suited to the developing wholesale clothing industry. With few if any skills, he fulfilled the requirements of what Alfred Marshall called 'Babbage's great principle of economical production',[156] the monotonous, sub-divisional process of manufacture which enabled the employer to pay precisely for the amount of skill required for each task rather than for the maximum skill level throughout. There was no economic or human wastage in the clothing sweatshops. In his evidence to the Select Committee on Sweating, James Sweeney described how the system of production operated in a medium-sized Leeds Jewish tailoring workshop after the bundles had been collected from the wholesaler and given to the fitter-up. (With allowances to be made for size and extremes of sub-division the following description, though not necessarily the wages, can be applied to the London tailoring workshops of the same period.)

> From the fitter-up he hands them to the machiner; from the machiner in some particular branches, it goes to the under-presser; some other parts of the garment go to the tailor, what they call a tailor, that is, a baster out, and a baster under him; then there is the lining maker that pieces linings before they are put into a garment, to be stitched together and made up ready to be sent to the presser. Then the presser presses the garments off ... and they have to go through the finishers, feller hands, and button-hole hands, and then they come to, what they term, a brusher off, the garments then being all ready for going to the warehouse.[157]

The exact division of labour was determined by the size of the workshop. The larger the unit the more extreme the sub-division. The 1894 Report on Eastern European Immigration into the United Kingdom provided a breakdown of the deployment of men and boys in the Leeds workshops. It clearly illustrates the way in which size determined skill and usage. In the 95 workshops visited 1,130 men and boys and 990 women were at work. In each case the process favoured by the alien was machining, an explanation for the paucity of their female counterparts. The machiner held the profitability of the workshop quite literally in his hands; this, and the degree of skill the job demanded, validate the title 'aristocrat' of the workshop. Second in the hierarchy was the presser, who required not so much skill as strength to lift irons which could weigh up to 25lb each. The tailor, in the sub-divisional workshop, was not a craftsman, merely a hand, versed in only one operation, basting-under or basting-over. On the bottom of the rung were the sub-contracted workers, the under-pressers and plain machiners employed and paid by the presser and machiner. Sub-contracting within the workshop was a major barrier to the cohesive organisation of labour. It lessened employer responsibility and divided loyalties. Such was the antipathy that the AJTMP refused membership to those who employed sub-contracted labour.[158]

Workshop status determined both the length of the working day and rates of pay. In a letter written in 1943 Joseph Finn recalled his experiences as a machiner in a workshop in Leeds in 1885. He worked a twelve-hour day for which he earned between 6s. 0d. and 7s. 0d. The presser worked a thirteen-hour day for anything betwen 5s. 6d. and 6s. 0d. Lower down the scale came the tailor who took home no more than 6s. 0d. for his fourteen-hour day. But it was the 'poor devil underpresser who was forced to rise at 5 a.m. to light the oven in which the irons were heated and then work through till 9 p.m.' who suffered worst.[159] He was totally dependent on the earnings of the presser for his income. Standing apart from the 'hands' was the fixer. He earned the most money for working the shortest hours. His job was that of overseer as, in almost every instance, he was a general tailor who could make a garment through. In the small workshop the master would carry out the fixer's task which was a job that combined management and craft, engendering loyalty to employers rather than employees. In the busy season, in the 1880s, a fixer's earnings were on a par with that of the machiner at as much as £1. 10s. per week.

Men employed in the workshops fared no differently to women in that their take-home pay was totally dependent on the length of the working day and the volume of output. Once again dexterity rather than skill was the dominant factor. The length of the working week in the Jewish sub-divisional tailoring workshops varied from between three and five days in the busy period, known simply as the 'busy', which traditionally lasted from March until July and from October until late December, to as little as one, or even half a day in the slack period. Wages were based either on a daily basic rate or on the piece. At the end of the nineteenth century the average weekly wage of an alien tailor was reported to be between £1. 10s. and £1. 15s.[160] As these figures were based on the busy period the average over one year was far less, ranging between 15s. 0d. and 17s. 6d. per week. It was only the aristocrat of the workshop who could hope to earn in excess of Charles Booth's poverty line, which, in 1889, he set at between 18s. 0d. and £1. 1s.0d., per week.

Payment on a daily rate enabled employers to exploit their workers to the full. Normal practice was to withhold work until mid-week, with the result that a hand was forced to toil far into the night to complete his load on time. In this way masters saved up to three day's wages and still delivered on time. The readiness of workers to comply with this iniquitous practice resulted from the promise of overtime – a promise which, according to Joseph Finn, was rarely kept. When pressured for outstanding overtime payments masters would reply, 'God will pay you.' Finn believed that it was because the Jewish hands tolerated this treatment and 'held their masters as God' that the 'Jewish workers were hated by the Christians'.[161] Jewish workers would 'bend down for the masters to sit on them' rather than join trade unions.[162] The flames of anti-alienism, never far from the surface, were constantly fuelled by this acceptance of low wages and long hours, which English trade unionists saw as a denial of the brotherhood of labour. It was not until 1911, and the Smith Award,[163] which followed the Leeds Jewish tailors' strike of that year, that the seventy-hour working week was reduced to one of fifty-four hours.[164] There was a downside to the agreement as the effect on profits was so severe that a number of middlemen and masters were forced out of business and almost 300 tailoring hands made redundant.[165]

The infrastructure of the Leeds wholesale clothing industry was based on a system which brought two distinct methods of production together. One utilised innovatory technology, enabling the employment of semi-skilled and unskilled females in large, sanitary, custom-built factories. The other mode of manufacture took advantage of the immigrant's need to subsist and his drive toward economic independence and thus his willingness to exert maximum effort, for minimum reward, for future benefit. Both fitted the late-nineteenth-century pattern of developing mass production; extensive sub-division, polarisation of skill, use of a reservoir of stagnant labour and the growth of new, eager and more easily satisfied consumer markets. The parallel systems of production in the wholesale clothing industry were separated by divisions of gender, skill, religion and culture. That they were able to unite was due to the eventual, mutual recognition that only a single union could wield sufficient power to unite the skilled, semi-skilled and unskilled in a concerted attack against threats posed by further technological advance and increased deskilling, sweating and non-organised labour.

In Leeds that unification was hard fought and hard won. In addition to problems of race and gender there were those endemic to the industry. Seasonality, though not as severe a problem in Leeds as in London, took its toll on a stratum of the work-force and acted as a disincentive to union membership. Variations in skill levels created stumbling-blocks, as did sectionalisation within the female tailoring work-force. But if there were divisions amongst the women there were chasms between the eastern European tailors and their English counterparts. It took time and patience to dispel the fears and superstitions that surrounded the alien population. Jewish workers had to demonstrate their preparedness to participate in the fight against the employers and become willing members of the English labour movement. In 1891, the *Arbeiter Fraint* warned that the Jewish tailors could not succeed alone, 'they must unite internationally and with the Christian workers fight the general enemy'.[166] It took several decades for the message to be accepted but, as the next chapter describes, in 1914, for the 19 per cent of tailoring workers in Leeds who were trade union members, it was.

NOTES

1. T. Fentiman & Co., *An Historical Guide to Leeds and its Environs* (1858), quoted in Fraser, op. cit., p. 143.
2. In the 1901 decennial census the textile industry was shown as employing a total of 18,307 male and female workers, less than 10 per cent of the city's total work-force. By comparison the clothing industry gave employment to 19,813 or 10 per cent of the city's employed. Engineering accounted for 25,000 male workers or 10 per cent of the total male work-force and just under 12.5 per cent of those employed in Leeds, the population of which numbered 198,000.
3. R. Redmayne, *Ideals in Industry: The Story of M. Burton 1900–1951* (1951), p. 85.

4. *Men's Wear*, 26 Sept. 1903.
5. I am grateful to Harold Pollin for bringing the history of the company founded by George and Henry Holloway to my notice. In spite of the company's early entry into wholesale manufacture it did not move to its own custom-built factory until 1914. The history of the company was recorded in the *Gloucestershire Chronicle* (4 Aug. 1923) and in the *Stroud Valley Industrial Handbook* of 1963.
6. Kelly's *Leeds Directory*, 1881.
7. Robinson's *Directory for Leeds*, 1911.
8. Fraser, op. cit., p.28.
9. *Decennial Census*, PP 1801, VI and *Decennial Census 1851*, op. cit.
10. Wholesale ready-made tailored garments for women were a later innovation (*see* Ch.4 below). They were not manufactured by John Barran's company in Leeds until 1927. E. Ewing, *A History of Twentieth Century Fashion* (1975), p.126.
11. Leeds Mercury, 25 Aug. 1878.
12. As Barran's Stock Book for 1845–52 (in Leeds City Archives) shows, stock held in 1845 was valued at £131.4s.4d., seven years later the stock was valued at £2,380.15s.0d.
13. *Leeds Mercury*, 15 March 1879.
14. *Yorkshire Post*, 4 May 1905.
15. A patented sewing machine first appeared in England in 1753. Subsequent models were developed in England, France and America but none proved commercially viable until the appearance of the 'practical' machine invented by Isaac Merit Singer. In 1851 the machine patented by the American Elias Howe was exhibited at the Crystal Palace Exhibition and drew the following comment from the *Economist* in June 1851: 'the astounding velocity of the new sewing machine will extinguish the race of tailors'. In fact Howe's machine was not commercially successful due to its lack of a lockstitch facility. In reality the sewing machine did not annihilate the tailoring work-force and by 1856 Singer's machine, which embodied all the facilities necessary for practical tailoring, was being used by tailors in Leeds, London and other provincial cities. In 1865 a machine could be purchased for £4.4s. or hired out at a weekly rate. During the 1860s the popularity of the sewing machine grew and it found its way into private homes as well as factories and workshops. A number of different companies began to manufacture models which had the facility to embroider, gather, hem and so on.
16. Barran's was not the first attempt to introduce technology into cutting. In 1813 a circular cutter was tried out and in 1853 an endless steel knife put into service. However, it was the bandknife that proved to be one of the most successful cutting tools in wholesale clothing manufacture.
17. *John Barran Story*, undated pamphlet, Leeds City Archives.
18. *Royal Commission on Aliens 1903*, PP 1903, X, qq 15144.
19. *Report of the Royal Commission on Aliens*, op. cit., qq 14320.
20. A proportion of trousers and vests were made by homeworkers but their number was small in comparison with the homeworking labour force in the London tailoring trade.
21. *Report of the Truck Committee 1906*, PP 1908, LIX, qq 7086.
22. *House of Lords Select Committee on the Sweating System 1889*, PP 1889, XIV, qq 30966.
23. *Men's Wear*, 23 Nov. 1912.
24. *Mercantile Age*, 1 Oct. 1884.
25. John Barran & Co. Balance Sheet, 1911, Leeds City Archives.
26. *Men's Wear*, 3 Aug. 1912.
27. John Barran & Co., Minute Book, 21 Nov. 1907, Leeds City Archives.

28. Redmayne, op. cit., p.85.
29. *Decennial Census 1861*, op. cit. and *Decennial Census 1871*, op. cit.
30. Tailors who were sufficiently proficient to make a garment through.
31. *Royal Commission on Labour 1892*, PP 1892, XXXVI, Part IV, p.402.
32. Barran, who was later knighted, was Liberal MP from 1876 until 1885. He was also twice Lord Mayor of Leeds.
33. *Leeds Mercury*, 15 Feb. 1879.
34. Hamish Fraser, op. cit., 1981, pp.85–93.
35. Ibid.
36. J.F. Barclay, *The Story of Arthur & Co. Ltd.* (1953), p.24.
37. *Leeds Mercury*, 22 Feb. 1888.
38. *Children's Employment Commission Second Report*, 1864, op. cit.
39. *Mercantile Age*, 2 Sept. 1884.
40. Ibid.
41. *Leeds Mercury*, 22 Sept. 1888.
42. Barclay, op. cit., p.104.
43. *Leeds Mercury*, 22 Sept. 1888, 23 July 1889 and 8 May 1890. *Yorkshire Factory Times*, 19 July 1889. *Royal Commission on Labour*, PP 1892–94, Vol. XXIII, p.402.
44. *Yorkshire Factory Times*, 5 July 1889.
45. Ibid., 19 July 1889.
46. *Men's Wear*, 22 Feb. 1902.
47. Ibid., 16 Jan. 1903.
48. Ibid., 18 March 1903.
49. John Barran and Co., Minute Book, 19 May 1906, loc. cit.
50. R.H. Tawney, *Establishment of Minimum Rates in the Tailoring Industry* (1915), p.2.
51. While this was common to second-class bespoke tailors the practice was never followed by the élite Savile Row craftsmen who rarely gave work out.
52. *Clothiers' and Outfitters' World*, 2 Nov. 1895.
53. *Men's Wear*, 17 Jan. 1903.
54. *Clothiers and Outfitters' World*, 7 Sept. 1895.
55. John Barran & Co., Minute Book, 25 Nov. 1904, loc. cit.
56. W. Blackburn Brochure (undated but circa 1900–14), Leeds City Archives.
57. Both Lloyd Gartner (op. cit., p.89), and Bernard Gainer in *The Alien Invasion* (1972), p.18, suggest that the Leeds sub-divisional workshops depended on production backlogs. This is a suggestion which the division of labour, whereby the females in the factories produced vests and trousers and the Jewish workshops coats and jackets, would appear to belie.
58. C. Roth, *A History of the Jews In England* (1978 edn), p.230n.
59. E. Krausz, *Leeds Jewry* (1965), pp.1–2, C. Roth, *The Rise of Provincial Jewry* (1950), pp.81–2 and L. Saipe, *A History of the Jews of Leeds* (1985 edn).
60. Fraser, op. cit., p.277.
61. For an explanation of the term 'Jewish *alrightnik*' and its application to the Jewish immigrant experience of the late nineteenth century see Bill Williams, 'East and West in Manchester Jewry 1850–1914', in Cesarani, op. cit., p.16.
62. Information about Goodman's trips to and from Poland from a conversation with Dr G. Raisman, 25 July 1985.
63. Mendelsohn, op. cit., pp.12–13.
64. Before the mass influx from eastern Europe some of the early members of the Jewish community, such as Herman Friend, were of German or central European origin. They were emigrés who, after the failure of the 1848 revolutions which

resulted in a re-emergence of anti-semitism and a clampdown on political freedom, sought their futures elsewhere – see H.M. Sacher, *The Course of Modern Jewish History* (1982), pp.107–12. Others were early eastern European immigrants who were making their way up the socio-economic ladder and were classified as the 'Aenglishers' or 'Englishers'. 'Grinner' (Greener) was the name given to the semi-skilled and unskilled, more recently arrived, eastern European immigrants.

65. V.D. Lipman, *A Social History of Jews in England 1850–1950* (1954), p.187.

66. During 1880–81 there were two secessions from Belgrave Street. The leaders of both made overtures to the Reform West London Synagogue of British Jews, to establish a Leeds branch. Both attempts failed and it is obvious, from the correspondence of the time, that it was internal synagogal politics, not ideology, that led to the rifts which were later healed. See A. Kershen and J. Romain, *Tradition and Change: A History of Reform Judaism in Britain, 1840–1994* (forthcoming 1995), Ch.3.

67. In 1837 the Earl of Cardigan sold the Leeds Jewish community a plot of ground for £2 in Gelderd Road. This became the Jewish cemetery but it took a public appeal for funds in the *Leeds Mercury* in September 1838 to raise the money to consecrate the land.

68. *Jewish Chronicle*, 13 Sept. 1878.

69. L. Saipe, op. cit., p.17.

70. Information from Mr H. Raisman, former member of the community.

71. In 1884 Joseph Finn reported the presence of 'two large synagogues, one small synagogue and some private prayer groups all of which were filled on Saturdays and Holy Days'. See *Poilishe Yidel*, 25 July 1884.

72. Jewish boy's coming at age, usually at 13.

73. Saipe, op. cit., p.18.

74. *See* Chaim Bermant, *The Cousinhood* (1971).

75. *See* Gartner, Lipman, Bermant *et al.*

76. Williams, op. cit., p.31.

77. Ibid., pp.327–40.

78. Saipe, op. cit., p.18.

79. *Lancet*, 16 June 1888, p.1146.

80. *Poilishe Yidel*, 25 July 1884.

81. For biographical details of Winchevsky, *see* W.J. Fishman, op. cit. pp.138–51.

82. M. Winchevsky, *Zi Aur* (1885), Rollin Collection, loc. cit.

83. Fishman, op. cit., p.50.

84. *Select Committee on the Sweating System, 4th Report*, PP 1889, XIV, Vol.I qq 31657.

85. Ibid., qq 31654.

86. *Arbeiter Fraint*, 11 May 1888 and *Leeds Evening Express*, 23 May 1888.

87. *Jewish Chronicle*, 9 Dec. 1881.

88. Saipe, op. cit., p.23.

89. *Poilishe Yidel*, 25 July 1884.

90. C. Collet, 'Women's Work in Leeds', *Economic Journal*, Vol.I (1891), p.469.

91. Letter from Joseph Finn to A.R. Rollin, dated 27 October 1943, Rollin Collection, loc. cit.

92. *Select Committee on the Sweating System, 4th Report*, op. cit., qq 31709.

93. For Sweeney's role in the organisation of the Jewish tailoring work-force of Leeds, see Ch.3 below.

94. Ibid. qq 30285.

95. *Report to the Board of Trade on the Sweating System in Leeds, 1887*, PP 1888, LXXXXVI, p.3.

96. *Lancet*, op. cit., p.1147.
97. *Yorkshire Factory Times*, 18 June 1888 and 29 Aug. 1890. *Select Committee on Sweating System, 5th Report, 1890*, PP 1890, XVII, qq 1509.
98. For a fuller account of conditions in the Leeds workshops in the 1880s and 1890s, see Buckman, op. cit., pp.45–86.
99. *Report of Inspector for Factories, 1910*, PP 1911, XVII, p.52.
100. This practice was exposed by Moses Sclare, the General Secretary of the Leeds Jewish Tailors' Union in a letter to the Leeds *Jewish World* published on 11 Sept. 1908.
101. Burnett, *Report*, op. cit., p.3.
102. *Lancet*, op. cit p.1147.
103. Burnett, *Report*, op. cit., p.3.
104. *See* Collet, op. cit, and Buckman, op. cit., p.1.
105. *Board of Trade Report on Volume and Effects of Recent Immigration from Eastern Europe into the United Kingdom*, PP 1894, LXVIII.
106. Buckman, op. cit., p.2.
107. *Jewish Chronicle*, 4 Feb. 1898.
108. The 1878 Factory Act changed the definition of a factory from one of 'rule of hand', that a place with over fifty workers being designated a factory, establishments with fewer workers being designated workshops, to one by means of power; any workshop which used machinery driven by mechanical means, that is, steam, gas or water (electricity was not in common use at that time), subsequently came within the category of a factory.
109. *Chief Inspector of Factories Report 1914–1916*, PP 1914–16, XXI.
110. *22 Annual Report: Leeds Branch AJTMP, 1915*, Rollin Collection, loc. cit.
111. *Decennial Census 1851*, PP 1852–3, LXXVIII and *Decennial Census 1911*, PP 1913, LXXVIII.
112. *Report of the Truck Committee 1906*, op. cit., qq 5446.
113. *Men's Wear*, 7 0ct. 1911.
114. *Decennial Census 1851*, op. cit.
115. *Decennial Census 1911*, op. cit.
116. The average female operative's wage was 11s. 6d.
117. *See* H. Braverman's debate on the place of women in the work force and in the deskilling process, Braverman, op. cit., pp.386–92.
118. *Lancet*, op. cit.
119. Collet, op. cit, pp.95–137.
120. *Royal Commission on Labour, 1892*, op. cit.
121. Ibid.
122. The Census Report for 1901 highlighted the increasing ratio of female to male workers in the 'tailoring, clothing and outfitting' category for England and Wales since 1861. In every 1,000 employed, the number of females was:

1861	208
1871	254
1881	330
1891	427
1901	471

This serves to highlight still further the structure of the Leeds industry and its dependence on female labour.
123. Collet, op. cit.
124. *Decennial Census 1891*, op. cit., and *Yorkshire Factory Times*, 19 July 1891.
125. *Royal Commission on Labour*, op. cit.
126. *Yorkshire Factory Times*, 20 April 1906.

127. Collet, op. cit.
128. *Yorkshire Factory Times*, 23 Aug. 1889.
129. A. Stafford, *A Match to Light the Thames* (1961), p.66.
130. Lewis, op. cit., p.165.
131. *Board of Trade Report into Earnings and Hours of Labour in the Clothing Trade 1906*, PP 1909, LXXX.
132. *Yorkshire Factory Times*, 28 June 1907.
133. Ibid., 23 March 1910.
134. *Men's Wear*, 7 Sept. 1911.
135. Ibid., 23 March 1912.
136. *Report on Volume and Effect of Recent Immigration into the United Kingdom from Eastern Europe, 1894*, PP 1894 LXVIII.
137. Burnett, op. cit.
138. It is commonly accepted, though no reason is given, that a *machiner* in the clothing industry was male and a *machinist* was female.
139. Burnett, op. cit
140. Collet, op. cit.
141. Lewis, op. cit., pp.149–54.
142. *Decennial Census 1901*, op. cit.
143. *Royal Commission on Labour 1892*, op. cit.
144. *Decennial Census 1901*, op. cit.
145. *Yorkshire Factory Times*, 7 May 1914.
146. Collet report in *Report on Volume and Effect of Recent Immigration*, op. cit. p.104.
147. *Royal Commission on Labour 1892*, op. cit.
148. *Leeds Daily News*, 28 Oct. 1888.
149. *Board of Trade Report into Earnings and Hours of Labour*, op. cit.
150. As no official statistics for the number of men working in the clothing factories of Leeds between 1881 and 1911 were published, a numerical overview was obtained by: (a) deducting the total of female clothing operatives from the estimated total factory labour force; and then (b) totalling the estimated number of alien tailors and the estimated number of bespoke tailors in the city and deducting the result from the overall total of male tailors shown in the decennial census tables for the years shown. It must therefore be stressed that the table (Appendix, Table 6) is only intended as a guide. Though the numbers were small they show a continuing pattern of growth until the outbreak of the First World War.
151. Thomas, op. cit., p.56.
152. *Decennial Census 1881*, op. cit.
153. *Decennial Census 1911*, op. cit.
154. Gartner, op. cit., p.49.
155. *Board of Trade Report on Volume and Effect on Recent Immigration*, op. cit., p.573.
156. Quoted in Braverman, op. cit., pp.80 ff.
157. *Select Committee on Sweating System 1889*, op. cit., Evidence of James Sweeney, qq 3029.
158. Minute Book of the AJTMP, 22 April 1907, Archives of the NUTGW (the Minute Book is now believed mislaid or lost).
159. Letter from Joseph Finn to A.R. Rollin, dated 27 October 1943, Rollin Collection, loc. cit.
160. *Leeds Trades Council Annual Report 1899*, Leeds City Archives.
161. *Poilishe Yidel*, 31 Oct. 1884.

162. Ibid., 15 Aug. 1884.
163. *Jewish Chronicle*, 17 March 1911.
164. Ibid., 7 April 1911.
165. *Yorkshire Factory Times*, 24 Nov. 1911 and 13 Jan. 1912.
166. *Arbeiter Fraint*, 11 Dec. 1891.

3 Organising the Tailors of Leeds, 1870–1915

> Dismiss from your minds all traditional prejudice of race, sex or difference of working conditions. The true aim is solidarity and a welding up of forces.
>
> Moses Sclare, Secretary ATJMP[1]

Writing in the last annual report of the AJTMP, its Secretary, Moses Sclare, highlighted the problems which had surrounded the discussions and negotiations leading up to the formation of the United Garment Workers' Trade Union in 1915. It had taken almost four decades for trade unionists employed in the Leeds wholesale clothing industry to put aside past differences in the name of union, years which were some of the most memorable in labour history. Whilst the country suffered long bouts of depression and recession, relieved by occasional, short-lived booms, the number of organised workers rose from 1,600,000[2] in 1876, the year of the formation of the first working tailors' union in Leeds,[3] to 4,335,000[4] in 1915, the year of the amalgamation. During those years the face of trade unionism was transformed from one dominated by the 'new model' variety,[5] subsequently shaken by the explosion of 'new unionism', to one forced to accept that if craft was to be preserved and the semi-skilled and unskilled protected, the two had at least to co-exist, at best to merge.

The story of the organisation of the wholesale clothing workers of Leeds in the years between 1876 and 1915 puts flesh on the bones of the trade union history of one major industry. It also illustrates the way in which political ideology and political activists influenced workers, many of whom had little time or regard for politics. For the vast majority the overriding priority was work, in conditions which, if not ideal, were at least tolerable.

The Early Stages of Jewish Unionism

It was the Jewish sub-divisional tailors who, in 1876, established Leeds's first union for wholesale clothing workers. Though conceived at the peak of 'new model' unionism it did not manifest all the characteristics associated with the craft societies which, according to the Webbs, set out to 'protect the interests of craftsmen, seek peaceful negotiation and employ full-time paid officials controlling branches from a centralised office.'[6] Indeed a number of unions which emerged in the 1860s and 1870s did not conform with the prescribed design. And though the Jewish tailors' union adopted a formal pattern and was clearly influenced by local craft unions, it was born out of a need for self-defence, not in order to preserve craft superiority. Sam Freedman, first full-time salaried secretary of the AJTMP recalled how, in the 1870s, Jewish tailoring hands were wickedly exploited by the masters and frequently forced to work a seventeen- or eighteen-hour day. As a consequence the tailors began 'thinking about trade unionism.'[7] Moses Sclare, Freedman's successor, described how, in addition to working the longest hours, for the lowest pay, in the worst conditions, those sweated hands were subjected to 'violent physical attacks' by their employers.[8] They did not counter violence with violence, however. Instead, in February 1876, they founded a working tailors' society with an initial membership of 'between forty and fifty men'.[9]

The alien workers' desire for protection was then fashioned into a model of an English trade union. Its formation was registered in the Report of the Chief Registrar of Friendly Societies for 1876,[10] the year in which the Trade Union Amendment Act was passed enabling any combination of workers, whether in restraint of trade or not, to adopt the term 'trade union'. One detects the influence of a local craft society in the behaviour of that new Jewish society; doubtless the Leeds branch of the AST which, whilst not prepared to admit alien sub-divisional workers, was keen to encourage them to take positive steps to eliminate undercutting and exploitation. Only three Leeds unions appear in the official Friendly Society and Trade Union Register for 1876, the Leeds Pattern Makers' Association, the Leeds and District United Tanners' Society and the Jewish Working Tailors' Trade Society.[11] All three, and the Leeds branch of the AST, had their headquarters within a half-mile radius of each other. Alien and English paths must have crossed, if not when buying needles and thread, then when 'putting money on the horses'.

The last years of the 1870s were difficult for small, embryonic trade unions attempting to establish themselves during the 'Great Depression'. The larger unions suffered reduced membership and funds; the ASE paid out £287,596 in unemployment benefit between 1878 and 1880.[12] The Jewish Working Tailors' Trade Society did well just to keep alive, even reaching an agreement with employers for a one-hour reduction in the length of the working day. However, as the decade drew to its close membership dwindled and the Society was able only to 'struggle on'.[13] Paradoxically, as others across the country were suffering the effects of unemployment, the Leeds Jewish tailors' society was weakened by the expansion of the wholesale clothing industry and the upward socio-economic mobility of its affiliates. In 1880 a group of members announced their intention to convert the society into a 'Sick and Burial Society for the Strictly Orthodox'.[14] The core membership of that first Leeds Jewish tailors' union was drawn from workers who evidently were eager to integrate with the host society as rapidly as possible, though the choice of title manifests a concern to retain, and no embarrassment in displaying, religiosity. At the first opportunity they made the transition from a body which reflected a proletarian image to one that aspired to that of the newly emerging middle class. In 1883 the society affiliated to the Ancient Order of Foresters, the second largest friendly society in the world, and adopted the title 'Court of Hope of Israel', so bidding farewell to 'orthodox'. In offering its congratulations on the change of status and title, the *Leeds Express* emphasised the Anglicisation process by classifying the new society 'English in concept'.[15]

Trade unionism amongst the Leeds Jewish tailors was not completely dead. In 1883 the Jewish Working Tailors' Trade Society was resurrected, offering trade protection only for a membership fee of 2*d*. per week.[16] It is at this point that the divisions of skill within the Jewish sub-divisional workshop, not overcome until 1891,[17] became overt. In the summer of 1884 the machiners and pressers founded their own separate unions.[18] The total membership of the three Jewish unions represented only ten per cent of the city's alien tailoring work-force. This was better than nothing and the foundation of the three societies was welcomed by a Liberal-dominated Leeds Trades Council, relieved at a move to reduce the threat posed by unorganised, sweated, alien labour. Following the announcement of the formation of the machiners' union an approving *Leeds Express* published the following editorial:

> I know of no class of worker in Leeds who needs protection more than the Jews. A great number come to Leeds with no knowledge of customs and wages and work the hours and accept the wages they have been accustomed to on the continent . . . it is a sign of the times that the people are willing to organise to get rid of the evil.[19]

Affiliation to the Leeds Trades Council was marked by the presentation of an award to one Mark Ries, 'in recognition of his dedication in instructing his fellow Jews in the value and benefits of trade unionism'.[20] However the association with the Trades Council was short-lived. The link was severed a year later and, although it was rumoured four delegates were appointed to the Council in 1887,[21] the Trades Council's Annual Reports for the years between 1885 and 1893 make no reference to the membership of Jewish tailoring trade unionists.[22]

Departure from the Trades Council coincided with the increasing influence of socialism on semi-skilled and unskilled workers. Virtually all the disciples of the new ideology were members of one or other of the emergent societies, the Social Democratic Federation (SDF), the Socialist League (SL) or the Fabians. Initially socialism in Leeds was manifest in the form of the SDF but when the split took place, at the end of 1884, between Henry Hyndman, the autocratic and eccentric founder of the SDF and William Morris,[23] the formation of the Socialist League by Morris, 'took away the SDF's Leeds Branch',[24] and replaced it, in February 1885, with a League branch which included amongst its founder members one Jew, an eastern European tailor's machiner by the name of Joseph Finn.[25]

The current of socialist thought which flowed through to the working class in the second half of the 1880s was to have a decisive impact on the future development of trade unionism. As would be manifested by the Leeds Jewish tailors, the non-confrontational philosophy of the 'new model' unions was replaced by one of action as a means of, not just wringing concessions from exploitive employers, but of disestablishing the capitalist system, an ideology supported by the scholarly Finn.[26] Bi-lingual in English and Yiddish, Finn was a bridge between the city's socialists and the immigrant work-force. As Leeds correspondent of the *Poilishe Yidel* he made it his duty to inform and educate Jewish workers in order to hasten worker fraternity and accelerate the as-similation process. It was not just the Anglo-Jewish establishment that was eager to integrate alien workers, socialist intellectuals such as Finn, together with his counterparts in London, believed it vital that im-migrant workers be Anglicised as a means of countering anti-alien tensions and furthering the campaign against capitalism. The *Poilishe Yidel* kept its readership up to date with events which directly, or even indirectly, affected them. Reports of the progress of the 1884 Reform Bill appeared regularly. Yet whereas in the capital Jewish tailoring trade unionists participated in demonstrations supporting the Bill,[27] in Leeds, in spite of Finn's declaration that the public demonstration to be held in Victoria Park was in order that 'the rights of the people would succeed', local Jewish workers took no part.[28]

At the same time as Joseph Finn was attempting to create a bond between his co-religionist workers and local socialists, an English bootmaker, James Sweeney, was devoting all his non-working hours to 'thoroughly investigating the Leeds tailoring industry' in order to forge another link between the host work-force and the exploited aliens.[29] Twenty-seven-year-old Sweeney, who had lived nearly all his life in Leeds, was a member of the local branch of the National Union of Operative Boot and Shoe Riveters and Finishers[30] and a dedicated socialist. He too believed it imperative for the Jewish workers of Leeds to organise, unite with their English brothers and fight the common capitalist enemy. His verbal attacks on workshop masters and his support of the Jewish tailors facilitated his acceptance and, as he explained to the House of Lords Committee on Sweating in 1889, his election as 'secretary of the Jewish Tailors' Society through organising the branches with the assistance of other gentlemen'.[31] The societies turned to Sweeney after an abortive strike in 1884. In a break with their tradition of peaceful and non-confrontational protest, in November 1884, the Jewish tailors, machiners and pressers of Leeds downed tools in protest at their increasingly harsh working conditions and terms of employment. The essence of the strike's failure was its bad timing. November was uncomfortably close to the slack period. Workers could ill afford to sacrifice income at a time when they needed to consolidate all their financial resources for the bleak winter months ahead. In the face of the stoppage the masters stood firm. Without strike funds there was little alternative but to return to work in conditions so severe they were rejected by the imported alien 'scab' labour from Liverpool.[32] Victorious, the masters played another card.

They formed a Master Tailors' Association (MTA) with the declared intention of driving the strike leaders from Leeds. The MTA then circulated a black list headed with the names of the societies' secretaries together with a warning that any master discovered giving out work to those named would be penalised.[33] Somehow, for the next few months, the strike leaders, including Joseph Finn, managed to stay put.

Writing of it nearly sixty years later, Finn called the Leeds Jewish tailors' strike of 1885, 'the first Jewish strike by the first Jewish trade union in the modern world'.[34] Even if one gives licence to his reminiscences, there is no doubt that the strike was a landmark in the history of the organisation of Jewish workers in England. In spite of Professor Gartner's assertion that the strike 'took place spontaneously',[35] it is clear that the lessons of the previous year had been learnt, as this time good timing proved the essence of success. The second Leeds Jewish tailors' strike in six months followed the MTA's refusal to reduce the length of the pressers', under-pressers' and tailors' working day, one exceeded in severity only by that of the slipper-makers.[36]

At the beginning of May the patience of the tailors, worn down by the knowledge that the middlemen were enjoying the good life at their expense,[37] had reached breaking point. Demands for a shorter working week, put forward on 26 April, went unanswered. It was time for action. At a meeting of over 300 tailors, pressers and under-pressers (according to Finn the machiners put forward no demands and supported the strike out of altruism), a call for a strike was approved. Some cautionary voices were raised. Isaac Myers, leader of the tailors' society, was all too aware of the aggressive nature of his membership. He was worried that violent action would lose them not only the support of the Trades Council but also that of sympathetic English socialists such as Sweeney. Myers appealed for the 'strike action to be kept within the confines of the law';[38] by and large it was. Once again the employers imported alien scab labour from the East End of London. This time Finn and his associates were ready. They met the would-be blacklegs at the railway station, 'gave them a brotherly talk and handed them pre-paid return tickets to London'.[39] Without substitute labour and under increasing pressure from wholesalers demanding the completion of urgently needed orders, as the busy season had only just begun, the masters had no option but to discuss a settlement. A tense meeting, attended by six hundred workers and representatives of the MTA, was held at the Belgrave Street Synagogue.[40] An agreement was finally reached which reduced the length of the working day by one hour for the pressers and two for the 'poor devil' under-presssers, with no accompanying wage reductions.[41] This still left the under-pressers with a sixty-five-hour working week. Those most exploited of sub-contracted workers remained the underdogs of the clothing industry. Over twenty years later, in 1906, they were still pleading for payment for time spent lighting stoves in the hours before dawn.[42]

As the economy fell further into recession and the pool of immigrant and female labour spread the masters had little need to adhere to the agreement. Finn, in common with the leaders of the tailors' and pressers' unions, was subject to constant victimisation. Unable to obtain work there was no alternative but to leave Leeds.[43] The MTA had won. Joseph Finn set sail for America. He settled in Boston, found work in the city's nascent garment trade[44] and, for a while, played an active role in the local socialist society.[45] Through the pages of the *Arbeiter Fraint*, despatched to him in America, he kept in touch with his old comrades. Upon learning of the Leeds tailors' strike in 1888 he sent back a 'few dollars' to boost their resources. In 1893 he returned to England, this time to London's East End and its burgeoning mantle (women's outer tailored garment) trade. In 1895 Finn became secretary of the London United Ladies' Tailors' Trade Union. In that same year, following the passing of the TUC Conference resolution calling for controls on pauper alien immigration, Finn published a pamphlet entitled *The Voice of the Alien*, in which he presented the aliens' case. Finn denied that the eastern Europeans were taking the jobs of Englishmen. On the contrary, as he clearly outlined, the picture was very different, and the aliens had made a significant contribution to the British economy.[46]

Bereft of leadership, in a climate of economic decline, workshop conditions in Leeds rapidly deteriorated. Three years passed before the Jewish tailors felt ready to mount another attack on the employers. Once again the Leeds experience 'bucked the trend'. As the economy climbed out of recession, in the summer of 1888, the match-girls of London's East End demonstrated that, with the help of the socialists, they could take on the bosses and win. In Leeds that May, at the height of the 'busy', with the guidance of the Socialist Leaguers, men who in the months to come would help organise factory operatives, general labourers and gasworkers, the working Jewish tailors took on the employers and lost.

In 1885, when the Leeds branch of the Socialist League was founded its members favoured revolution as the solution to the iniquities of capitalism. By 1888 the ideological pendulum had swung towards support for the organisation of labour as a weapon in the battle against the capitalist employers. The leadership of the three Jewish tailors' societies was now in the hands of men with strong socialist convictions[47] under the guidance of a trio of Socialist Leaguers, one member, of course, being James Sweeney. The second was Tom Paylor, secretary of the Socialist League and a man who, in contrast to Ms Collet, firmly believed that sweating was rampant in Leeds. At one socialist meeting he openly declared that the Jewish masters were 'villains' whose aim it was to 'squeeze as much life as they could out of their men'.

The third musketeer was Tom Maguire, a legend in Leeds labour history.[48] Born in 1864, the son of Irish parents, he was brought up in East Leeds where he became a photographer. A romantic figure, who died a young man, Maguire was an early convert to socialism and a founder member of the Leeds branch of the Socialist League. Though he spoke out in favour of controls on pauper alien immigration[49] he was sympathetic to the cause of those who, having settled in England, were then used and abused by middlemen and masters. The song he wrote at the time of the Jewish tailors' strike in May 1888 illustrates his compassion and the moral dimension of his political beliefs.

1

Up in the morn, at break of day,
To the Sweater's den we go;
We sweat our health and strength away,
And pale and sickly grow,
That the sweaters may dwell in mansions fair,
And wear the costliest clothes,
Whilst our children starve in hovels bare
Where the sunlight seldom goes.

Chorus
So we strike for our babes,
We strike for our wives.
Together we stand or fall,
Determined to win true manly lives
For the workers one and all.

2

Surely a man has a right to live,
If he be honest and true,
If for his bread he'll freely give,
The best his hands can do,
Why should he toil starving the while,
Driven and bullied by men
Who never were fitted for honest work,
But are fit for a sweating den?

Chorus

3

We hope with best of all good men
Better days yet to see,
When hand in hand all over the land
United we all shall be,
When every worker in every trade,
In Britain and everywhere,
Whether he labours by needle or spade
Shall gather in his rightful share.

Chorus[50]

With the strengthening of political and ideological bonds between the alien proletariat and the English socialists the stage was set for battle.

The catalyst for the Leeds Jewish tailors' strike of 1888 was the employers' use of non-union labour imported from London and other provincial tailoring centres. Their aim was to increase profits by reducing the length of the busy season. The workers' response was to call for a closed shop. The MTA rejected that out of hand, calling it 'a form of dictatorship'.[51] They also refused to consider demands for a fifty-eight hour working week and overtime payment at time and a half. With no possiblity of negotiation in view, on 5 May 1888, 3,000 Jewish tailors downed tools, calling for a general strike by all those employed in the sub-divisional workshops. Four days later, at a rally held in Victoria Square, attended by over 5,000, Sweeney, Paylor and Maguire spoke out powerfully and persuasively in support of the tailors' cause. The lonely voice of a compassionate employer, that of David Lubelski, made an emotional appeal on behalf of the workers. Other master tailors were neither as sympathetic nor as forthright. In a move to destroy the strikers' credibility they circulated a rumour that the tailors intended to 'throw the women out of the workshops'. In a letter to the *Leeds Evening Express* Maguire refuted the allegation. In the same issue Lubelski explained that, in truth, the strikers wanted a 58 hour week for the tailoresses as well as for themselves.[52] In confirmation of this the three tailoring societies passed a resolution to open a branch for all females, Jewish and Gentile, employed in Jewish workshops.[53] It has to be said that once the strike was over the idea seems to have been dropped and we hear no more about it. In the vibrant and volatile atmosphere of those first few weeks in May membership of the three societies doubled.[54] As the days passed, with a settlement no nearer, the gloves were removed. Sweeney accused the middlemen and masters of obtaining orders through bribery, maintaining that the Jewish workshop hands were forced to 'pay for corruption as well as making garments'.[55] The accusation was well founded. Lubelski, in his evidence to the Select Committee on Sweating the following year explained that, in order to ensure work for his employees, even he had been forced to bribe the foremen of the wholesale warehouses.[56] The practice of 'greasing the palm' of those with the power to provide work and profit for labour and capital is one which, even towards the end of the twentieth century, has not been totally eradicated.

In London, as we shall see,[57] the Jewish tailors' strike which took place the following year was settled after the intervention of Samuel Montagu and Lord Rothschild. In Leeds there were no such luminaries prepared to bring their power, and money, to bear in order to reach agreement over a difference which seemingly was of little interest to anyone beyond the city's boundaries. In the three issues of the *Jewish Chronicle* published during the strike only five lines were devoted to the Leeds tailors' dispute, whilst at a demonstration held in London, in support of the strikers, the grand total of nine pounds was collected.[58] Passions ran higher in Leeds. During the first fortnight of the strike the SL held fifteen meetings at which members of the local Trades Council and labour movement voiced their support for the alien workers.[59] The employers were unmoved by a report which appeared in the *Leeds*

Evening Express suggesting that Beatrice Potter was travelling north to mediate.[60] (There are no reports of her actually visiting the city.) They remained obdurate even when the directors of Rhodes and Hepworths, concerned over the breakdown in production, put pressure on them to negotiate.[61] Hepworths even offered to open a 'Jewish workshop with one hundred machines',[62] if a settlement was reached.

After three weeks there was still no sign of concessions from employers whose position was strengthened by the 'presence of a number of unscrupulous blacklegs'[63] and the refusal by local provision merchants to allow strikers credit following an announcement by the MTA that the workshop hands would receive no further work and therefore would be unable to meet their commitments.[64] It was funds, or the lack of them, which proved the decisive factor. Without money for food the men gradually returned to work and the strike collapsed.[65] The masters' victory left the workers and their societies weak and divided. Union membership plummeted as employers again issued a black list. Those most loyal to the cause found themselves without work. A co-operative workshop was set up in Briggate to help those worst affected but, though it started off with 125 orders, after a few weeks it was no more.[66]

The strike exposed the ideological divisions extant within the Jewish tailoring work-force of Leeds. Support had not been unanimous. There were those who had argued for conciliation whilst others considered such a move 'humiliating and debasing'.[67] Some held socialism responsible for failure, declaring that the strike had been 'accelerated by socialist propaganda ... carried on by a few leaders'.[68] Was this a case of ideology outweighing pragmatism? The financial imperative certainly appears to have been overlooked. Without reserves to stave off hunger, disillusion and political dissension were bound to follow. Membership of the three societies, which at the height of the strike had soared to 800,[69] dwindled to zero. There had been no victors amongst the men, only amongst the masters.

For almost a year attempts at resuscitating the tailoring unions failed.[70] Conditions in the workshops became even more wretched. In May 1889 a small group of Jewish socialist tailors, including John Dyche and Lewis Franks, reconstituted the Jewish tailors' union with a manifesto to 'reduce hours of labour, improve workshop conditions and increase wage rates', all for a membership fee of one penny per week.[71] The 'new' style union was open to pressers, machiners and tailors alike. However the sub-divisional workers were not yet ready for the more general nature of 'new unionism' emerging elsewhere. Separations of skill and religiosity still ranked high. For the non-politicised, socialism was considered analagous with atheism,[72] and a small clique of observant tailors, determined to maintain the tenets of traditional Judaism, founded their own, short-lived, 'Orthodox Union'.

But change was on its way, precipitated by the new spirit manifest in labour organisation. The example set by the match-girls, gasworkers and dockers proved that those previously considered unorganisable could be organised. The 'first forward march of labour' had begun. Nine months after the match-girls formed their union in Bow, Will Thorne successfully organised the Beckton gasworkers and won an eight-hour day. That union became the Gasworkers' and General Labourers Union (GGLU). Its branches blossomed all over the country. In Leeds, as a result of the labours of Maguire, Paylor and Sweeney, the building labourers established a union in July 1889.[73] In the December it became the Leeds branch of the GGLU with a 'general' membership which included builders, gasworkers, maltsters, draymen, general labourers and dyers.[74] Urged on by the Socialist Leaguers the Jewish tailors' union, now including the pressers, affiliated to the local GGLU,[75] thus providing the first example of a fusion between a Jewish and an English trade union. The machiners retained their independence for a year: was this craft protection or obstinacy? Then they too 'threw in their lot' with the Gasworkers and General Labourers and became part of the phenomenon of 'new unionism'.

Organising the Male and Female Factory Operatives

The Jewish working tailors of Leeds worked their way painfully through various forms of trade unionism until they reached a point at which they adopted a more 'effective form of organisation than before'.[76] It was not until the last quarter of 1889 that the vibrations of 'new unionism' reached male and female wholesale clothing operatives in the city of Leeds. Once again the Socialist Leaguers proved largely responsible for persuading men and women working in the clothing factories to combine. Until then few, if any, attempts had been made to organise the male operatives. Their small number, varying skill levels and aristocratic status deterred those who had more urgent cases to deal with, such as that of the female clothing operatives. Continuing exposure to the truck system and correspondingly low take-home pay made the girls a prime example of a group of semi-skilled and unskilled workers who should have been in search of a union.

The first attempt to organise the Leeds factory tailoresses was made by Emma Paterson, founder of the Women's Protective and Provident League (WPPL). Mrs Paterson, a 'new woman' of the Victorian era, first encountered a successful example of organised female labour whilst on a visit to New York in 1874.[77] On returning to London she determined to improve the lot of British working women. Emma Paterson placed particular emphasis on raising low wages, as she believed that if rates of pay were increased women would automatically work shorter hours. The way to achieve this was through the creation of trade unions which would have the added benefit of taking women out of isolation in the workplace. However, although the Webbs credited Mrs Paterson with having been responsible for the formation of a number of small unions for women, in general her efforts were ineffectual and, for the most part, short-lived. From her middle-class vantage point Mrs Paterson neglected, or was unaware of, two major factors; one, continuing male chauvinist opposition to the organisation of women and two, the fickle nature of the working female. In July 1884 she visited Leeds and, apparently, awakened some interest as shortly after her departure a union for English females employed in the sub-divisional workshops was founded by the machinists. (It is not clear whether Jewish tailoresses were excluded or uninterested.) The union offered sickness and unemployment benefit for a weekly contribution of 2d.[78] In the tradition of female labour organisation, by the end of 1885 the union was no more. Three years later Mrs Paterson's successor, another 'new woman', one of the earliest female factory inspectors, Clementina Black, visited Leeds in a further attempt to improve the lot of the female clothing factory operatives. She was joined by the daughter of a prominent Leeds Quaker family, Isabella Ford. Miss Ford's philosophy was that moral standards would be raised if working conditions were improved. In pursuit of that ideal she devoted much of the 1880s and 1890s to the development of textile and clothing unions for female workers. Following the WPPL's transition to the Women's Trade Union League, Miss Ford was appointed Leeds representative, a role she combined with her support for female suffrage and membership of the ILP. The Misses Black and Ford set out to encourage female trade unionism in Leeds through the formation of a society which provided sickness benefit for female workers. This appealed to the tailoresses as, by 1889, they represented the majority of the society's 105 members. Here was the evidence needed to persuade the Socialist Leaguers that the female clothing operatives could be persuaded to develop their desire for benefit into the creation of a full-scale trade union.

The combination of middle-class Victorian 'new women' and working-class socialists brought about the creation of the first female clothing operatives' trade union in Leeds in 1889. Their vehicle was that thorn in the side of the tailoresses, the truck system. One of the worst offenders was the company of Messrs. Arthur. Its list of fines and charges deducted from the girls' weekly wages was impressive; one penny in every shilling earned, whether or not the work was completed at home, was deducted for the use of steam power; bobbins were to be purchased from the company at a cost of 5d., irrespective of their availability elsewhere for 3d.; one penny per week was deducted for cooking facilities, whether used or not and one penny for the sick club. In addition arbitrary fines were imposed for late arrival and damaged work. Even though other companies in the city imposed financial penalties Arthur's were the most severe. For example, Barran, Rhodes and Bainbridge made no charge for power, Buckley paid a higher rate and made no charge for power. The other companies limited the amount deducted to sixpence per week.[79] Aware of the heightening tensions at Arthur's the crusading Miss Ford organised a series of meetings, to be presided over by Tom Maguire, with the intention of persuading the female operatives of the benefits and power of organised labour. Eventually, at a meeting held on 16 October 1889, the girls passed a resolution to form a Leeds Tailoresses' Trade Union.

The force in the early success of the tailoresses' union was the refusal of Arthur and Co. to end the truck system. When negotiation failed a militant solution was sought. On 22 October 1889 a strike was called. Immediately 900 of the company's female operatives downed tools.[80] Within a week membership of the Tailoresses' Union had risen to one thousand, a figure which accounted for virtually the entire female labour force of Arthur & Co. A series of strike meetings were organised by Maguire and Ford, some drawing crowds of over 3,500 tailoresses,[81] though how many came through camaraderie and how many to satisfy curiosity is not recorded. The city's press called for the girls to stand firm. Caught up in the euphoria, the Jewish tailors instantly agreed to Tom Paylor's request not to accept work left unfinished by the girls at Arthur & Co.

Female solidarity was short-lived. Though collections on behalf of the strikers brought in some money the new union was unable to offer much in the way of strike benefit. Within a few weeks rumours were rife that some girls had arranged for their parents to collect work from the factory for them to finish at home. By the end of the first week of November ten per cent of the strikers were back at work. Some had taken jobs with rival companies, others had travelled as far as Manchester, Middlesbrough and Huddersfield for employment. All attempts made by the strike committee to reach a negotiated settlement failed. Arthur & Co. magnanimously announced its willingness to re-employ any striker who wished, provided they signed a document denying the veracity of any public statements made against the company. No concessions were made on charges for power. But Christmas was coming and with it the seasonal demand for ready-made clothing; job availability increased. Ideals of trade unionism were replaced by thoughts of the expense of the festive season. Before the end of December, with trade brisk, all the girls had resumed work.

Though they had stood firm in the face of the strike the management of Arthur & Co. learnt from the experience. Not prepared to concede while the pressure was on, after a few months, in February 1890, when the tensions receded, they announced that no further charges would be made for the use of power or cooking facilities. Despite the fact that this change was allied to a reduction in the price list, the overall result was an increase in the girls' take-home pay. The disruptive and costly nature of the strike was a clear warning to other wholesale clothiers. They too dispensed with power charges. As Isabella Ford reported to Leeds Trades Council: 'We regret the girls were unsuccessful in their efforts; but have reason to believe the conditions of the workers in the said firm, and in others, has been materially improved through the said dispute, which can only be maintained by strengthening their union.'[82]

The pattern of the strike and its backwash illustrate the ephemeral nature of female trade unionism in the years before the First World War. The excitement and glamour of the early days of the strike resulted in a membership of 1,800. However, as the *Yorkshire Factory Times* carried reports that new members were 'rolling in to the Leeds Tailoresses' Union', on another page it highlighted the problems of organising and retaining female membership.[83] A state of affairs not ameliorated by the behaviour of fathers and brothers who, together with male trade union leaders, did little to encourage female trade unionism. For example, AUCO did not appoint a female organiser until 1914, by which time its female membership outnumbered that of the males by 2:1. Isabella Ford openly stated that men did not 'seem to think it worthwhile to encourage their daughters to join (the tailoresses' union)',[84] while that self-styled champion of the county's working class, the *Yorkshire Factory Times*, adopted a middle-class male Victorian attitude to the organisation of female labour. The paper's editor showed himself keen to stress the domesticity of the female, and advocated that pre-marital job experience should be domestic as 'the best wives for working men are those drawn from the ranks of domestic service'.[85] Protective and confrontational action was permissible for men, but was to be discouraged amongst females, as was work itself. As Eric Hobsbawm has shown, even when their union was unable to pay benefits, 'out-of-work bricklayers would not let their wives go out to work'.[86] Women did little to counter the male view as female operatives continued to regard union dues as burdensome unless a strike was in progress and strike benefit was in sight.[87]

Unlike their female counterparts, once won over to the ethic of trade unionism, male clothing factory operatives remained true to the cause. Until 1889 there had been little incentive, or pressure, to combine. But once the forward march was under way the Socialist Leaguers refused to let the male operatives miss the parade. National and local events had shown that organised labour was for the common good, or so the men were told. The peaceful and successful strike of London dockers, concluded in September 1889 with the creation of the dockers' union, served to underline the point. There was no doubting the worth of benefits and protection. After much discussion, meeting and debate, on 1 November 1889 the male clothing operatives of Leeds announced their decision to form a Leeds Wholesale Clothing Operatives' Trade Union (LWCOU).[88] Even here divisions of skill and race were in evidence. At first the cutters refused to agree to the creation of any union which included the pressers. This was not just craft snobbery, elements of the rising tide of anti-alienism are detectable. During the 1880s the number of eastern European immigrants escalated as more and more fled Tsarist oppression. In Leeds it was estimated that the number of alien residents had doubled in the decade. In London, Leeds and Manchester, indeed wherever there was a significant eastern European presence, as is always the case at times of high unemployment and economic hardship, the indigenous population held the immigrant responsible for shortages of jobs and homes. At a time when working Englishmen were calling for controls on pauper alien entry it is not surprising that, as the *Leeds Daily News* suggested, as a number of pressers employed in the factories were Jewish, the objections raised by the cutters were in part anti-semitic:

> What was the reason the cutters wanted to be separated from the pressers, was it because the latter included Jews? If it was so it was a great mistake, they should all work together and while a feeling of wishing to be kept separate from the Jews existed, they could do no good whatsoever.[89]

In spite of pressure from the socialists for the creation of a multi-racial union the cutters stood firm. They would agree to unite with the pressers only if Jews were banned. On their part, the English pressers expressed a reluctance to fuse on the grounds that they had 'no wish to be involved in any action that might be taken by the cutters'.

The Socialist Leaguers, prepared to ignore the expressions of anti-alienism, did not let the matter end there. After 'a group of socialists delivered handbills at all the wholesale clothing establishments in Leeds',[90] the pressers called a meeting to discuss the formation of a union. According to A.H. Mills, a founder member of the LWCOU, 'It was a tremendous meeting', the outcome of which was the formation of the first male clothing operatives trade union in Leeds.[91] A major factor in the union's formation had been the concentration of workers in large-scale units of production. Common purpose was facilitated by common work-place. The ability to propagandise large numbers of male clothing factory operatives on one site saved time, cost and energy whilst, at the same time, stimulating debate and encouraging unity of action.[92] The LWCOU was founded for, and supported by, workers in the large clothing factories, many of whom retained an unbroken membership until the 1915 amalgamation. If the Socialist Leaguers had planned to follow up by converting the new trade unionists to their cause they were disappointed. As Mills explained, 'everything went well until our friends proposed we should affiliate with their London Society, but good judgement by Yorkshiremen came out on top and we decided to join up with Leeds Trades Council'.[93] Even at that early stage in its history the LWCOU demonstrated a preference for moderate, rather than radical, politics.

By 1889 all those employed in the manufacture of wholesale clothing in Leeds, with the exception of the Jewish tailoresses, had representative trade unions on offer. The next five years fashioned both unions and unionists. In Leeds, as everywhere else in the country, 'new' unionists and those of the more pacific, 'new model' breed had to face up to the future and each other. Some 'new' unions fell by the way, others recognised the need to work in conjunction with the older 'model', a minority of both varieties retained their autonomy, survived and prospered.

1889–1894

Jewish Tailors, Jewish Unions?

For the Jewish tailoring trade unionist of Leeds, as for so many of the new unions born in the passion-filled months of 1888 and 1889, the years between 1889 and 1894 were traumatic. The honeymoon of the Jewish tailors and the GGLU was one of goodwill and growth. Maguire, Sweeney and Paylor organised numerous public meetings at which they appealed to alien workers to forget past differences and work towards the common good of labour. Their words fell on receptive ears. Within three months the Jewish tailors' branch of the GGLU had grown from 900 to 2,000,[94] a figure that represented almost 50 per cent of the recorded alien tailoring work-force in the city and one not equalled again.

The marriage between the tailors and the GGLU was, however, short and tempestuous. In the early days the gasworkers were staunch and persuasive allies. When, in August 1890, the tailors launched what the *Yorkshire Factory Times* christened the 'Revolt of the Israelites', in protest against a seventy-seven-hour working week, Tom Paylor and William Cockayne visited the masters and *recommended* that agreement would 'avoid further trouble'. The refusal to negotiate was followed by an immediate strike call and picketing. The powerfully built gasworkers and labourers were more than a match for the physically weaker employers. Within twenty-four hours 75 per cent of the masters had capitulated, in a matter of days there was total agreement.[95] Impressed by this show of strength, less than two weeks later the machiners joined the Jewish Tailors' Branch of the Leeds GGLU.[96] For several months any demands put forward by the Jewish tailors were hastily agreed to by employers scared to do otherwise. However, the tailors outstayed their welcome. The gasworkers were soon disenchanted by the increasingly selfish demands of the alien workers. Neither the GGLU nor the *Yorkshire Factory Times* looked with favour on the solitary worker who asked for 200 pickets for three weeks to support his claim against a workshop master. Nor did the paper approve of strike action taken in protest at an employer's refusal to provide money for gambling.[97] 'They are always running to the Gasworkers for support for everything they want right or wrong.'[98] This was not just an anti-alienist blast by the *Factory Times*; thirty years later Moses Sclare recalled with shame that 'no matter what breach was perpetrated by a member (of the Jewish tailors' branch of the GGLU) at his work he expected to be personally protected, right or wrong, irrespective of the cost inflicted upon his fellow members.'[99]

The alliance between the alien trade unionists and the English executive of the GGLU, heralded with such optimism at the outset,[100] deteriorated into petty squabbling. The Jewish tailors criticised the executive for their drinking and excessive bureaucracy whilst the aliens were castigated for the irrationality of their behaviour.[101] But the fissures went far deeper, the ideological rift between parliamentarians and Anarchists – the Leeds Socialist Leaguers were all staunch parliamentarians[102] – that was dividing socialists nationally resulted in the Anarchist faction of the Jewish tailors' branch breaking away. They strongly resented the bureaucracy of the union which the Anarchist Jewish tailors' leader, Jacob Caplan, believed had an anti-alien bias. He felt stifled by the GGLU and said that 'workers should be able to breathe freely in their own union'.[103] Thus he departed, taking with him all but 40 members of the Jewish tailors' branch. His successor as leader of the Jewish tailors' branch of the GGLU was a Russian-born Jewish socialist, John Dyche, who would later make his name in London, as the second secretary of the mantle-makers' union, and in America as General Secretary of the International Women's Garment Workers' Union between 1904 and 1914. In spite of all the efforts of the Socialist Leaguers and Dyche, by June 1892 the number of affiliated tailors had dropped to twelve. It was not just the Jewish tailors who had lost faith in the union, seven other local GGLU branches completely disappeared.[104] A national increase in unemployment was resulting in a drastic reduction in union membership. General unions felt the pinch most. In the two years between 1890 and 1892 membership of the GGLU fell by almost 50 per cent whilst others such as the Dock, Wharf, Riverside and General Labourers' Union and the Sailors and Firemen dropped by over 60 per cent.[105]

Though disillusioned by his experience with the GGLU Jacob Caplan held fast to the ideals of trade unionism and brotherhood, albeit in Anarchist form. At a heated meeting of Jewish tailors Caplan warned that, 'if Jews don't belong to a union they will be considered the enemy of the English worker'. In spite of opposition from Orthodox Jewish tailors a Leeds Independent Jewish Tailors', Machiners' and Pressers' Trade Union was founded with Morris Goldstein as chairman and Jacob Caplan as secretary.[106] Its exact life span is not recorded, but reports in the *Arbeiter Fraint* suggest that it survived 1892 but was gone by 1893. There remained a core of support for Anarchism, as Rudolf Rocker discovered when he spent a year in Leeds during the autumn, winter and spring of 1901–2. The political freethinkers, together with the Social Democrats, were outcast by the 'official Jewish Community', who 'hated us and all our activities'.[107] The Leeds Anarchist Group, based in Roundhay Park, were active throughout the 1900s. They published a number of radical socialist and communist writings including Rocker's Yiddish translation of Bakunin. Little had changed by 1912 when the English Anarchists held their conference in Leeds.[108] They were refused accommodation and, in spite of the cold of winter, were forced to hold their meetings outdoors in Victoria Square. The non-sectarian conference drew forth expressions of anti-alienism from the Conservative *Yorkshire Post*, which criticised Jewish radicals for 'ill-paying the refuge we have afforded their race'.[109]

With the exception of the Anarchists, 1892 and 1893 were wilderness years for the Leeds Jewish tailors. Unemployment was on the increase. In Leeds the number of jobless stood at over 8,000.[110] Some Jewish tailoring workers began to re-evaluate organisation and the protection it offered. Perhaps it was not such a bad thing after all. At the end of 1893 the Amalgamated Jewish Tailors', Machiners' and Pressers' Union was founded, with an initial membership of one hundred. In spite of early hiccoughs, including a short-lived breakaway by the pressers, at the end of 1894 the AJTMP was all set to take on board the best of both the 'new' and the 'new model' varieties of trade unionism and follow a course which would lead to the amalgamation of 1915.

English Operatives, English Unions

Although established in 1889 the Leeds Wholesale Clothing Operatives' Union exemplified the 'new model' unions of the 1850s, 1860s and 1870s. The new union lost no time in appointing Joseph Young, formerly a Leeds clothing factory operative, as its full-time salaried General Secretary. Young's ambition was to see his union operate on a nationwide basis. Shortly after its formation the LWCOU published a manifesto announcing its intention to acquire new members locally, open branch offices in nearby manufacturing towns and cities and, in due course, amalgamate with smaller unions in the provinces. To achieve this end the union avoided confrontation whenever possible. Following the announcement of the formation of the LWCOU, the Leeds wholesale clothiers counter-attacked by announcing that any male operative known to be a member would be refused employment. The union's executive responded by opening a 'still book' in which to record membership in secret. This conciliatory policy came under the critical eye of the editor of the *Factory Times* who considered that the union's leaders were 'soft in their dealings with management'.[111] However, it was the employers who finally weakened and, once out in the open, the union's membership rapidly rose to four hundred. The depression of the early 1890s was felt in the factory as well as in the workshop and union affiliation reduced by almost 60 per cent. Young put his recruitment programme into top gear and by March 1893 membership had trebled.[112] At the same time negotiations were under way for an amalgamation with the Bristol Clothing Operatives' Trade Union. These proved successful and, on 1 January 1894, Joseph Young became General Secretary of the newly created Amalgamated Union of Wholesale Clothing Operatives.

One item on the agenda during the amalgamation talks had been the organisation of women in the factories. Male chauvinism won the day. It was decided not to admit women, and they were left to their own devices. Organised female operatives were doubtless viewed as a threat to jobs and wage rates. Whether fusion with their male counterparts would have made any difference is yet another matter for conjecture. Left to stand alone, the Leeds tailoresses' union followed a downhill path. The excitement of the 1889 tailoresses' strike was followed by a return to work and a drop in membership from 1,000 to 98. A successful strike in 1892 saw the membership rise to 212,[113] but, as the depression deepened, only 61 (English) tailoresses, out of a work-force conservatively estimated to total 10,919, stayed true to the ethic of trade unionism. Female membership did not rise above double figures[114] until 1909, nine years after the eventual fusion with AUCO. However, a major breakthrough came in 1911, following the passing of the National Insurance Act when nine thousand women joined the Union. State sickness benefit had acted as a magnet and the new female members overwhelmed the union with claims. An exhausted Joseph Young told the *Factory Times* that, 'having become an approved society for state insurance purposes has created more work than is worthwhile'.[115] Twenty-two years after the tailoresses' union was established women still put income above ideals.

The male tailoring trade unionists of Leeds learnt their lessons well. The factory operatives, neither militant nor radical, built on their policy of moderation and grew strong. The alien tailors painfully discovered that extreme radicalism, irrationality and volatility did not reduce anti-alienism, help the cause of union or provide a regular income. Fusion with an English union had been tried, but had failed. The years ahead would not be easy, as the legality of unions and their members was again put to the test through bouts of economic boom and bust. Overt anti-alienism, at the TUC and on the streets, made Jewish trade unionists think long and hard about the brotherhood of workers. In the face of all this, and more, the Amalgamated Union of Wholesale Clothing Operatives and the Amalgamated Jewish, Tailors', Machiners' and Pressers' Union survived.

1894–1915

The Route to Amalgamation

The excitement and passion of the 'first forward march of labour' gave way to the prosaic reality of recession. If trade unions were to endure and prosper there had to be a *rapprochement* between the 'new model' and the energetic, restless 'new'. In the West Riding the conjunction was facilitated by the failure of the Manningham Mills strike in Bradford in 1891. Trade unionists faithful to Liberal ideals were disillusioned with, and disappointed by, local party members who took the part of the mill owners. At the same time many of those who had marched behind the socialists in the balmy months of 1889 were grown weary of the ideological wranglings. They too were moving towards the idea of an independent labour party. The latter became reality in Bradford on 13 January 1893, close to the spot where the Manningham strikers had staged their protest two years earlier.[116] The centre of gravity of labour politics had moved to the industrial north. Indeed, south-east Leeds was one of the handful of constituencies that returned a member of the newly formed Labour Party in the General Election of 1906.

Fear of a take-over by the socialists and the disproportionate strength of the 'new' unionists forced the Parliamentary Committee of the TUC to re-examine its aim and direction. The narrowing of the divide between old and new was cemented at the 1899 TUC Conference when a resolution to provide the 'ways and means for securing the return of an increased number of labour members to parliament' was formally approved,[117] and the Labour Representation Committee (LRC) established. The decision was supported by the leaders of both Leeds male tailoring unions who regularly sent delegates to the annual conference. Between 1895 and 1915 the AJTMP was represented at every TUC conference, except that held in 1898 when it clashed with the most holy of Jewish festivals.

The years leading up to the outbreak of the First World War were marked by oscillations in the legal status of trade unions. The secure foundations of AUCO and AJTMP, unlike those of many of their counterparts in the capital, enabled them to steer a steady course through the stormy waters of the first decade of the twentieth century and the 'second forward march of labour'. Even though the AJTMP had a touch of strike fever there was little evidence of the Syndicalist bias manifest amongst some of its London counterparts.[118] The secret of the survival and growth of the tailoring unions of Leeds in the third phase of their history lies with the ability of their secretaries, the 'de facto leaders of trade unions'.[119]

When we come to examine the strengths and weaknesses of the tailoring trade unions of London and Leeds it becomes obvious that one of the most important factors in their success or failure was quality of leadership. Joseph Young led the factory operatives of Leeds on a path which enabled it to grow and prosper. His experience as a clothing operative made him all too conscious of the needs of the worker and the problems of labour. From 1894 he dedicated himself to the well-being of his union and the welfare of its members. Within months of the creation of the Amalgamated Union of Clothing Operatives its future came under threat. During 1894 the recession bit hard into the clothing trade. In order to counter the harsh economic repercussions Arthur & Co. announced that factory pressers would be subject to wage reductions. Cutters were exempted as they provided the flow of production for the tailoresses. In the tradition of the 'new model' union and in spite of its non-confrontational policy AUCO was prepared to defend its members with strike action when necessary. In February 1894 the union's executive thought it necessary. The cutters did not. They refused to support their brothers in the factory and some even resigned from the union. Support came from an unexpected quarter, the Jewish tailors' union. The AJTMP immediately announced its intention to 'get out of the factory' any non-union blackleg Jewish pressers.[120] Here was a template for the future. And, when factory operatives went on strike in the Broughton Wholesale clothing factory in 1899, the Jewish tailors' union once again gave them full backing. As Sam Freedman explained, his policy was to 'bring about better understanding between the AJTMP, the AST and AUCO'.[121] Throughout February and March 1894 an air of confidence surrounded the strikers and their union. Public meetings were organised by James Sweeney, Isabella Ford — both now members of the ILP, the Socialist League having descended into chaos — and Joseph Young. Tom Mann even made a special journey from London to address the strikers.[122] All the while the price of militant action was rising. The pressers, sticking to their demand for three times the amount offered by Arthur and Co.,[123] were receiving 15s. 0d. per week strike pay; with 36 men on strike the cost to the union was £27 a week. The *Factory Times*, believing all was well, publicised the fact that the union had 'money in the bank'.[124] The truth was very different. Bankruptcy was only a whisper away.[125] Fortunately the strike ended in May. Of the 36 who originally went on strike only seven stayed through to the end. With a depleted membership and reduced funds AUCO struggled into 1895. The lesson was clear; strike only when the finances of the union were sound and when the economy was in growth. The union backed a dozen small strikes in the years leading to the First World War but never again was its security or reputation placed in jeopardy.[126] Its most impressive gains were achieved by negotiation.[127]

In keeping with its manifesto AUCO began its expansionary programme following the amalgamation of 1894. At the close of the nineteenth century it had fourteen branches. The development was noted with concern by the AST executive in Manchester which, some years earlier, had voted to admit the 'dishonourables' of the trade, recognising that an élitist policy weakened its bargaining position. It now suggested a merger with AUCO.[128] This can be read as a defensive move intended to maintain control of the workplace through the membership of factory operatives. AUCO's executive gave the request serious thought. After cogitating for a year they rejected the suggestion.

The reasons were various; the factory union considered the AST to be old-fashioned, too 'set in its ways'; 'the 1,000 members of AUCO would be outnumbered and outvoted by the 15,000 members of the AST'. However, as Joseph Young explained, the determining factor was that AUCO 'would lose both its individuality and its autonomy'.[129] The craft union's response was to circulate damaging literature intended to blacken AUCO's name and capture its members.[130] Was all fair in trade union war?

The membership of AUCO, with just a few minor setbacks, rose steadily and at the time of the 1915 amalgamation numbered 4,000 male and 8,000 female operatives, a ratio indicative of the continuing trend of deskilling and use of the reservoir of female labour. By 1915 the union had established 36 branches covering the map from Yarmouth to Glasgow, from Dublin to Newcastle-on-Tyne and points north, south, east and west.[131] It made two attempts to enter the capital. The first, in 1904, was thwarted by the London Clothiers' Cutters' Union which vetoed a proposed merger between the two. The next year AUCO opened an independent London branch, hoping to attract the support of some of the capital's 400 unorganised stock cutters. It did not succeed, but the *Yorkshire Factory Times*, ever eager to bolster AUCO's morale, referred to the move as 'highly prestigious'.[132] The cost of growth, of quiet and hard-working dedication, of regular attendance at TUC, LRC and Labour Party conferences and meetings, of endless factory visits and negotiations was high. Joseph Young's health was failing but even so he accepted the role of General Secretary of the newly created UGWTU and steered it through the exciting and troublous war years. Following the amalgamation of 1920, which resulted in the creation of the Tailor and Garment Workers' Union, Young took on the treasurership of the TGWU and handed over the reins of the general secretaryship to Andrew Conley, the pugnacious, jovial, powerfully built Boer War veteran. Conley, previously a branch secretary of AUCO, was appointed the UGWTU's first National Organiser. He remained General Secretary of the national clothing workers' union until his retirement in 1948.

Between 1894 and 1915 the Jewish tailors of Leeds were led by just two full-time secretaries, Sam Freedman and Moses Sclare. Both men's work ethic, political beliefs and personalities proved central to the growth and development of the AJTMP. Sadly, in 1905, personal problems prematurely ended Freedman's term of office and almost brought about the collapse of his union.

Sam Freedman arrived in Leeds from Kovno in 1883. A typical unskilled young immigrant, he began his working life as a greener, making his way up the ladder to become a tailor's machiner. The ethos of trade unionism appealed to the young socialist and Freedman joined the machiners' union shortly after it was established in 1884,[133] learning at first hand the hardship of strike action. Membership of the Jewish tailors' branch of the GGLU also left its mark. Following his appointment as Secretary of the AJTMP in 1895 Freedman determined to follow a moderate path. Even though he was not scared of standing up to employers when necessary, he avoided confrontation when possible.

In spite of the sour taste left by association with the GGLU, Freedman recognised that his members, indeed tailoring workers in general, would be best served by a harmonious and supportive relationship with other tailoring unions in the city. It was he who advocated the AJTMP's standing behind the factory workers in 1894 and 1899. Following his example, in the late 1900s, his successor, Moses Sclare, together with Joseph Young, in a demonstration of unity between Jewish and English unions, visited factories and workshops on a recruitment drive.[134] These examples of brotherhood were applauded by the autocratic, long-time chairman of Leeds Trades Council, and branch secretary of the AST, William Marston. He was convinced that the sub-divisional system and the production of jackets by alien tailors in the workshops 'benefited English labour in the factories',[135] and that 'Jewish trade unions worked harmoniously with our trade unions.' This contemporary view conflicts with Clegg's theory that differences between trade unions in the wholesale section of industry and in the sub-divisional workshops 'weakened such trade unionism as existed within those two groups'.[136]

Freedman and Young appreciated that it was only through interaction that real progress could be made, a policy Sam Freedman upheld even under pressure. In 1893, and again in 1903, at the height of economic recession and alien immigrant entry, Leeds Trades Council adopted an anti-alien stance. Freedman refused to secede from the Council. Instead he set out to prove that his members were true supporters of the labour cause and would 'stick to our guns and show we are disciplined trade unionists in every way'.[137]

As we know, Freedman supported his words with action in the national, as well as local, arena. When the General Federation of Trade Unions was established in 1899, the AJTMP was amongst the first to affiliate in order 'to unite with all other trade unions of Great Britain'.[138] That ambition was not fulfilled due to the general paucity of support for the GFTU.

The first half of the 1890s was a difficult period for Jewish trade unionists and their unions. The indigenous work-force was pointing the finger of blame for unemployment at the alien. Annually between 1890 and 1895 resolutions requesting the limitation or total prohibition of pauper alien entry were laid down at the TUC conference.[139] In 1895 the resolution was approved. Significantly, in the period leading up to the First World War, 1895 marked the sole year in which a delegate from a London Jewish union attended a TUC conference. The executive of the AJTMP ensured that its TUC voice was regularly heard on topics which ranged from those which specifically affected Jewish trade unionists, such as the appointment of Yiddish-speaking factory inspectors and reductions in the cost of naturalisation, to wider issues such as the introduction of the closed shop by co-operative societies and the abolition of bedroom workshops.

Following his appointment Sam Freedman undertook what some thought impossible and others considered unnecessary, the organisation of Jewish tailoresses employed in the workshops. According to the *Arbeiter Fraint* this was an impossible task, as the women were 'the right hands of the masters'.[140] The Anarchist paper avoided, or ignored, traditional female apathy, choosing instead to highlight what it saw as the capitalist bias. Freedman made several attempts to organise a Jewish tailoresses' union and in January 1896 succeeded.[141] Against all odds the union thrived, managing to retain the allegiance of 50 per cent of the Jewish tailoresses of Leeds[142] until the merger with the AJTMP in 1908. The indomitable Miss Ford was so impressed by the success of the 'powerful and progressive' Jewesses that she advocated an amalgamation with their sister factory operatives' union.[143] The suggestion did not find favour and membership of the female operatives' union continued to decline whilst that of the Jewish tailoresses' remained stable at 225,[144] a figure which represented between 30 and 50 per cent of the Jewish female labour force. The history of the Leeds Jewish tailoresses' trade union is unique and, in some ways inexplicable, running contrary to local and national trends. What stands out is the apparent aversion to amalgamation with the men. By 1910 membership of the female branch of the AJTMP was registered as zero.[145] The branch was revitalised in the early months of the First World War when the demand for increased labour to produce military uniforms drew women back to the workshops.

As trade union secretary and member of the executive of Leeds Trades Council Sam Freedman devoted himself to the cause of the AJTMP and to its integration with the local and national labour movement. In his evidence to the Aliens Commission in 1903, Freedman stressed how beneficial the Jewish tailors and their union had been to the industrial development of Leeds. In an editorial in the *Factory Times* Joe Burgess came out firmly behind the AJTMP, stating that he did not 'know a finer trades union than the Jewish tailors' union'.[146] During 1903 and 1904 trade and industry were exposed to yet another severe depression. Reports in the *Factory Times* highlighted the suffering of the Leeds Jewish tailors and the large amount their union was having to pay out in benefits.[147] As the months passed concern mounted over the financial position of the AJTMP. Rumours were buzzing that members were 'asking questions about the balance sheet' and had requested that the books be 'exhaustively audited'.[148] Reading between the lines of the *Factory Times* and the Minutes of the AJTMP – nothing specific was ever published – it becomes clear that Sam Freedman was in extreme financial difficulty and had been borrowing from the union's meagre resources. In October 1905 the *Factory Times* announced the resignation of the secretary of the AJTMP. In a moving editorial Joe Burgess recorded how Sam Freedman had built his union's membership up from 20 to 800; he was a man who had served his union, and his trade, with distinction and dedication, 'the union cannot get a better secretary than Sam has been', Burgess concluded.[149] The extent of the shortfall was not disclosed, the union's Minutes for early March 1906 simply record that Sam was to be granted '£50 as a testimonial, thus negating (part of) the debt' and that the men be 'notified of their generosity to their old secretary'.[150] Unhappily, the saga does not end there. In May the same year, with £15 still outstanding and (apparently) having no knowledge of his whereabouts, the union's executive put out a warrant for Sam's arrest.[151] In fact Sam had fled to New York and was working as a tram conductor.[152] Just under a year later Sam's wife was told that if her husband repaid his debt the AJTMP would not pursue charges and he could return to Leeds, but in no circumstances would Sam Freedman be allowed to rejoin the union or its club. The disgraced ex-secretary of the AJTMP returned to Leeds in 1907 and started up 'a business in the clothing trade'.[153] It is a tragedy that Sam Freedman's reputation as a dedicated and hard-working trade union official and supporter of the labour cause was ruined as a result of his financial mismanagement. His failing appears to have been a characteristic endemic amongst Jewish trade unionists of the period, as the career of the charismatic yet flawed Lewis Lyons reveals.[154]

The AJTMP survived the misfortunes of 1905 and under the direction of its newly appointed secretary, Moses Sclare, went from strength to strength. Moses Sclare was born in the Ukraine and it was there that his interest in socialism began. Whilst working as an apprentice engineer in the Black Sea he met a group of Scottish engineers working on a contract for the Russian government. They encouraged Sclare to emigrate to Glasgow where, on his arrival in 1889, he found work as a marine engineer. It was a natural progression to join the ASE and within a short time Sclare was appointed secretary and president of his branch. Through his devotion to socialism and the labour cause Sclare met a number of activists including Keir Hardie, Kropotkin and Stepniak.[155] A curriculum vitae which included fluent Yiddish, socialist politics and trade union branch leadership were recommendations the AJTMP could not ignore. With the appointment of Moses Sclare the executive of the AJTMP demonstrated their rational and pragmatic approach to trade unionism and their determination to put their union back on course.

Moses Sclare's appointment as secretary of the AJTMP, which he took up in May 1906, was applauded by a Leeds Trades Council heavy with members of the engineers' union. But the Council meeting which welcomed Sclare echoed with anti-alienism when Alderman Buckle advised the Jewish tailors to 'conduct their union business in English'. Seeking to reduce the tension, Councillor Shaw urged the Jewish tailors to rally round their new secretary, who was a 'good union man'.[156] These were prophetic words, as almost immediately membership took an upward course and within a year had risen from 490 to 900. There was definitely 'an improved union spirit under Mr. Sclare's secretary-ship'.[157]

Though Sam Freedman's career had ended in ignominy the pattern he laid down was followed by his successor. A good working relationship continued with AUCO; Sclare was appointed an executive member of Leeds Trades Council; membership of the TUC and the Labour Party were maintained and delegates regularly attended conferences. In addition the new secretary set out to improve facilities for members. By 1908 those who wished could benefit from kosher food, burial and prayer facilities.[158] The crowning glory was the opening of the union's newly built Labour Hall in 1911, the cost of which was covered by donations from 'working tailors, a number of workshop masters and some manufacturers'. However, the 'good feeling between masters and men' jubilantly reported by the *Jewish Chronicle*[159] was only a blip between two fierce bouts of industrial action.

As soon as he was appointed secretary of the AJTMP Sam Freedman began a crusade against a system which favoured the speedy and the dextrous as against the skilled, that of payment by the piece. Numerous employers kept their hands in ignorance of current piece rates – an illegal act – the intention being to extract maximum output from desperate and hungry workers. Payment by time, by the hour, day or week, regulated workflow, standardised production and benefited employee as opposed to employer. Payment by piece was a licence to sweat. In 1897 Freedman led his union in a six-month strike against the piece system. At the strike's conclusion the AJTMP announced that it 'had practically broken down the system of piecework in Leeds'.[160] A presumptious statement as, in 1901, 1904, 1907 and 1908 the Jewish tailors of Leeds struck in protest against the iniquity of payment by the piece. Upon assuming the mantle of secretary, Moses Sclare was determined to eradicate the system. The tool in his first major attempt was master tailor Benjamin Joseph, a man who treated his workers 'as though they were machines'.[161] Joseph's policy was to dispense with hands in the 'slack' season and dismiss those who did not complete their work quota in the 'busy'. In January 1908 after a worker was dismissed, supposedly unfairly, Joseph's hands went on strike, 'not just for better conditions but for the general abolition of piecework'.[162] Joseph used every weapon at his disposal, threats, police protection and the importation of scab labour, all to no avail. In the end he was forced to concede to the workers' demands. His trade had suffered severely during the strike and in order to satisfy the terms of his agreement Joseph had to take smaller premises and dismiss a number of workers.[163] As had been proven so often before, industrial action during a depression was rarely profitable. Neither employer nor employees could claim victory. Sclare was determined to prevent such a situation recurring. Where was the benefit of payment by time if there was no work? After protracted discussion the AJTMP and the MTA signed an agreement intended to 'prevent disputes ... and encourage the adoption of the principle of union shops'.[164] Harmony lasted until two months after the opening of the new Labour Hall.

Whilst there is no doubt as to the outcome of the Leeds Jewish tailors' strike of March 1911, its origins are unclear. The *Factory Times* reported that the strike was called by fifty-five hands in protest at their employers' 'unfair practice of working at the same bench ... but doing the easiest work'.[165] Here was a demand for equality of treatment if not equal pay. The *Arbeiter Fraint*'s version of the dispute was very different. That paper reported that the masters were becoming increasingly worried at the strength and presence of the union in the workshops. When attempts to resolve a small dispute failed, the MTA proclaimed that the AJTMP 'had no right to dictate what to do with the workers ... if the union is not in agreement then the MTA will see who is stronger'. On 25 February 1911, after two further attempts to reach a settlement ended in deadlock, the masters announced 'an unexpected lockout' and 'threw over 2,000 men on the streets'.[166] According to the *Arbeiter Fraint*, the Jewish tailoring workers of Leeds were in a state of turmoil with no alternative but to call a strike.

The strike that followed involved 705 men, 402 women and 56 workshops.[167] Timing was again of the essence. The economic depression was lifting and wholesale clothiers were rumoured to be considering increasing the number of their indoor tailoring units. A long-drawn-out dispute would benefit no one. For once the MTA adopted a pragmatic course and applied to the Board of Trade for an independent arbitrator. Since the passing of the Trade Boards Act the Board of Trade had played an increasing role in conciliatory arbitration in the sweated trades. Agreement, followed by an immediate return to work, was reached in less than two weeks. On 13 March, 'an award of considerable importance to the great Jewish clothing industry' was announced.[168] The award, arrived at through the skilful intercession of the arbitrator, Alderman Smith of Leicester, marked the most significant amelioration in wages, hours and conditions since the formation of the first Leeds Jewish working tailors society in 1876.[169] The *Arbeiter Fraint* triumphantly announced the news in the simplest of language, 'the masters made a mistake and the workers have found a victory'.[170]

The Anarchists saw only a successful battle in the Syndicalist war against the capitalists. They did not appreciate that a shortened working week, without accompanying wage reductions, would make inroads into profits. A number of masters were brought to their knees, economically. Appeals for the wholesalers to increase manufacturing prices and for the union to delay the second stage in the reduction in working hours were ignored. By the end of the year, as a result of employers' bankruptcies and workshop closures, over 300 workers had been made redundant.[171] The masters held the wholesalers and the union responsible. But the main culprit was the system, one ignored by the recently formed Tailoring Trade Board, which failed to link minimum rates of pay to prices paid by the wholesaler. Without co-ordinated agreements which flowed from the top of the chain of production downwards, industrial action could only bring about redundancy for the worker and bankruptcy for the small employer. The outcome of the 1911 strike left its mark. No further reports of strikes by the Leeds Jewish tailors appear in the English or Yiddish press, or in government reports. One should not assume that no minor skirmishes took place, but at a time when in London, Manchester and Liverpool thousands of English and alien workers were once again marching forward, little is heard from the clothing workers of Leeds.

As early as 1907 Moses Sclare had announced his intention of opening branches of the AJTMP in other tailoring centres.[172] At that time his ambitious statements appear to have fallen on deaf ears. The key to expansion proved to be his leadership of the 1911 strike. Writing in the last (1915) report of the AJTMP, Sclare explained how 'disorganised tailoring workers in provincial towns appealed to (the AJTMP) to open branches ... the first being Stockport followed by Glasgow and Manchester'.[173]

By 1915 AUCO and the AJTMP had come of age, born after the explosion of 'new unionism' but spawned whilst its shock waves were still being felt around the country. The clothing workers of Leeds, male and female, Jew and Gentile, were indebted to the Socialist Leaguers for their determination to organise – or keep organised – those dismissed by others as unorganisable. The leaders of the AJTMP, like so many others, replaced the mantle of radicalism with one of a more moderate fabric, steering through the years ahead with common sense and compassion. (In this context we must put to one side Freedman's crisis of 1905 as a tragic aberration.) Freedman and Sclare withstood the pressures of mounting anti-alienism, unemployment and the spectre of war in order to build a stronger union, even if it was one that women chose to avoid. Joseph Young, a true supporter of the working man and his independent political representation, soon learnt the economics of trade union success and the pressures of female membership. The leaders of both unions recognised the dangers of isolating craft and race, though, as discussions with the AST highlighted, there were limits to the cost of fusion. During the first decade of the twentieth century it became clear that trade unions needed secure foundations if they were to survive the years ahead. If this meant subordinating ethnic, gender and skill differences for the common good then, for the wholesale clothing workers of Leeds, so be it.

NOTES

1. *Amalgamated Jewish Tailors', Machiners' and Pressers' Trade Union, 22 Annual Report: 31 December 1914–31 December 1915*, p.5, Rollin Collection, loc. cit.
2. Laybourn, op. cit., p.39.
3. A Leeds craft tailors' union was founded in the 1860s. In 1866 it affiliated to the AST. Due to its low membership, and the marginal role of the bespoke tailor in the wholesale clothing industry, the Leeds branch of the AST does not play a significant part in this history.
4. H. Clegg, *A History of British Trade Unions Since 1889*, Vol.II, *1911–1933* (1985), p.568.
5. Though not to the exclusion of others which did not quite fit the Webbs' definition of those unions which surfaced in the years between 1850 and 1888, *see* Webbs, op. cit., pp.204 and 216–24.
6. Ibid.
7. Sam Freedman writing in the *Trade Unionist*, July 1899, p.449.
8. M. Sclare, speech to members of the Leeds Branch of the Tailors and Garment Workers Trade Union, 1923, in the Rollin Collection, loc. cit.
9. *Trade Unionist*, op. cit.
10. *Report of the Chief Registrar of Friendly Societies 1876*, PP 1877, LXXVII.
11. Ibid.
12. Webbs, op. cit., p.348.
13. *Trade Unionist*, op. cit.
14. *Leeds Mercury*, 12 April 1880.
15. *Leeds Express*, 2 April 1884.
16. *Report to the Board of Trade on the Sweating System in Leeds*, op. cit., p.561.
17. In that year a short-lived Anarchist-inspired Leeds Independent Tailors', Machiners' and Pressers' Society was founded *Arbeiter Fraint*, 25 Dec. 1891.
18. *Leeds Express* 15 Aug. 1884.
19. Ibid., 5 July 1884.
20. *Leeds Weekly Express*, 17 Jan. 1885.
21. *Arbeiter Fraint*, 9 Dec. 1887.
22. Leeds Trades Council Annual Reports, 1885–1893, Leeds City Archives.
23. For a detailed account of the events and differences which led to the split within the early socialist camp, *see* Thompson, *William Morris*, op. cit., pp.331–65.
24. C. Tsuzuki, *H.M. Hyndman and British Socialism* (1961), p.67.
25. Socialist League Foundation Certificate, dated February 1885, Leeds City Archives.
26. Joseph Finn's daughter in an interview with the author in 1989 said that her father eschewed his radical views after his departure from the United Ladies' Tailors' and Mantle Makers' Trade Union in London at the beginning of the twentieth century, *see* Ch.6.
27. *Poilishe Yidel*, 22 Aug. 1884 and *The Times*, 14 July 1884.
28. Ibid., 10 Oct. 1884.
29. *House of Lords Select Committee on Sweating 1889*, op. cit., qq 30204.

30. Ibid.
31. Ibid, qq 30187 and *Leeds Daily News*, 13 May 1885. It must be assumed that Sweeney's reference to 'branches' was in fact to the three separate unions.
32. *Leeds Express*, 15 Nov. 1884.
33. Ibid.
34. Letter from J. Finn to A.R. Rollin dated 27 October 1943, Rollin Collection, loc. cit.
35. Gartner, op. cit., p.118.
36. Buckman, op. cit., p.69.
37. *Yorkshire Post*, 4 May 1885.
38. Ibid.
39. Finn letter to A.R. Rollin, loc. cit.
40. *Yorkshire Post*, 14 June 1885.
41. *Leeds Weekly Express*, 13 May 1885.
42. AJTMP Minute Book, 17 Sep. 1906.
43. *Select Committee on Sweating 1889*, op. cit., qq 30884.
44. For an old, but finely detailed account of the American garment industry, *see* Louis Levine, *The Women's Garment Workers* (1924).
45. Information from meeting with Finn's daughter, 1989.
46. See *The Voice of the Alien*, Rollin Collection, loc. cit.
47. *Arbeiter Fraint*, 2 March 1888.
48. *See* Thompson, 'A Homage to Tom Maguire' op. cit.
49. *Labour Chronicle*, 6 May 1894.
50. Taken from *The Garment Worker*, May 1948.
51. *Leeds Evening Express*, 7 May 1888.
52. Ibid., 10 May 1888.
53. Ibid., 18 May 1888.
54. Ibid., 10 May 1888.
55. *Leeds Evening News*, 7 May 1888.
56. *Select Committee on Sweating System 1889*, op. cit., qq 31567.
57. *See* below, Ch.5.
58. *Leeds Weekly Express*, 2 June 1888.
59. *Commonweal*, 19 May 1888.
60. *Leeds Evening Express*, 23 May 1888.
61. *Yorkshire Post*, 13 May 1888.
62. *Arbeiter Fraint*, 18 May 1888.
63. Ibid.
64. *Select Committee on Sweating 1889*, op. cit., qq 31785.
65. *Trade Unionist*, op. cit.
66. *Arbeiter Fraint*, 29 June 1888.
67. *Leeds Evening Express*, 11 June 1888.
68. Ibid.
69. *Arbeiter Fraint*, 9 Dec. 1888.
70. On 29 June 1888 the *Arbeiter Fraint* announced the formation of an Amalgamated Tailors' Union. No further information about the union appeared and it must be assumed it died a rapid death.
71. *Leeds Daily News*, 28 May 1889.
72. *Yorkshire Evening News*, 21 Jan. 1925.
73. Thompson, op. cit., p.528.
74. Thompson, in Briggs and Saville, op. cit., p.296.
75. The Jewish Slipper Makers affiliated at the same time.
76. Laybourn, op. cit., pp.75.

77. Webbs, op. cit., p.175 ff.
78. *Leeds Weekly Express*, 17 Jan. 1885.
79. Ibid., 19 Oct. 1889.
80. Ibid., 26 Oct. 1889.
81. Ibid.
82. Leeds Trades Council Report, May 1889–May 1890, p.7.
83. *Yorkshire Factory Times*, 7 Dec. 1890.
84. Minutes, Leeds Trades Council Meeting, 28 April 1897, Leeds City Archive.
85. *Yorkshire Factory Times*, 5 Dec. 1890.
86. Hobsbawm, *Worlds of Labour*, op. cit., p.239.
87. *Yorkshire Factory Times*, 13 March 1891.
88. Ibid., 1 Nov. 1889.
89. *Leeds Daily News*, 29 Oct. 1889.
90. Letter dated 20 Feb. 1931 from A.H. Mills, member of the first executive of the Leeds Wholesale Clothing Operatives' Trade Union, to H. Bullock. Archives of GMB – the National Union of Tailors and Garment Workers fused with the GMB in 1991 and is the clothing section of that union.
91. Ibid.
92. Ibid.
93. Ibid.
94. *Yorkshire Factory Times*, 9 May 1890.
95. Ibid., 29 Aug. 1890.
96. Ibid., 11 Sept. 1890.
97. Ibid., 24 Oct. 1890.
98. Ibid., 7 Nov. 1890.
99. *7th Annual Report, Amalgamated Branch of the Tailors' and Garment Workers' Trade Union*, April 1923, Rollin Collection, loc. cit.
100. *Yorkshire Factory Times*, 9 March 1890.
101. *Arbeiter Fraint*, 11 December 1891.
102. Thompson, *William Morris*, op. cit., p.560.
103. Ibid., 25 Dec. 1891.
104. Leeds District GGLU Financial Statement, 25 March 1893, Leeds City Archive.
105. E. Hobsbawm, *Labouring Men* (1979 ed.), pp.158–230.
106. *Arbeiter Fraint*, 25 Dec. 1891.
107. R. Rocker, *The London Years* (1956), Ch.13.
108. For details of the Anarchist Conference held in Leeds in 1912, see J. Buckman, 'The 1912 Anarchist Conference in Leeds', *Bulletin of the Society for the Study of Labour History*, 47, p.13 (Autumn 1983).
109. *Yorkshire Post*, 26 Feb. 1912.
110. *Yorkshire Factory Times*, 12 Jan. 1894.
111. Ibid., 17 July 1891.
112. *Yorkshire Factory Times*, 12 March 1893.
113. June Hendricks, unpublished M.A. Thesis, 'The Tailoresses in the Ready-Made Clothing Industry in Leeds 1889–1899', University of Warwick, 1970.
114. Membership of the Leeds Tailoresses' Union 1894–9: 1895–40, 1896–53, 1897–20, 1898–31, 1899–50. June Hendricks, op. cit.
115. *Yorkshire Factory Times*, 7 May 1914.
116. H. Pelling, *Origins of the Labour Party* (1976 edn), p.115.
117. B. Pimlott and D. Cook (eds), *Trade Unions in British Politics* (1982), p.48.
118. *See* Ch.5 below.
119. Sam Freedman, first secretary of the AJTMP, as we will see below, put ten valuable years into his union, until tragically, personal folly led to his departure.

Fortunately, he was followed by Moses Sclare, whose guidance was such that Sam's lapse was overcome.

120. *Yorkshire Factory Times*, 9 Feb. 1894.
121. Ibid., 21 July 1899.
122. Ibid., 23 March 1894.
123. Arthur & Co. were offering between 1*s*. 3*d*. and 1*s*. 9*d*. for a jacket and from 6*d*. to 1*s*. 3*d*. for trousers whilst the pressers were demanding 3*s*. 0*d*. for working on jackets and from 1*s*. 6*d*. to 2*s*. 0*d*. for trousers. *Yorkshire Factory Times*, 16 Feb. 1894.
124. Ibid. 2 Feb. 1894.
125. The union had taken out some form of insurance by asking all the strikers to sign a promissory note which guaranteed that if they acted contrary to the wishes of their union they would return all monies received and accept no further benefits.
126. *AUCO Monthly Gazette*, May 1899, 41/T/Board of Trade Library Collection, Modern Record Centre, University of Warwick, *Report of the Truck Committee*, 1906, op. cit., qq 5541 and *Report on Strikes and Lockouts 1912*, PP 1914, XLVIII.
127. In 1913, following the publication of the wage rates laid down by the newly established Tailoring Trade Board, AUCO negotiated a settlement on behalf of its Leeds and Huddersfield members which provided a ¾*d*. increase on the minimum rate for women aged 19 and over and one of between 2¼*d*. and 3½*d*. for men, with an accompanying work week of forty-nine and one-half hours (*see* Tawney, op. cit., pp.93–5).
128. *AUCO Monthly Gazette*, Aug. 1898, loc. cit.
129. Ibid., May 1899.
130. Annual Reports of the TUC Conference for 1901 and 1903, Archives of the TUC, Congress House London.
131. *Report of Trade Unions, 1902–1904*, PP 1906, CXIII, United Garment Workers' Trade Union, First Annual Report, 8 June 1915–31 Dec. 1916, Archives GMB.
132. *Yorkshire Factory Times*, 25 Aug. 1905.
133. Freedman's Evidence to the *Royal Commission on Alien Immigration 1903*, op. cit., qq 20366.
134. *Yorkshire Factory Times*, 18 Oct. 1907.
135. *Royal Commission on Alien Immigration, 1903*, op. cit., qq 14310 and qq 14376.
136. Clegg, op. cit., p.181.
137. Leeds Trades Council, Minutes, 8 Feb. 1893, loc. cit and *Yorkshire Factory Times*, 3 April 1903.
138. *Yorkshire Factory Times*, 10 March 1900.
139. Annual Reports of the Conference of the TUC 1892–1915, Archives of the TUC, London.
140. *Arbeiter Fraint*, 31 Jan. 1896.
141. Ibid.
142. *Jewish Chronicle*, 9 Aug. 1901.
143. *Yorkshire Factory Times*, 5 March 1897.
144. *Report on Trade Unions 1906–1908*, PP 1908 LXXXIX.
145. *Report on Trade Unions 1908–1910*, op. cit. Some Jewish females loyal to the ethic of trade unionism might have transferred to AUCO when they moved from workshop to factory in the first decade of the twentieth century.
146. *Yorkshire Factory Times*, 3 April 1903.
147. *See Yorkshire Factory Times*, 27 Dec. 1903, 15 Jan. 1904, 4 March 1904, 10 March 1905.
148. Ibid., 4 Aug. 1905.

149. Ibid., 6 Oct. 1905.
150. Minute Book of the AJTMP, meeting of 4 March 1906.
151. Ibid, 5 May 1906.
152. *Yorkshire Factory Times*, 23 March 1906.
153. Ibid., 24 April 1907.
154. *See* Chs. 4 and 5 below.
155. *Leeds Weekly Citizen*, 28 March 1941.
156. *Yorkshire Factory Times*, 18 May 1906.
157. Ibid., 1 March 1907.
158. *Jewish Chronicle*, 29 May 1908.
159. Ibid., 21 Jan. 1911.
160. *Yorkshire Factory Times*, 3 Sept. 1897.
161. The Minute Book of the AJTMP has frequent references to the disputes between Joseph and his employees, nearly all of whom were members of the AJTMP.
162. *Arbeiter Fraint*, 24 Jan. 1908.
163. Leeds Trades Council, Minutes for 13 March 1908.
164. *Yorkshire Factory Times*, 25 Dec. 1908.
165. Ibid., 2 March 1911.
166. *Arbeiter Fraint*, 3 March 1911.
167. *Leeds Mercury*, 8 March 1911.
168. *Jewish Chronicle*, 13 March 1911.
169. The recommendations of the award were: no victimisation of union members; no union involvement in the running of workshops; no forced employment of 'difficult' union members; accusations of victimisation to be referred to arbitration; wage payments to be made no later than Friday; payment by piece to be mutually agreed and to be no less than time payment; the reduced working hours to be without a reduction in income. The reduction in hours was to take place in three stages, reducing from a sixty-one-hour week to a fifty-four-hour week by 31 December 1911. The award was to be valid for two years.
170. *Arbeiter Fraint*, 10 March 1911.
171. *Yorkshire Factory Times*, 13 Jan. 1912.
172. Ibid., 18 0ct. 1907.
173. 22 *Annual Report of the AJTMP*, Dec. 1915, op. cit. For a comprehensive list of branches of the union *see* Appendix, Table 24.

4 The Structure of the London Tailoring Trade, 1870–1915

By the mid-1870s Henry Poole, Savile Row court tailor, was a London institution. His premises were more like a club than shop with the great and wealthy flocking between 3.30 and 5.00 p.m. to partake of his fine Claret and Hock and to puff 'Pooley's' cigars.[1]

E. Moses & Son brought about a wholesome and important revolution in our trade when we originated new yet ready-made clothing a Beau Brummel would have been proud to wear at prices a mechanic could afford to pay.[2]

For the 'Kaffir trade' East End workers produced garments of a cheapness and shoddiness almost unknown to the consumer in this country.[3]

The above quotations illustrate the diverse nature of the London tailoring trade in the second half of the nineteenth century. It covered a spectrum which embraced wealthy aristocrats and industrialists, representatives of the emerging professional and middle classes and the more affluent members of the working class. Overseas customers included diplomats, civil servants and liberated 'slaves' working for white masters in South Africa. As varied as were the consumers so were the skills that satisfied demand. At one end of the scale was the Savile Row craftsman at the other were the exploited semi-skilled eastern European tailor, breaking under pressure from the sweatshop master, and the starving English tailoress, praying she would not have to sell her body in order to survive. Even the centres of production were distanced, geographical separation engendering an industrial snobbery all its own. The divide between West End and East End was far greater than the few miles shown on the map, for, as was said in 1867, 'From the East End...it would take a long while for a man to walk to the West End.'⁴ Upward mobility of skill was possible, but only just.

London had been a centre of clothing production since Tudor times. By the middle of the nineteenth century, Savile Row, in the Mayfair district at the west end of the metropolis, had established its reputation as the headquarters of the finest quality bespoke tailoring in the land. The concentration of high-level craftsmanship gradually extended, so that by 1870 it was bounded by Bond Street, Regent Street, Oxford Street and Piccadilly. As demand for tailored garments increased, barriers were broken and lower-quality bespoke manufacture spread eastward into Soho, where there had been a colony of Polish/Jewish tailors since the eighteenth century, and north-west into the parishes of St Giles and Marylebone.

The East End of the city had long had a reputation as a source for second-hand clothing and it was a natural progression to poorly made clobbered or 'soaped' together new garments which were in increasing demand as the range of consumers expanded. Gradually the concentration of Jewish tailors in Spitalfields spread west into Houndsditch and east along the Whitechapel and Commercial Roads. Boundaries to the north and south were formed by the Great Eastern Railway and Cable Street.

With such a complex structure of industry, diversity of skills and division of locations, the organisation of the tailoring workers of London was considered an almost impossible task.

MARKETS AND MANUFACTURERS

One of the principal determinants in the structure of the capital's tailoring industry was the diversity of consumers and markets served. London, unlike Leeds, whose clothing industry was geared to the sale of medium-priced ready-made men's clothing for home and foreign markets, served the wealthiest, the poorest and all points between. It was the increase in demand for middle and lower-quality garments that was most impressive.⁵ The artisan and working man looking for their best suit and working trousers were catered for by what Beatrice Potter categorised, rather disparagingly, as the 'common and very common' section of the London tailoring trade.⁶ At the same time the new stratum of white-collar workers employed in government, commercial and financial institutions were stimulating demand for made-to-measure[7] and 'stock' ranges. If Industry boosted the clothing trade then so did Empire. Between 1861 and 1891 the number of civil servants employed to administer colonial affairs rose dramatically.[8] All wore suits for work.

In addition to servicing home markets, workers in the East End of London produced garments for what was considered to be the very lowest level of tailoring, the manufacture of trousers for the native (kaffir) workers of South Africa. In 1887 John Burnett reported to the Board of Trade that of the '£2,600,447 of Apparel and Slop' exported from the Pool of London the bulk was destined for the Kaffir Trade.[9] After the Boer War the native and immigrant South African market expanded still further. However, the bulk of the male export trade to the Colonies, North America and Europe remained the province of the Leeds wholesale clothiers.

Native workers in Africa were little concerned with the location of their tailors. Londoners were. Depending on the thickness of their wallets the choice ranged from discreet bespoke tailors' establishments in Mayfair which served emperors, dukes and prime ministers, to the glass-fronted emporiums of E. Moses & Co. in Aldgate, Minories, Oxford Street or Tottenham Court Road where, by the 1860s, ready-made or made-to-measure garments could be purchased in a variety of styles at a variety of prices.[10] For those with less to spend there were always the open-fronted cheap and slop shops in the East End where clothes were displayed on poles suspended from outside rails. Higher-quality garments could be bought from city merchants including Hope Brothers and Cook & Son. The increase in surplus income manifest in the 1850s led to a burgeoning of single and multiple retail tailoring outlets in the following decade.[11] Competition forced a change in the system of pricing. While it was standard practice for high-class tailors to offer varying discounts to their illustrious clients,[12] the increased sale of ready-made clothes necessitated pre-determined pricing. Shop windows were filled to overflowing with clearly priced goods. The power of the multiples to cut prices in order to attract custom forced the small wholesaler, and those lower down the chain of production, such as middlemen and sub-contractors, to rely increasingly on the cheapest, and often the least skilled, sweated labour.

In 1863 a new style of consumer outlet appeared on the map when William Whiteley opened his 'universal provider' in Bayswater.[13] The location chosen indicates that it was intended to attract the growing number of middle-class suburbanites settling in Maida Vale and the surrounding areas. But the working class was not overlooked. The Wholesale Co-operative manufactured working men's suits in their own factories and workshops for sale in their retail outlets. Indeed, by the end of the nineteenth century London catered for all categories of male customers in shops and stores fed by sweated workers in the East and West Ends of the city, the gradually diminishing number of craft journeymen tailors and the married, widowed or spinster home-workers.

During the first part of the nineteenth century it was the needs and whims of the male consumer that influenced the aim and direction of the nation's clothing industry. From the 1850s women took a hand. A 'New Woman' was emerging in Victorian England, one who con-sidered her role to be somewhat different from that of her elder sister. Life held more than childbearing, domestic management, tea parties and huge, awkward crinolines. Sport, radical politics, 'hands-on' charitable work, votes for women, teaching and clerical work beckoned. In order for her to participate fully in the new order, efficient, business-like tailored garments were a necessity.

Until the 1850s and 1860s the rare examples of tailor made garments to be found in the female closet were a lady's riding habit and/or her cloak (or mantle). The former was necessarily tailormade, often by London-based craftsmen for fashionable women living in the country; dressmakers were unable to cope with the weight and cutting of 'good, stout cloth'.[14] As the century progressed commercial and social freedoms, together with new modes of transport, made it imperative for the liberated female to dispense with the unwieldy clothes of earlier years. Though ladies now participated in hockey, golf and cricket the major craze was bicycling, a pastime which was certainly not in tune with the crinoline. 'Radical dress' was the order of the day and women attired in roomy knickerbockers, topped by a 'frantic frock-coat' and a 'Robin Hood' hat were seen flying down the roads.[15] Females donned the 'tailormade' costume for shopping trips to the increasing number of department stores[16] and to take tea in ABC tea shops, which opened in the early 1880s in response to the need for public restaurants where women, unaccompanied by male companions, could take a meal at ease. Navy blue tweed and serge jackets and skirts were far more suited to rent collecting in the East End and lecturing on the virtues of socialism and female suffrage than were the frills and flounces of the drawing rooms of Maida Vale and Mayfair.

But who was to supply the New Woman with her new wardrobe?

The development of retail and wholesale outlets for women's tailored garments ran parallel to transitions in style. During the early part of the nineteenth century women either made their own clothes or had them made up by dressmakers. Fabrics and trimmings were sold by drapers and haberdashers. As styles changed retail outlets enlarged their premises in order to offer an increasing range of goods. By the century's end a number of originally small shops, such as Swan & Edgar, Dickins & Jones, Bentalls and Harrods,[17] had metamorphosed into department stores in which women's tailored clothes, bespoke and ready-made, and, in certain instances, partially made for completion at home, were sold in departments adjacent to those selling linens, hosiery and millinery. The department store remained largely female territory[18] until 1909 when Gordon Selfridge opened his impressive custom-built emporium in Oxford Street. As one titled shopper described the experience in 1896:

> What an amount of trouble and expense is avoided where one can order one's New Zealand mutton downstairs, buy one's carpet on the ground floor, and deck oneself out in all the glory of Worth or La Ferrier, on the top floor, to all of which one is borne on the wings of a lift, swift and silent.[19]

Sadly, only a small proportion of the female population could shop in the style of Lady Jeune.

In order to satisfy provincial demand for women's tailored garments, warehouses in the City of London, such as Hitchcock Williams and Pawsons & Leafs, both of which were opened in the 1820s to sell linens and haberdashery to retailers at home and abroad,[20] extended their ranges, glamorised their premises and opened their doors to retail custom. Proximity both to the docks and to the centre of mantle manufacture in London's East End facilitated overseas trade and by the turn of the century export markets included Europe, the Americas and the Colonies. In this way the fashion trends of London society were made available to those whose appetites were whetted by the increasing number of women's journals in circulation, with titles such as *The Lady's Gazette of Fashion*, *La Belle Assemblée*, *The Lady's Treasury* and the *World of Fashion*,[21] the latter offering a free pattern service to its readers.

The demand for women's garments was there but where were the producers? As in the case of riding habits, women's tailored outerwear was, initially, only available from gentlemen's outfitters. In the 1850s

'Ladies Ventilating Waterproof Travelling Cloaks' were on sale in such male precincts as Aquascutum (which did not have a ladies' garments department until the beginning of the twentieth century) and Scott Adie.[22] One of the earliest companies to specialise in the wholesale manufacture of women's tailored garments was that started in 1857 by Charles Selincourt, a tailor of Huguenot descent. His small factory in Pimlico, using hand and treadle machines, produced costumes, mantles and shawls for a number of retail outlets which included Harvey Nichols, Marshall & Snelgrove, Dickins & Jones and Peter Robinson in London, as well as for shops in Bath, Reading, Torquay and Edinburgh.[23]

An eastern European tailor, Morris Cohen, claimed to have introduced mantle manufacture on a large and profitable scale to England. Selincourt's share of the market was small but, as a result of his entrepreneurial and manufacturing skills, Cohen built up a corner of the tailoring trade which proved highly beneficial for Britain's balance of trade. It is therefore fitting to recount his story as told to the Royal Commission on Alien Immigration in 1903 and recorded in the family archives.[24]

When Cohen landed in England in 1877 he was not the conventional greener but a trained gentleman's tailor, 'having slight knowledge of ladies tailoring'.[25] These qualifications enabled him to bypass the miserable sweatshops of Whitechapel and take up employment with Hope Bros., bespoke tailors in the City. He stayed there for three years until, having become restless, he answered a newspaper advertisement for 'a tailor to make up ladies' jackets'. It was the break he needed. Cohen then made up a number of sample garments from his own designs and showed them to a selection of tailoring masters that he knew were keen to take advantage of the newly emerging female market. In his evidence to the Aliens Commission, Cohen stressed that at that time there were 'no English ladies' tailors. All the ladies' tailoring...was then done abroad, principally in Germany and France.'[26]

In less than ten years Cohen's business had reached a point at which, in 1895, he was able to open his, indeed the country's, first 'custom-built' mantle-making factory in Spital Square. By then the mantle-making industry in the East End of London was well established and providing employment for over one thousand workers.[27] According to his evidence, by 1903, Cohen's factory employed '180 persons indoors, about 50 English Christians, about 50 English Jews and the remainder

8 Morris Cohen (courtesy Clive Moss and the London Museum of Jewish Life)

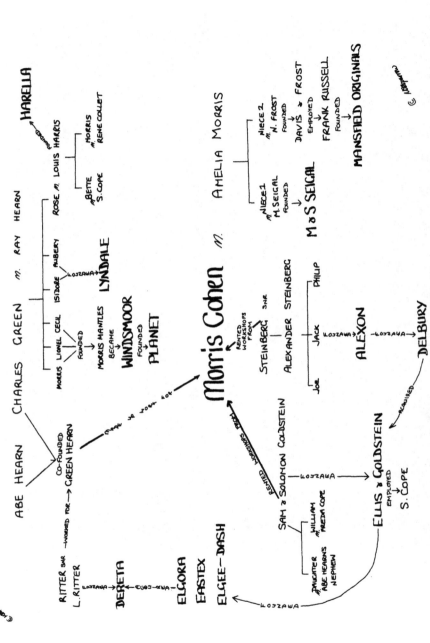

9 Chart showing Morris Cohen's contribution to the mantle-making trade and the kinship and company connections that developed, 1895–1988 (Maxine Sparrow)

10 Morris Cohen's mantle factory under construction in 1895 (Clive Moss and the London Museum of Jewish Life)

SYNAGOGUE PARADE.

A PROCESSION

OF

Jewish Unemployed & Sweaters' Victims

will be held on

SATURDAY, MARCH, 16th, 1889,

and will proceed to the

GREAT SYNAGOGUE

where the Chief Rabbi will deliver a Sermon to the Unemployed & Sweaters' Victims.

THE PROCESSION WILL START, WITH MUSIC, AT 12.30 FROM 40, BERNER STREET, COMMERCIAL ROAD, E.

We demand work to buy bread, and the hours of labour to be 8 per day.
We mean to effect this without nonsense.

COME IN LARGE NUMBERS AND BRING YOUR FRIENDS WITH YOU!

LEWIS LYONS,
PHILIP KRANTZ,

Secretaries to the Unemployed Committee

40, BERNER ST., COMMERCIAL RD., E.

Worker's Friend Printing Office, 40, Berner St., Commercial Rd. E.

11 Procession to the Great Synagogue of 'Jewish Unemployed and Sweaters' Victims', 1889

TAILORS' STRIKE, 1889.

RESOLUTION to be submitted to a Meeting to be held at the Jewish Working Men's Club, Great Alie Street, Whitechapel, on Monday, September 30th, 1889.

That this mass meeting of Tailors on strike pledge themselves to continue the Strike until the following demands are conceded—

(1) The hours of labour to be from 8 o'clock in the morning until 8 o'clock in the evening, with one hour for dinner and half-an-hour for tea.

(2) All meals to be had off the work premises.

(3) Only four hours overtime may be worked in a week.

(4) Not more than two hours overtime to be worked in any one day.

(5) The first two hours overtime to be paid for at the ordinary rate, and the second two hours to be paid for at the rate of time-and-a-half.

(6) That the hour system be not introduced.

Further, that an agreement be drawn up to this effect, to be signed by the Chairman and Secretary of the Strike Committee, Representatives of the West London District of the Amalgamated Society of Tailors, Chairman and Secretary of the Jewish Branch of the Amalgamated Society of Tailors, Chairman and Secretary of the Machinists Society, Chairman and Secretary of the Pressers Society, and the Chairman and Secretary of the Master Tailors' Association.

TO TAILORS AND TAILORESSES ! ! !

GREAT
STRIKE
of
LONDON TAILORS
& SWEATER'S VICTIMS.

FELLOW WORKERS,

You are all aware that a Commission of Lords have been appointed to enquire into the evils of the Sweating System in the Tailoring Trade. The Revelations made before the Commission by Witnesses engaged in the Tailoring Trade, are a Disgrace to a Civilised Country. The Sweaters' Victims had hoped that this Commission, would have come to some satisfactory conclusion as to an alteration in the condition of the Sweated Tailors. Finding they have just put off their deliberation until Next Session, we have decided to take Immediate Action.

It is too long for us to wait, until Next Session, because the hardships inflicted upon us by the Sweater are unbearable. We have therefore decided to join in the CENERAL DEMAND FOR INCREASED COMFORT AND SHORTER HOURS OF LABOUR. Our Hours at present being on an average from 14 to 18 per day, in unhealthy and dirty dens.

WE DEMAND:

(1) THAT THE HOURS BE REDUCED TO 12 WITH AN INTERVAL OF ONE HOUR FOR DINNER AND HALF-HOUR FOR TEA.

(2) ALL MEALS TO BE HAD OFF THE PREMISES.

(3) GOVERNMENT CONTRACTORS TO PAY WAGES AT TRADE UNION RATES.

(4) GOVERNMENT CONTRACTORS AND SWEATERS NOT TO GIVE WORK HOME AT NIGHT AFTER WORKING HOURS.

We now Appeal for the support of all Tailors to join us and thus enable us to Successfully Enforce our Demands, which are reasonable,

Tailors & Tailoresses support in joining this General Strike.

We Appeal to all Tailors, Machinists, Pressers, Basters, &c. to meet, EN-MASSE, on THURSDAY, FRIDAY & SATURDAY MORNINGS, at 10 o'clock, (outside the Baths) GOULSTON STREET, WHITECHAPEL, E.

Piece Workers Finish Up, Week Workers Give Notice at Once,

ALL WORK TO CEASE ON SATURDAY AFTERNOON WHEN THE STRIKE WILL BE DECLARED.

Signed, STRIKE COMMITTEE,

				M. Rosenthall,
Lewis Lyons, Chairman	Richard Roskeliy,	Annie Goodman,	Jacob Sydler,	Harris Frank
J. Green	Phillip White,	L. Goldstein,	J. Margolis,	Lewis Perlburg,
J. Silverman	Simon Cohen	Charles Mowbray,	D. Greenbaum	W. Wess, Secretary.

Tailors Strike Committee Room " White Hart," Greenfield-st., Commercial-Rd. All communications to be addressed to the Secty

P.S. We appeal to those engaged in the Trade to at once join either of the following Societies:

" JEWISH BRANCH, AMALGAMATED SOCIETY OF TAILORS." Meets on Sunday Evenings, from 8 till 10, at the " White Hart," Greenfield Street, Commercial Road, E.
" PRESSER'S SOCIETY," Meet Sunday Evenings, from 8 till 10, at the " Man in the Moon," Plough Street, Commercial Road, E.
" MANTEL MAKERS, TAILORS AND MACHINISTS SOCIETY " Meet Saturday Evenings, from 7 till 10 at the " White Hart," Greenfield Street, Commercial Road, E.

AUGUST 27th, 1889

T. G. SAWYER, PRINTER, 227, BETHNAL GREEN ROAD

13 Poster advertising the Great Strike of 1889

aliens who do the principal parts of the work...which I cannot get done by English workers'.[28] This was, or so Morris Cohen wished the Commission to believe, a working environment in which Jew and Gentile, Englishman and alien, worked in harmony for the benefit of themselves, their employer and the country's balance of trade.

The image projected by Morris Cohen in his evidence to the Aliens Commission was of the positive contribution made by the Jewish immigrants to the English tailoring trade. Major Evans-Gordon, anti-alienist and founder member of the British Brothers' League, set out to undermine this view. He suggested that Cohen's claims were based on a false premise. He asked the Commission to consider the example of Hitchcock Williams, the well-known suppliers of ladies' tailored garments. According to Evans-Gordon they employed no more than '10 foreign tailors and three assistants', not the 50 to 60 Cohen suggested.[29]

> The witness says there are few firms in the trade who could possibly carry on their business without foreign labour. My point is that there is a very large firm to my knowledge which carries on a very large business in this identical ladies' tailor-made clothing, supplying the whole country, all over England, who employ only 10 foreigners in a very large factory.[30]

Cohen countered this by explaining that it did not pay the St Paul's Churchyard wholesalers to employ foreign indoor labour when they could buy garments more cheaply from himself and other manufacturers who in turn employed alien tailors. Evans-Gordon continued to press the point, clearly unaware of, or perhaps choosing to ignore, the letter written by the managing director of Hitchcock Williams to the Editor of the *Jewish Chronicle* in 1898. The letter succinctly sums up the alien contribution to the mantle-making industry, one stressed by Joseph Finn in his pamphlet, *The Voice of the Alien*, written three years earlier.

> Foreign Jewish tailors introduced new methods of manufacture and created a trade which has become a distinct gain to the country's commerce. We [Hitchcock Williams] were the first wholesale mantle manufacturers to employ foreign Jewish tailors in a factory. Prior to 1889 women's mantles imported amounted to the sum of £150,000 per annum as English female factory workers were unable to produce them. British instead of German material was used and money previously exported went to British

firms. Other English firms followed the example and Germany admits loss of trade to Britain. These foreign Jews do a class of work which our workers cannot undertake with success and they earn a high rate of pay.[31]

Morris Cohen's expertise was not restricted to the manufacture of women's clothing. 'Within 15 to 20 years of his arrival in this country he had become a considerable property investor in the East End of London.'[32] In addition to buildings in Spitalfields, which included a synagogue, and Stepney Causeway (sold to Dr Barnardo) he purchased Albert Square, in the Commercial Road area – now Albert Gardens – which contained thirty-nine houses built between 1830 and 1840. He supervised the building of additions onto the rear of the properties, which he then rented out to furriers, capmakers, dressmakers and, of course, mantle-makers. Amongst those who began their mantle-making days in Albert Square were Alexander Steinberg who founded Alexon, Shyer Green, whose sons created Windsmoor, and Solomon Goldstein of Ellis & Goldstein, all success stories of the 1930s and after. Morris Cohen's financial expertise went beyond the clothing and property worlds; he was an early investor in the cinema industry and acquired a substantial interest in the 'Purple Picture Palaces'.[33] Cohen became a rich man and enjoyed the delights of travel. The family photograph album shows a dapper Mr Cohen and an elegant Mrs Cohen enjoying the pleasures of Madeira. Shortly before the outbreak of the First World War Cohen retired to Brighton where he led the life of a respected gentleman and benefactor; he even made his motor car available for the mayor. Ever conscious of trends and fashions, shortly before he handed over control of the business to his elder son, Cohen supervised his company's prestigious move to Goswell Road, within the boundary of the City of London. Morris Cohen died in 1927. The business survived a further ten years then closed following the death of his eldest son who had taken over the reins of business. Morris Cohen represents the stereotypical successful, hard-working Jewish immigrant, using initiative and perspicacity to identify consumer patterns and develop their potential to the full for the benefit of himself, his work-force and, in spite of Major Evans-Gordon's attempts to prove otherwise, his newly adopted country.

TECHNOLOGY

The London tailoring trade served consumers and markets separated by class, gender and location. Three variations bred an industry the landscape of which was dominated by small-scale units of production relieved by the occasional large-size workshop and the rare factory. It was located in a metropolis the west end of which was dedicated to the manufacture of high-class finished goods, accessories and services while its east end had seen the departure of large-scale industries northwards to be replaced by those dominated by seasonality and casuality. Bespoke and sub-divisional tailoring was an industry which required little in the way of sophisticated plant and machinery. One of the few common denominators in the East and West Ends was the machinery used to produce tailored garments. The sewing machine represents the finest example of a technological innovation which made its impact on both production loci. The new machine, which could be operated by hand or treadle in a small space, accelerated both the deskilling and production processes. What could be more appealing to masters and middlemen catering for markets unaffected by demands for high-level craftsmanship? During the 1860s sewing machines for use in the home and the workshop were manufactured by at least half a dozen English companies.[34] But the undoubted leader in the field was the Singer Sewing Machine Company which, by 1877, operated 160 shops throughout the country selling or hiring out machines.[35] The price of a new machine, complete with accessories, ranged between £3. 10s. and £5. 10s.[36] Very few customers could afford to buy their machines 'right out', most paid by weekly instalment. Indeed it was from the returns of the thirty Singer Sewing Machine Company collectors based in the East End that Beatrice Potter collated her statistics on tailoring workshops for Charles Booth's survey.

The sewing machine revolutionised the London tailoring industry, enabling workers of both sexes, with little or no skill, to find employment in a previously demarcated zone. In the 1860s those lacking the manual dexterity of the craftsman could, by using the sewing machine, earn up to three times as much in a week as hand workers.[37] The considerations which facilitated the growth of a plethora of small-scale workshops producing poor-quality goods included the financial and physical ease of installation, a reliance on cheap, sweated man- or woman- power rather than fuel, and the use of domestic as opposed to industrial locations. (Even in the 1930s the workshop masters of east London were reluctant to install electrically operated sewing machines. As one retired salesman told the author, 'if they saw me coming they would lock the doors and pretend to be out'.) The trade unionist and socialist tailor James MacDonald, writing in 1889, was convinced that the hiring and installation of sewing machines in small commercial or domestic workshops, or in the outworkers' own homes, weakened the capital's stronghold of craft tailoring. MacDonald stressed that the expansion of the outworker system in London's West End was a direct result of the arrival of the sewing machine and its ease of acquisition.[38] The *Jewish Chronicle* had noted this as early as 1872 in an article which criticised the Jewish Board of Guardians' practice of hiring out sewing machines to the immigrant poor. The criticism was anchored to a more ominous theme, the fear of increasing anti-alienism. The *Chronicle* believed that providing fuel for the labour pool of 'an already full industry' was dangerous and to be undertaken with caution.[39]

There were few other areas of innovative technology visible in London's tailoring workshops before the First World War. Pressing was done by hand using heated irons, weighing anything between 16 and 24lb., which were lifted many thousands of times a day. No wonder pressers were identified by the length of their pressing arm. It was not until the late 1920s that the more sophisticated steam presses were generally introduced. These were operated by placing the garment between two boards which, when pressed together, effused steam, thus reducing the physical strain whilst increasing the speed of production. However, nothing could replace the old-fashioned hand-presser's skill at easing out, or easing in, a misshapen garment.

In London, unlike Leeds, not all cutters took advantage of 'labour saving machinery'.[40] Bespoke gained its name and reputation for individuality of cut, cloth and finish. Bandknives had their uses in London but to a more limited extent. In general wholesalers, sub-contractors, middlemen and masters made the fullest use possible of the capital's reservoir of semi-skilled and unskilled workers in units of production where cheap and expendable sub-divisional labour was substituted for labour-saving machinery.

WORKSHOPS AND WORKERS

From the beginning of the nineteenth century London experienced unprecedented dock development, road, railway and canal building, demolition and change of use of the housing stock. In the poorer parts of the capital the needy and mendicant, the casual workers and the residuum were increasingly forced in upon themselves. In a city which was the nation's centre of government, finance and commerce, space was at a premium, labour was not. The sweated tailoring trade was forced to use whatever accommodation it could afford, and it would afford very little. In both the East End and the West End, with the few exceptions mentioned below, tailoring workshops were small-scale and, frequently, insanitary. Bedrooms, back rooms, attics, workshops built on to the backs of existing buildings and large single Huguenot residences converted into extremes of multi-occupancy, all were commissioned into use. Any available space was turned into a workshop. Overcrowded conditions were intensified as warehouse foremen insisted that workshops be located within a specific radius, usually no more than half a mile away, before they would agree to give work out.[41] These stipulations created conditions under which the highest rents could be charged for unsafe and sub-standard accommodation.

EAST END

By the 1880s the *laissez-faire*, self-help philosophies of the mid-Victorian era were being questioned. As the depression deepened unemployment increased and with it expressions of protest which culminated in Bloody Sunday – 13 November 1887. Tensions were further heightened by the continued influx of thousands of aliens from eastern Europe who gave a new meaning to the term 'overcrowding' in the East End; in Spitalfields it was estimated that there were now more than one thousand people per acre, the average, even for east London, being two hundred and fifty. New political ideologies such as socialism and anarchism were seen by some as the solution to the nation's ills and the East End became a meeting place for refugee and English radical intellectuals.[42] The icing on the cake was the Ripper murders, which took place in Whitechapel between 6 August and 9 November 1888. The perverse brutality of the crimes stunned the nation and the world. The East End became a focal point of public and private concern, its layers of abysmal poverty open for all to see. Procrastination was no longer acceptable, the issue of poverty, its cause and effect, now headed the agenda of public and private investigation and a whole stream of government commissions and committees were established to investigate sweating, volumes of immigration and emigration, housing, policing, the Poor Law and old-age pensions.

Even before the Ripper and his knife became active the East End had been put under the spotlight of investigation. However, it was Charles Booth who was credited as having 'drawn the curtain behind which East London had been hidden'.[43] The newspaper reviews of the first volume, in what was to become the *Life and Labour* series, conveniently overlooked the earlier warnings of Mayhew, Mearns, Stead, Besant, Sims and Sala, all of whom had exposed the horrors of the 'city of darkest night'. But it was Booth, England's first social scientist, and his team of investigators who collected the enormous quantity[44] of original, and thought-provoking, data on east London[45] which was to provide the foundations from which the welfare legislation of the 1900s would emerge.

One of those eager, young, middle-class researchers was Beatrice Potter (later Webb), a cousin by marriage of Booth. In 1888, she collected material on the size, type, number and nature of tailoring workshops in the East End. Given the nature of the trade and the obscure location of cellar, attic and domestic workshops, we must not assume that Miss Potter carried out an all-inclusive survey. The territory she covered stretched from Mile End Old Town and Poplar in the east, through to Hackney, Shoreditch and Bethnal Green to the north, covering Whitechapel and Stepney. In all a total of 1,272 workshops were visited. Her statistics reveal that, as in Leeds, coat and jacket manufacture was the province of the male and was carried out in 958 of the workshops investigated, all but 57 of which were located in Whitechapel. Of the 167 workshops visited in its West Ward, 153 housed alien tailors producing coats, in one street alone there being 30 tailoring workshops. In workshops where English and Jewish women were employed, a wider range of garments was produced. Miss Potter discovered 11 shops in which vests (waistcoats) were made up, 72 producing juvenile garments and 158 in which trousers were manufactured. Lighter-weight and simpler garments which required lower levels of skill were made up by women working at home or were made in the clothing factories of Leeds.

While a cheap option was available there was little incentive for London middlemen and masters to operate large workshops and factories which, as illustrated by the Leeds example, required substantial capital investment. One of Beatrice Potter's most often-quoted comments is that which describes the ease of setting up a tailor's workshop in east London.

> The ease with which a man may become a master is proverbial in the East End. His living-room becomes his workshop, his landlord or his butcher his security; round the corner he finds a brother Israelite, whose trade is to supply pattern garments, to take a sample of his work to the wholesale house; with a small deposit he secures on the hire-system both sewing machine and presser's table. Altogether it is estimated that with £1 in his pocket any man may rise to the dignity of a 'sweater'... if he is successful, day by day, year by year, his profit increases and his labour diminishes relatively to the wage and labour of his hands.[46]

As we know only too well, in the years before the First World War only the few, Morris Cohen among them, were able to enjoy what Beatrice Potter termed the 'Characteristic love of profit of the Jewish race'.

There were some medium and large-scale units of production in the East End, though what was considered large in London would have be been labelled medium or even small in the West Riding. In 1887, John Burnett, investigator for the Board of Trade, reported that 'tailoring workshops in which ten, twenty and even thirty and forty are employed (in the East End) are numerous. There are even some where the numbers are more than fifty.'[47] Burnett refers to one workshop in which 100 hands were employed in 'factory-like' conditions. Beatrice Potter detailed 892 workshops in which under ten workers were employed, 266 in which there were between ten and 20 hands and 42 in which 25 workers were employed. As early as 1864 the Children's Employment Commission referred to one Whitechapel workshop in which 30 hands were compelled to work in bleak, overcrowded and unhealthy conditions.[48] For a few months in 1886 Lewis Lyons, as part of his campaign against the sweating system, published the *Anti-Sweater*, a journal dedicated to the exposure of that most vilified class of employer. Lyons pinpoints two large clothing factories in the East End, Lottery & Co. and Schneider & Son. In each case, '400 female hands operating steam powered machines were employed in very poor conditions'.[49] But for the most part, as economic history confirms, the belief prevailed that 'small was beautiful'.

The reality was far from beautiful. Those who made expeditions into the hell that was the sweated workshop invariably found conditions unbearable. In 1883 one of Her Majesty's Inspectors of Factories unearthed a mantle and costume workshop in which nine hands worked in a room where the temperature never dropped below 86°F. In the busy season work began before light and ended after dark. Natural daylight was a rare phenomenon as, in so many instances, workshops were windowless cellars or the windows contained panes so filthy that the outside world was invisible. For the benefit of the nation's health the *Lancet*, rightly convinced that clothes made in unhealthy conditions by unhealthy workers spread disease to the better classes, despatched a reporter to investigate sanitary conditions in Jewish tailoring workshops. These were found to be 'appalling'. Amongst the other evils the reporter discovered were filthy and inefficient water closets, housed indoors in cupboards adjacent to coal boilers. In addition to the obvious discomforts, the water closets constantly overflowed. The workshop environment was hardly improved by the common practice of glazing poor quality fabrics with urine![50]

John Burnett believed that these unacceptable conditions persisted because of the 'alien's preparedness to accept sub-standards in return for employment at rates no Englishman would accept',[51] an opinion which supports the anti-alienist critique of wage undercutting. In common with the *Lancet*, Burnett recorded the filthy and insanitary state of the small workshops, often no more than nine feet square. In poky rooms a dozen or more workers would slave away in intolerable temperatures created by the gas jets and coke fires used to heat the irons. In these hellholes hands worked and ate at the same time; nothing was permitted to halt production in the busy. It is a delusion to believe that the English-run workshops were any better. Though these were equally insanitary, investigators and commentators paid little attention to them. It was the eastern European immigrant who was deemed culpable for the perpetuation of the sweatshop.[52]

Between 1851 and 1911 the total number of tailors and tailoresses recorded as working in London rose by over 100 per cent, from 30,773 to 64,993. The largest increase occurred in the twenty-year span between 1881 and 1901, the high point of alien immigration, when the rise was just over 50 per cent. The arrival of the sewing machine and the continual deskilling of the tailoring trade is highlighted by the increasing number of females employed as tailoresses. Overall the ratio of male to female tailoring workers gradually reduced from 3:2 in 1851 to almost level sixty years later, tailors outnumbering tailoresses by only

1,557. London thus was different from other large manufacturing centres. In England and Wales as a whole, in 1911, there were 122,352 tailors to 127,115 tailoresses.[53]

Tailors and tailoresses working in London's East End produced garments which ranged from all but the highest quality bespoke down to the poorest slop. In a multiplicity of commercial and domestic workshops and the several clothing factories, hands were employed as basters, pressers, fitters, machiners, tailors, plain machiners and under-pressers. In contrast to the West End, where the tailoring work-force reduced by over 60 per cent, the number of those recorded as employed in the trade in the years between 1871 and 1911 altered by less than one thousand.[54] (It must be assumed, however, that a proportion of the tailoring work-force evaded the eyes, and forms, of the census enumerators.) But statistics simplify a history which, when examined, can be seen to have been fashioned by a multiplicity of factors which included fluctuations in demand, variations in the labour supply and economic peaks and troughs.

In addition to her data on the East End tailoring workshops, Beatrice Potter provided an analysis of the internal structure of the sub-divisional workshop.[55] Though dependent to a large extent on the information provided by the collectors of the sewing machine company, school board visitors, wholesale houses and a combination of labour contacts and workpeople, Miss Potter did carry out some field work. As recorded in her diary, on 14 and 15 April 1888 she worked as a trouser hand in Mr Marks's tailoring workshop at 198 Mile End Road.[56] By London standards it was a large workshop, employing thirty tailoresses making up trousers and vests. Beatrice's diary for those two days contains the expected descriptions of stuffy, over-crowded working conditions, low pay, meals eaten at the work bench and the constant pressure to finish orders before the Sabbath commenced on a Friday night. What comes through too is the workshop *bonhomie* which combined good humour and bad language, the apparent absence of any antipathy between Jewish and Gentile workers and the cheeky behaviour of the pressers who responded to the 'missus's' rebuke for lateness by drawing attention to her unfortunate gambling [sic] habits. Beatrice Potter's account of her days in the workshop provides some support for the view put forward in the *Arbeiter Fraint* that the Jewish tailoresses sided with the employers rather than with their male counterparts.[57] In London discontent fashioned into labour organisation was a male prerogative.

The various classes of work produced in the tailoring workshops of London's East End were classified by Beatrice Potter as Best Bespoke, Bespoke and Stock, Stock and Common and Very Common. Best Bespoke went against the trend through the use of a small, skilled work-force which received high wages: tailors earned between 7s. and 10s. for a thirteen to fourteen-hour day while tailoresses earned between 4s. and 6s. for a twelve-hour day. In the Bespoke and Stock workshops the spectrum of skills was widest. Two grades of general tailor (those who could 'make a garment through') machiners, pressers, sub-contracted workers and a general hand were paid from 8s. 6d. down to 5s. 0d. for working a thirteen to fourteen-hour day. General tailors, machiners and pressers all received the same hourly rates. The services of the general tailor were dispensed with for the manufacture of garments at the bottom end of the market. Here machiners and pressers headed the scale of wages, earning between 6s. 0d and 7s. 0d a day. Miss Potter described a garment produced in that sector of the trade as, 'not a coat at all' but 'a balloon...bagged together'.[58] In common with their brothers in Leeds the 'poor devil' plain machiners and under-pressers worked 'indefinite' hours for below starvation wages of between 1d. and 2½d. an hour. With no excess available for board they 'took their rest on a stake-down between the pressers' table, the machines and scattered garments'. Menials of the workshop were rarely paid overtime. Jewish masters avoided this by classifying unskilled hands as 'convenience workers', making up time lost as a result of Sabbath observance or some other 'convenient' reason. As one union spokesman complained in 1907, 'What has *Shabbos* [the Jewish Sabbath] got to do with the economic life of the Jewish worker?'[59]

The statistics compiled by Charles Booth's cousin Beatrice were drawn from the 'gents' sector of the East End tailoring trade. In his evidence to the Aliens Commission, Morris Cohen stressed that higher standards of skill were required in the manufacture of mantles. 'A man who has not been taught the trade cannot start getting a living at mantle making', and whilst there were any number of unskilled 'greeners' about Cohen admitted he had problems hiring skilled labour.[60] When he did wages were as high as £1. 15s. to £3 a week for tailors and £1. 10s. a week for tailoresses. It may well have been Cohen's figures which resulted in the exclusion of mantle-making from the sectors of the industry which came under the first Tailoring Trade Board established in 1911 following the Trade Boards Act of 1909.

During the mid-1900s the import of mantles once again rose. The economic repercussions of this change in pattern were hardfelt by the ladies' tailors whose earnings fell by as much as 50 per cent.[61] The gents' trade was unaffected. There machiners continued to earn up to 7s. 6d. a day,[62] some taking home over £1. 10s. per week.[63]

Beatrice Potter's table of wages was based on payment by time rates. But this must not be taken as the norm, for the debate over piece-payment as opposed to time-payment continued long after the First World War. Priority was net take-home pay, the determining factors being speed and agility, not skill. In 1888 the London Tailors' and Machinists' Society, in common with so many other workers' organisations, appealed, without success, for an eight-hour day to run from 9 a.m. to 6 p.m. with a one-hour break for lunch.[64] In 1906 the mantle-makers went on strike, unsuccessfully, for a twelve-hour day.[65] Even in 1912 a twelve-hour day was the best the mantle-maker could hope for.[66] While the system of payment by the piece remained profitable, unanimous support for a shorter working day was impossible. Those paid by the piece were convinced that the only way to achieve a living wage was by working long into the night. Trade unionist Sam Dreen, writing in the *Arbeiter Fraint* in 1906, reported on the debate being held by the mantle-makers over a proposal to substitute day-rates for piece-rates. Those in favour believed that day-rates would eliminate sub-contracting in the workshop, would provide for a more regular working week and would strengthen the hand of labour organisation by ending divisions within the work-force. Those opposed stressed that it was not in the worker's best interests, and that time payment would lead to 'organisation going under'. The most powerful argument for piece-work came from the worker who told the *Arbeiter Fraint* that under the piece-work system he earned £2. 10s. per week, a sum impossible under day-rates.[67]

Whether paid by time or piece-rates life was hard and bitter for all but the most skilled of East End tailors. The *Arbeiter Fraint*'s graphic description of the life of the tailor during the depressed years of the 1900s tells all:

> It is heartbreaking to see how people, fathers of children, workers, good craftsmen work, so hard, such long hours with heads bent, tremble for their bosses, the majority caterers, shoe-makers or drivers and all for what, for a slice of bitter bread in the busy time barely just to keep alive and, in the slack time so little....[68]

Tailoresses in the East End fared little better. The Socialist League's journal *Commonweal* focused on the exploitation of tailors' machinists in the 1880s and 1890s. Those poor girls were paid 1½*d*. for sewing the seams of a jacket, binding the bottom, attaching two facings and making and inserting the sleeves and collar.[69] Girls unfortunate enough not to have the requisite skill for mantle manufacture took home just one shilling for making a shoddy garment 'right through'.[70] Ten years on Black and Meyer discovered that some tailoresses earned only 5½*d*. for making a 49-inch-long woman's coat of such complexity that only one could be made in a day. In certain unsavoury instances rates of pay were determined by the 'mood of the male fixer in charge', a whim with hints of immorality. Pay differentials were vast. Some women earned as little as 4*s*. 6*d*. a week, others an average of 14*s*. 9*d*.[71] In Selitrenny's portrayal of the tailoring workshop we find none of the warmth of 198 Mile End Road. His reports reveal abominable conditions. Unmarried Jewish females, required to return to the workshop three or four times per day so as not to lose any job opportunity, became 'morally, sexually and intellectually apathetic'.[72] Calls were made for 'a staff of Jewish factory inspectors to enforce the law', though Inspector Raskin in Leeds appears to have done little to increase local respect for the Factory and Workshop Acts. Labour organisation seemed to offer little hope. According to Selitrenny the Jewish tailoress in London 'dreads unions, they mean strikes and she has slack times enough'.[73]

Homework provided the cheapest form of tailoring. By 1911, 11.4 per cent, or 3,632 of the capital's 32,000 tailoresses were believed to be working at home.[74] They lived, as R.H. Tawney explained:

> in a world of naked motives...governed by work, hunger and fear, fear that there may be less work and more hunger, the wives of men who are paid starvation wages, or who are irregularly employed, snatch work for the sake of their children as a wild animal forages for its cubs...[75]

Tawney, as so many before him, makes the analogy between the savagery and barbarity of the jungle and the lives of those who inhabited the twilight world of poverty and desperation in the most modern and successful example of the civilised world.

Two-thirds of tailoring homeworkers were engaged in finishing garments, a task which required little training, no machinery and consequently received the lowest pay. For example, a woman making up trousers at home could expect to earn no more than ten shillings a week. Homework wages were rarely sufficient to support more than one human being. Those forced to accept that irregular and unsatisfactory style of employment tended to be the widow, the ageing spinster, the married woman subsidising the family income during those all too frequent periods of spouse unemployment or the young mother tending to the babies with one hand whilst making trousers or sewing seams with the other. Homework offered little improvement on the verminous and filthy working conditions of the workshop while the mental boredom and misery would surely have resulted in an even greater degree of apathy.

In the West End during the 1900s the number of homeworkers increased as unprofitable workshops closed down. In the East End numbers actually fell. This was due to a variety of factors, the increased production of medium-quality, cheap and special order garments in the Leeds clothing factories, the establishment of a Tailoring Trade Board in 1909, the introduction of National Insurance (providing sickness benefit) in 1911 and the alien presence. Eastern European tailors were speedier and more efficient than English homeworkers who were given work only when demand was high and time was short. Alien male labour was far more attractive, the men worked long and hard in order to get on and out of the ghetto and took every advantage of female kin who, though 'not considered as worthy of wages', provided extra hands in the workshop[76] – a cost-effective method indeed.

WEST END

Whilst the East End was bathed in the searchlight of investigation the West End remained in the shadows. Yet it had more than its fair share of sweatshops, overcrowding and insanitary conditions to which could be added a multi-ethnic cocktail of Germans, Poles, Italians, French men and women and central and eastern European Jews. Charles Booth's map of poverty[77] clearly illustrates that, in addition to its gleaming gold mosaic of wealth, the West End of London was punctuated by the dark blue of poverty. Frith Street, the spine of Soho was, and remained until well into the second half of the twentieth century, renowned for its overcrowded and cramped tailoring workshops. No crusading surveys were carried out in the nether regions of the West End. Neither Beatrice Potter nor John Burnett sallied forth into the workshops of Brewer Street and Berwick Street in order to provide first-hand information.[78] Therefore, in order to compensate for the paucity of information, a selection of primary and secondary sources have been used to provide an outline sketch of the structure of the tailoring trade in London's West End.

Until the turn of the nineteenth century the West End tailoring trade was devoted to the production of varying grades of male bespoke garments. The emphasis was on quality clothes produced by a work-force which, until the early 1900s, was male dominated and essentially English. The foreign presence was small, restricted to a few highly skilled German and Swedish craftsmen[79] and the colony of Jewish craft tailors resident in Soho since the late eighteenth century.[80] The number of eastern European Jews employed in the West End of London before the First World War was small. The 1881 Decennial Census records the presence of just 68 tailors of eastern European origin in the West End. Twenty years later their number, supplemented by 52 Jewish tailoresses, had increased to approximately 421. The alien proportion of the 6,360 work-force[81] was thus less than ten per cent. In 1890 James MacDonald, caught up in the rising tide of anti-alienism, warned that, 'the Jews have got a firm foothold in the West End tailoring trade and it is greatly to be feared with no good result to the Gentile workers'.[82] The burgeoning East End trade was gradually encroaching on the cheaper end of the bespoke market. There was no territorial threat, as the high level of West End craftsmanship and the Anglicised nature of the Jewish community deterred the semi-skilled and unskilled new alien arrivals; they were far more at home in the *stetl* that was Whitechapel.

The nature of the West End tailoring trade, with its concentration on the bespoke garment, encouraged small-scale production, whether behind the portals of the high-class craft establishment or in the domestic or rented workshops and sittings[83] in and around Soho where, by 1909, the rent for a single room could be as high as between 9s. 0d. and 11s. 0d. per week.[84] In the West End, as in the East End, there were some medium-sized production units. In the 1860s and 1870s these took the form of workrooms directly attached to bespoke tailors' establishments, their exact size and that of the work-force determined by market forces. Mathison and Co. of Conduit Street, Mayfair, supplied clothes of the highest quality and retained a permanent team of 'on-the-premises' journeymen who could produce bespoke garments to order. These were either made throughout by one craftsman or made by journeymen working in pairs, one making the right side and one the left. During the busy season the company took on extra gangs of journeymen tailors, whenever possible from the same House of Call.[85] The illustrious company of Henry Poole and Son, established in 1806, tailored garments for notables such as the Prince of Wales, Disraeli and Napoleon III. When necessary the company could call upon the services of up to 300 craftsmen, the majority journeymen tailors working in their own workshops. Nicolls and Co. of Regent Street was another company using both in-house and workshop tailors. They employed thirty men on their own premises and in addition contracted work out to workshops in the East and West Ends of London.[86] It was the perceived immorality of the company's use of sweated labour that led to Henry Mayhew's resigning his position as Metropolitan Correspondent of the *Morning Chronicle* in October 1850. In the tradition of newspapers which depend on advertising for revenue, the *Morning Chronicle* published a laudatory article about Messrs. Nicolls stressing the 'contented and happy' conditions of employment and the 'good wages' earned.[87] In reality Nicolls had refused Mayhew access to any information. The Metropolitan Correspondent was not prepared to have his name associated with what was evidently a biased, sycophantic and inaccurate article. He demanded that the *Morning Chronicle* publish a statement to that effect. When they refused he resigned and called a public meeting at which he exposed the falsehoods contained in the article.[88]

At the outset of the twentieth century the number of tailors and tailoresses in the West End of London had fallen by over 60 per cent in a period of ten years, from 18,092 to 6,360 owing to fundamental changes in male purchasing and outfitting habits. Personal preference and economic necessity had driven many away from the bespoke or 'made-on-premises' tailors to outlets which were serviced by the special order or stock departments of the Leeds wholesale clothing factories or the East End workshops. The very highest level bespoke retained its custom and, even at the end of the twentieth century, with prices for a bespoke suit ranging from between £1,500 to £9,500, remains.[89]

Initially, the arrival of the wholesale manufacture of mantles made little impression on the structure of the West End tailoring trade. Changes began to take place with the opening of underground stations at Oxford Circus in 1900 and Regent Street in 1907, and the increased usage of the omnibus. The West End department stores had thus become accessible to those who did not have ready access to the horse-drawn carriage or chauffeur-driven limousine. The result was a significant increase in the sale of mantles and the migration of some East End tailors westwards. Small-scale mantle-making factories, employing between fifty and one hundred tailoresses, began to appear immediately to the north and south of Oxford Street.[90] Improved transportation benefited workers as well as consumers. But it was not until after the First World War, when the wholesale manufacture of dresses, coats and suits really took off, that the area became a centre of clothing production.

In his chapter on the tailoring trade for Charles Booth's *Life and Labour* series, James MacDonald refers to the very highest level of craftsmanship as 'Best Bespoke', in which the aristocrats of the trade either singly, or in pairs, worked on the garment right through, rarely, if at all, using a sewing machine; even the trousers and vests were made by 'a single individual workman'. Bespoke craftsmen worked a minimum of twelve, but up to as many as sixteen, hours a day for wages ranging from between £1. 10s. a week in the slack to £4 a week in the busy.[91] Slightly lower down the craft scale, though still answering to the call of 'made on the premises', garments were produced by a team. This usually comprised 'a skilled tailor, two skilled tailoresses, a machinist and several apprentices', or if on a larger scale, 'a foreman, two tailors, two machiners, two finishers, one presser and one apprentice'.[92]

Throughout the handicraft sector of the tailoring trade, the production of male and female garments was costed by 'time-log', a complex system of piece-work based on a time-scale in which, for reasons unexplained, forty minutes equalled one hour. Log-rates were subject to regional variations and often did not conform to any set standards or rules. For example, during the 1880s, London handicraft tailors appealed for 5 ½d. per log hour but, as a result of the depressed economy, were forced to accept an increase of only 2d. per log hour. In 1891, during the brief period of prosperity, James MacDonald, as secretary of the West End branch of the AST, negotiated a uniform increase in the log-rate with the Master Tailors' Association. From that time until 1908, when it was increased to 9d., the London log rate was 6d. per hour.[93] By 1910 the annual average national earnings of bespoke tailors was reported to be 22s. 1d. per week.[94] Taking account of the fact that the London rate was slightly in excess of this figure – in 1891 the difference was 1d. – the real wage of the West End tailor had actually fallen to a level barely above Charles Booth's 1889 poverty line. The other aristocrat of the West End tailoring trade was the cutter.

The 1892 Royal Commission on Labour reported that there were 1,500 cutters in London. The secretary of the London Clothiers' Cutters' Trade Union told the Commission that working conditions and wages for the almost totally English work-force were 'fairly good' and rarely subject to the vicissitudes of seasonality. In the tradition of the old 'new model' union, the LCCTU imposed a five-year system of apprenticeship as a means of preserving the highest levels of craftsmanship. A skilled cutter, on a piece-rate basis, could expect to earn at least £2 per week,[95] with the addition of a 'bonus' log-rate which, in the 1880s, was 15s. 0d. per month.[96]

Sub-divisional tailors employed in the workshops of London's West End were rarely paid by the log-rate. They worked to a time- or piece-rate based on the quality of garment produced. As a result, their average weekly wage, calculated on the basis of between 4s. 0d. and 5s. 0d. a day for a four-day week, differed little from that of the craftsman referred to above.[97] Thus, whilst skill commanded a higher base rate, at the lower end of the trade, speed and dexterity ironed out the financial if not the craft divisions.

The West End tailoresses provide us with a clear example of the dividing line between the higher and lower levels of bespoke manufacture. Technological innovation accelerated the deskilling process and at the same time reduced demand for the mid-quality bespoke ranges and therefore the numbers of tailors and tailoresses. For those who satisfied the tailoring desires of the wealthy élite came the economic rewards of craftsmanship. The Inspector of Factories and Workshops for the Central Metropolitan District reported that in the mid-1880s women working for English or German craftsmen earned as much as 1s. 9d. for making a pair of trousers. At those rates a handworker averaging three pairs of trousers per week, working a four-day week, was paid a minimum weekly wage of £1.[98] In the early part of the next century the Misses Black and Meyer revealed that skilled tailoresses producing bespoke waistcoats took home more than £1 per week. At the other end of the scale wages had been pushed down to little more than 5s. 0d. per week.[99] Sixty years after Henry Mayhew's distressing account of the plight of the starving needlewomen, the place of prostitution in the fight for survival had not been eradicated.

The most significant alteration in the system and level of wage payment and bargaining in the tailoring trade resulted from the passing of the Trade Boards Act in 1909. The Act was part of the package of early social legislation delivered in the first decade of the twentieth century. The Trade Boards Act was a legislative attempt to control sweating in those industries in which the worst conditions prevailed. The sweating system had been under the microscope since the 1880s. The 1891 Fair Wages Resolution, a tepid response to the House of Lords Select Committee on the Sweating System, marked the first attempt to introduce some form of legislative control, but applied only to those who were contracted to provide government clothing. The resolution ensured that wages paid by contractors were equal to the local standard rate and that employers had no recourse to undercutting. By the early 1900s it was clear that tougher measures were needed to ensure the welfare of the most abused members of the nation's workforce, who in so many instances were poorly served by representative trade unions. Social Darwinists and Eugenists, concerned that women working in sweated conditions were producing enfeebled infants, joined with the increasing numbers of those calling for the introduction of 'limited socialism' in order that the individual and the nation could look forward to a secure future.

By the dawn of the twentieth century support for a form of government wage control was growing. The most powerful influence was that of George Cadbury, the cocoa manufacturer, who, as owner of the *Daily News*, was the force behind that paper's mounting the impressive and shocking Sweated Industries Exhibition in 1906. To a large extent the Exhibition concentrated on homework but examples of exploited outdoor labour in industries such as chain-making and nail-making were also on display. Public outrage at the extremes of human degradation and exploitation resulted in the formation of the Anti-Sweating League (ASL) founded, by amongst others, the leader of the Women's Trade Union League, Mary McArthur. The warden of Toynbee Hall, J.J. Mallon, was appointed secretary of the ASL. The follow-up to the Exhibition was a Conference on Minimum Wages in 1906 and a House of Lords Select Committee on Homework in 1908. Support for the idea of a Wages Bill grew. Reference was made to the Australian example, where in the State of Victoria controls had been in place since 1896. Opposition to the Bill was raised on the grounds that if wages were set above market level unemployment would follow. However, those intent on dealing with the problem of sweating won the day, to a degree. Government did not gain the right to set an actual minimum wage but to ensure that representatives of employers and workers in the appointed industries, together with independent persons, would agree a minimum wage which would then be legally enforced.[100]

The Trades Board Act of 1909,[101] passed in the same year as that which created state labour exchanges, covered chain-making, lace-making, box-making and certain, though not all, sections of the clothing trade. Retail manufacture was excluded because, according to Dobbs, 'the authorities were deceived by the high rates of hourly wages which characterised this section of the industry',[102] as was mantle-making for 'though organisation was not wide it was unclear how general low wages were and its complexity made demarcation difficult'.[103] Both these omissions were rectified after the Trade Boards Act was extended in 1918 to include 'all industries insufficiently organised to render collective bargaining ... effective'.[104] Except when there were rare surges of membership stimulated by strikes or strike action, the clothing trade would always be 'insufficiently organised'. The Tailoring Trade Board was composed of an equal number of representatives of employers' and employees' organisations[105] plus independent members appointed to 'represent the public economic conscience'.[106] The Board's first 'proposal to fix' minimum rates of pay was arrived at after much debate and counter-debate. It recommended that men and women working a fifty-hour week should receive respectively £1. 5s. and 13s. 6½d. per week.[107] It was firmly stressed that these were minimum rates which should not endanger the wages of those who were paid at a higher level. In addition the Tailoring Trade Board stipulated that all wages paid should be 'free and clear of all deductions'. By this it was hoped, first, to eradicate the system of fines and penalties which had been so oppressive to women workers and, second, to ensure that those covered by the Act were paid for time spent at the workplace waiting for work, rather than solely for the period actually working. This last aimed at eradicating the 'bunching' of work. The Act was a clear attempt to ameliorate conditions for those employed in the sweatshops and factories of the tailoring trade. It was also an attempt by some to ease women out of the work-force by reducing their economic viability and, as argued by Jenny Morris, a covert means of social control.[108] Although the first Board sat in 1911 its findings and proposals did not really take effect until 1914, by which time a new and vastly more threatening factor had appeared on the horizon, war, which brought with it demands for manpower and military clothing.

Between 1870 and 1915, with the exception of that 'ruthless few', life for the capital's semi-skilled and unskilled tailors and tailoresses was grim and showed little prospect of improvement. The structure of the London industry, its divisions, sub-divisions, gradations of skill, diversity of markets and differences of gender and race presented a daunting problem to those intent upon solving industrial problems through labour organisation. There was little chance of worker cohesion, the different sectors spawned independent representative bodies which too often opposed each other rather than jointly confronting employers and the system. In Leeds pragmatism and leadership overcame these difficulties, in London it was often the case that good leadership was absent.

NOTES

1. *Henry Poole* (pamphlet) (London, 1983).
2. E. Moses, *The Growth of an Important Branch of British Industry* (1860).
3. Tawney, op. cit., p.6.
4. Quoted in Hobsbawm, *Worlds of Labour* op. cit, p.139.
5. Between 1851 and 1901 the population of Greater London rose by over 130 per cent, from 2,685,000 to 6,586,000, B.R. Mitchell and P. Deane, *Abstract of British Historical Statistics* (1962), p.26.
6. C. Booth, *Life and Labour of the People of London*, First Series, Poverty, Vol.4 (1902 edn), p.50.
7. The difference between made-to-measure and bespoke was that the former was a garment made from the customer's measurements without any fittings whereas the latter was made to fit exactly as the result of as many fittings as were required.
8. The number of clerical workers alone rose by 175 per cent between 1861 and 1891, see Stedman Jones, op. cit., pp.358–9.
9. *Report to the Board of Trade on Sweating 1887*, op. cit., p.18.
10. By this time the company had opened outlets in a number of Yorkshire towns.
11. J.B. Jeffreys, *Retail Trading in Britain 1850–1950* (1954), p.299.
12. *Henry Poole*, op. cit.
13. Hamish Fraser, op. cit., p.131.
14. A. Adburgham, *Shops and Shopping 1800–1914* (1989), pp.53 and 77.
15. Ibid., p.228.
16. *See below* pp.101–2.
17. Jeffrey, op. cit., p.307.
18. *See below* p.101.
19. Lady Jeune's article in the *Fortnightly Review*, Jan. 1896 is quoted in Adburgham, op. cit., p.236.
20. Information from a meeting with Mr G. Williams, Managing Director of Hitchcock Williams in July 1984.
21. Women's fashion magazines were available from the first half of the nineteenth century but their number increased significantly during the last two decades of the century. See Jeffreys, op. cit., p.301.
22. Adburgham, op.cit., p.85.
23. Ibid., pp.125–6 and Ewing, op. cit., p.26.
24. I am extremely grateful to Clive Moss, Morris Cohen's grandson, and other

members of the family for the biographical information and photographs supplied which broadened the author's knowledge of the man who 'claimed' to have introduced mantle-making to England.

25. *Royal Commission on Alien Immigration 1903*, op. cit., qq 18968.
26. Ibid.
27. *Labour Gazette*, April 1895.
28. *Royal Commission on Aliens*, op. cit., qq 18968.
29. Ibid., qq 19007–14.
30. Ibid., qq 19016.
31. *Jewish Chronicle*, 22 April 1898.
32. Letter from Cohen's grandson, Clive Moss, to the author, dated 3 Nov. 1993.
33. Ibid.
34. Adburgham, op. cit., p.114.
35. Jeffreys, op. cit., p.401.
36. *Jewish Chronicle*, 19 March 1872.
37. *Children's Employment Commission, 1864*, op. cit.
38. Booth, *Life and Labour of the People of London*, Second Series, Industry, Vol.3 (1903 edn), p.44.
39. *Jewish Chronicle*, 10 May 1872.
40. *Royal Commission on Labour, 1892*, op. cit.
41. *Royal Commission on Aliens, 1903*, op. cit., qq 2211658.
42. *See* Fishman, *East End Jewish Radicals*, op. cit.
43. *The Times*, 15 April 1889.
44. These are housed in the archives of the London School of Economics and Political Science and University of London Senate House library.
45. For an account of Booth's work *see* A.J. Kershen, 'Henry Mayhew and Charles Booth', in Alderman and Holmes, op. cit., Ch.6. pp.94–117 and T.S. and M.B. Simey, *Charles Booth* (1960).
46. Booth, *Life and Labour of the People of London*, First Series, Poverty, Vol.IV, op. cit., pp.60–1.
47. *Report to the Board of Trade on the Sweating System at the East End of London, 1887*, PP 1887, LXXIX.
48. *Children's Employment Commission 1864, 4th Report*, op. cit.
49. *Anti-Sweater*, Sept. 1886.
50. *The Lancet*, 5 March 1884.
51. *Report on the Sweating System at the East End of London*, op. cit.
52. By the beginning of the twentieth century rent and rates were so high that a number of East End tailors were forced to migrate north to the suburb of Hackney and open workshops in better surroundings but further from the heart of the industry.
53. The ratio of tailoresses to tailors was higher in Manchester, Bristol, Essex, Norwich and, of course, Leeds: *see* decennial census reports for 1871, 1881, 1891, 1901 and 1911.
54. The number of tailors rose by 4,000 in the forty-year period whilst the number of tailoresses fell by 3,500.
55. *See* Appendix, Table 29.
56. *See* N. and J. MacKenzie, *The Diary of Beatrice Webb: One* (1982), pp.239–49.
57. Ibid.
58. Booth, *Life and Labour* First Series, Poverty, Vol.IV, op. cit., p.40.
59. *Arbeiter Fraint*, 1 March 1907.
60. *Aliens Commission*, op. cit., qq 19024.
61. *Select Committee on Homework 1906*, PP 1907, VI, qq 3335.

62. J. White, *Rothschild Buildings* (1980), p. 285.
63. Dobbs, op. cit., p. 108.
64. *Arbeiter Fraint*, 10 Feb. 1888.
65. Ibid., 31 March 1906.
66. Ibid., 16 Aug. 1912.
67. Ibid., 22 June 1906.
68. *Arbeiter Fraint*, 19 March 1907.
69. *Commonweal*, 5 May 1888.
70. *The Journeyman*, 23 March 1896.
71. C. Black and C. Meyer, *Makers of Our Clothes* (1909), p. 15.
72. Selitrenny, op. cit.
73. Ibid.
74. D. Bythell, *The Sweated Trades* (1978), p. 75.
75. Tawney, op. cit., pp. 192–3.
76. *Select Committee on Homework*, op. cit., qq 801.
77. Charles Booth produced a 'map of poverty' in which levels of affluence and distress were indicated by the colouring of the streets of London in gradations ranging from gold for the upper and wealthy classes down to black for the criminal, vicious members of the residuum.
78. As we have seen above, Beatrice Potter spent two days working in a trouser making workshop in the East End.
79. Dobbs, op. cit., p. 43.
80. Pollin, op. cit., p. 69.
81. As there are no available statistics on the number of aliens in the West End tailoring work-force betwen 1881 and 1911 the author has used the following method to arrive at the figures quoted: a ratio of 1:10 male eastern European to English tailors has been used for the years between 1881 and 1901 and for the following ten years a ratio of 1:6. The number of eastern European tailoresses is estimated by taking a base ratio of 1:8. It may be noted that the ratio of tailors to other occupations among eastern Europeans was reported as 1:3 in the *Summary of Census Results* for the County of London in 1901.
82. Booth, *Life and Labour of the People of London*, Second Series, Industry, Vol. 3, op. cit., p. 156.
83. The practice of renting sittings intensified during the 1900s as the cost of accommodation in London's West End made it increasingly unviable for small masters to maintain permanent premises. *See* Black and Meyer, op. cit., p. 20.
84. Ibid., p. 23.
85. Evidence of M. Trelawney to *Children's Employment Commission 1864, 4th Report*, op. cit.
86. Ibid.
87. *Morning Chronicle*, 4 Oct. 1850.
88. For a more detailed account of this episode *see* Kershen, 'Henry Mayhew and Charles Booth', op. cit., pp. 96–8.
89. Information on the price of bespoke suits given to the author by Harrods Men's Tailoring Department on 19 Nov. 1993. The fabric for the £9,500 suit is so fragile that a model is made up from a cheaper fabric and when this is considered to be perfect the Australian merino wool suit is made up and the customer given the model free. In the words of the manager of Gieves and Hawkes, 'he gets two suits for the price of one'.
90. *Annual Report of Chief Inspector of Factories 1910*, PP 1911, X11, p. 112.
91. Booth, *Life and Labour of the People of London*, Second Series, Industry, Vol. 3, op. cit., p. 145.

92. Dobbs, op. cit., p.108.
93. See Justice, 6 June 1891 and Dobbs, op. cit., p.108.
94. Labour Gazette, Jan. 1910.
95. Royal Commission on Labour, 1892, op. cit.
96. Commonweal, 8 Oct. 1887.
97. Dobbs, op. cit., p.108.
98. Report on the Social Conditions of Factory and Female Operatives in the Central Metropolitan District 1887, PP C.5328, pp.93–105.
99. Black and Meyer, op. cit., p.28.
100. See F.J. Bayliss, British Wage Councils (Oxford, 1962), pp.1–12.
101. For a detailed study of the debates surrounding the passage of the Trade Boards Act see J. Morris, Women Workers and the Sweated Trades (Hampshire, 1986).
102. Dobbs, op. cit., p.86.
103. Ibid., p.87.
104. Ibid., p.83.
105. In certain instances this necessitated the establishment of employers' representative bodies to fulfil the requirements of the Act, for example the Wholesale Clothing Manufacturers' Association, which was only established in 1910.
106. Tawney, op. cit., p.35.
107. See Tawney, op. cit., pp.36–47 for the process of negotiation and the changes that took place.
108. Morris, op. cit., Ch.7.

5 Organising the Tailors of London

In London... the number of trade unionists is exceedingly small.[1]

Though the historian G.D.H. Cole was writing in 1918 his words were as true of the past as they were of the present. The small-scale, seasonal and casual nature of London industry, with its dependence on a reservoir of semi-skilled and unskilled English and alien labour, did little to encourage support for the concept of organisation. In the years before the First World War it was a struggle to persuade skilled workers in London to join a trade society. For example, in 1911 only just over eight per cent of the capital's engineers were registered members of the Amalgamated Society of Engineers.[2] Therefore it would be natural to assume that it was even harder to encourage tailors and tailoresses to join a trade union. That assumption would be wrong. Of the capital's recorded 64,993 tailoring workers[3] 8,310, or 13.5 per cent, were organised.[4] Even more surprising was the ratio of Jewish to English[5] tailoring trade unionists which, in 1914, was 2:1. Thus 65 per cent[6] of the organised tailors of London were Jewish. In spite of their reputation for unreliability, one with justifiable historic foundations, by the outbreak of the First World War London's Jewish tailors were manifesting stronger support for union than their English peers.[7] Increase in, and stability of, membership was of a recent nature; union activity and, in certain instances, militancy, had been heightened by economic advancement, welfare legislation, such as the Trade Boards Act and the introduction of sickness and unemployment benefit and, to a lesser extent, anarcho-syndicalist activists. However, as Cole suggests, there was, and remains at the end of the twentieth century, plenty of room for improvement.

Until 1905[8] tailoring trade unionism in London could be divided between the AST, which opened its first branch in the capital in 1870, the small and élitist London Clothiers' Cutters' Union (LCCTU) established in 1889, and the various independent Jewish unions which represented the different branches and skills of the industry and the temperaments and antagonisms of the eastern European workers. In 1905 the West End branch of the AST broke with its parent over the issue of centralised, as opposed to local, control. For a short period the departure of almost one thousand West End tailors was compensated for by an influx of alien trade unionists fearful of the ramifications of increased anti-alienism and aggressive trade union legislation. It was a fusion which neither side could tolerate. The following pages explore the history of the organisation of the tailors of London in order to establish what factors were responsible for the growth of support referred to above.

ORGANISING THE JEWISH TAILORING WORKERS OF LONDON

Between 1872 and 1915 thirty-six independent Jewish tailoring trade unions were formed, and if the London Jewish branches of the AST are included that figure rises to over fifty. Some unions lasted only a few months, most no more than two years, only two survived for a decade.

Before the 1870s exploited alien Jewish workers employed in the sub-divisional sector of the trade had no inclination or direction towards organisation. The first attack on the iniquitous plight of the alien Jewish work-force of London was made by a Polish intellectual refugee, Louis Smith, who had made his way to London via the Paris Commune of 1871.[9] The liberal policies of England enabled Smith to pursue and promote his political beliefs in freedom in the East End of London, an area which, in the decades ahead, would provide a home for refugee Socialists, Anarchists and Russian revolutionaries – Stepniak and Kropotkin were esconced by the 1890s. Smith's intention was to organise 'the exhausted and worn out working tailors of London'.[10] In his eyes combination was the only means of overcoming the excesses of the capitalist employer. However, his view of trade unionism differed considerably from that of his contemporary, 'new model' English trade unionists. Shortly after his arrival, in 1872, Smith founded the Lithuanian Tailors' Union in Whitechapel. In spite of an initial membership of seventy-two the union collapsed within weeks as a result of its members' naïvety and their employers' duplicity. According to the account given by Isaac Stone in the *Poilishe Yidel*, published in August 1884, the masters, concerned at the emergence of an organised body of opposition, lulled the workers into a false sense of security by misleading them into believing that improved conditions and higher wages were 'just around the corner'. Membership dropped, no worker wanted to pay dues unnecessarily, until, 'there was no trace of a union, no money, no members and the tailors were once again working all night in the "busy" time while in the "slack" they went hungry all day'.[11] Smith, disillusioned by the apathetic response of all but a small number of the union's members, left for America. He had not understood that the indigent alien tailors of London's East End wanted bread today not jam tomorrow. However, Smith had set a precedent for the intellectual inspiration and leadership of Jewish working-class movements in London. Four years later that form of leadership revealed the antagonisms that existed amongst the eastern European alien immigrants.

In August 1876 a second Jewish tailors' trade union was formed. It was an offshoot of the Hebrew Socialist Union founded by ten Jewish socialists, including Isaac Stone, in a house in Gun Street, Spitalfields in May 1876. The driving force was the 'founding father' of Jewish socialist organisation, Aaron Lieberman[12] whose intellectual training combined the religiosity of the *stetl* with the radicalism of the rabbinical seminary of Vilna.

The Socialist Union's stated aim was to: 'spread Socialism among Jews as well as non-Jews...to support organisations recognised by it and to unite all workers in the fight against their oppressors...to unite with workers' organisations from other nations'.[13] From its base in east London the Union called on the 'working masses of the Jewish People' to shake off the shackles of tyranny and oppression. The Anglo-Jewish establishment viewed the creation of this radical society with concern, believing that its newly emancipated status would be blemished by the activities of the anarchic, intellectual Jewish refugees. Attempts were made to undermine the authenticity of the socialists and cast doubt on their Jewishness. The 'organ of Anglo-Jewry', the *Jewish Chronicle* published an article which suggested that the socialists were not Jews at all but 'missionaries or enemies'.[14] Such warnings published in a journal which was circulated within middle- and upper-class Jewish circles had little influence on the exploited East Enders with their limited knowledge of English. The Hebrew Socialist Union continued to gather support. At a packed meeting of the union held on 26 August 1876, requests for the formation of a tailors' union, as a means of overcoming the brutal treatment meted out by the masters, were acceded to and the second Jewish tailors' union in the history of the Jewish East End was established.

The events surrounding the rise and fall of that short-lived tailors' union, as told by Isaac Stone in the *Poilishe Yidel* eight years later, spotlight the division between the Jews from Lithuania and those from the region of Galicia. The Litvaks considered the Galicians their intellectual inferiors while they in turn were eyed with suspicion by their less well-educated co-religionists. The article in the *Poilishe Yidel* emphasised the dichotomy by referring to the 'problem' Lieberman and his associates had in persuading the Jewish tailors of the East End to attend the peoples' assembly on 26 August:

> What was this problem? The Litvaks wore brille [Yiddish for glasses]. Everyone had a different opinion about the brille [as Lieberman's group was nicknamed]. One said they were missionaries, others said that they were almost entirely simple murderers who carried loaded rifles in their trouser pockets, everyone was in doubt about the little Litvaks.[15]

The ridiculing of the glasses was a means of highlighting the intellectual distance between the two groups and of stressing the workers' lack of confidence in the ability of those early socialists to improve their conditions of work. The newly founded tailors' union held two subsequent meetings on 2 and 16 September during which time membership rose to nearly three hundred.[16] By the end of November personal and methodological differences, as opposed to pragmatic solutions to the everyday problems of the workshop, had exasperated an increasingly dissatisfied and volatile rank and file. Discontent exploded at what proved to be the last meeting of the union. A fight broke out between the socialists and the more religious members of the union. Lieberman was physically assaulted and, with his glasses smashed, was forced to take cover under a table until the arrival of the police restored peace. The final straw came when the treasurer absconded with the union's funds.[17] By the end of the year the Hebrew Socialist Union had collapsed, brought down by the ideological and personal differences of its founders and the onslaught by Rabbis, concerned at the emergence of what they perceived as an iconoclastic organisation. It was only afterwards that the Anglo-Jewish élite and the workers themselves recognised that the Litvaks had not been missionaries or murderers but 'friends who had offered to unite them'.[18] Aaron Lieberman left

England on 19 December 1876.[19] In 1879 he returned to the East End. It was here that fate and affairs of the heart took a cruel twist. In spite of having a wife and children in Vilna, Lieberman fell for 'an exotic though overblown young lady'[20] in the East End. His love was unrequited and early in 1880 he sailed for America. Shortly after landing in New York he committed suicide.

In 1883 one of the founders of the Hebrew Socialist Union, Isaac Stone, a tailor by trade, attempted to overcome the problems inherent in organising the alien tailors in London's East End. Idealistically, he believed that the Jewish proletariat could be converted to socialism through combination. But the new union, founded in 1883 at a time of high unemployment, economic recession and increased immigrant settlement, collapsed within months.[21] A disillusioned and despondent Stone, writing in the first edition of the *Arbeiter Fraint* two years later, pronounced his views on contemporary trade unionism. He considered that the role of the union as a body that organised strikes in order to improve the condition of the workers and a friendly society which provided benefits at times of strikes or illness was, as he wrote, 'damaging and useless'. Under the existing capitalist system the best the worker could hope for from a strong trade union was to keep his family from starving. He went on:

> Trade unions alone cannot end the wretched life of the worker ... they lead workers off the right road with their belief in self-help ... we socialists say that the role of the union should not be only to make strikes but to completely rebuild society.[22]

Unions had to be harnessed to the movement to overthrow capitalism; if members were concerned only with immediacy this would never happen. Once again ideology was in opposition to the workers' priority, the rapid amelioration of conditions of employment. The inability of those early intellectual Jewish radical refugees to capture and maintain the support of the Jewish proletariat was largely due to their reluctance to acknowledge that the exploited worker regarded the provision of food, warmth and clothing for his family and himself as more urgent than devotion to socialist dogma. Reality as opposed to idealism was something recognised by Morris Winchevsky, co-founder (with E. W. Rabbinowitz) and editor of the *Poilishe Yidel*. Winchevsky was a socialist and littérateur, though unusually for one of such persuasion, he was also in steady employment in a City merchant bank.[23] The aim of the *Poilishe Yidel* was didactic, to teach the greeners, in their own language, Yiddish, the ways of their new homeland. It was also intended to accelerate the assimilation process to the point at which all workers, alien Jewish and Gentile English, could progress toward common unity and brotherhood. To this end the journal and its editor acknowledged that English and Jewish unions had to interact. Referring to the demise of Stone's union the editor of the *Poilishe Yidel* remarked that, 'as it did not fuse with other trade unions (clearly the AST which, in 1884, had opened a Jewish branch) so in London it could not exist'.[24] As Fishman argues in his book on East End Jewish radicals, the popularity and success of men such as Rudolf Rocker in the early part of the twentieth century,[25] was due not only to their political ideology and charisma but to their open recognition of the proletariat's need for immediate and tangible amelioration of conditions. Even though in the years after 1883 socialist ideology remained very much part of East End Jewish trade unionism, dogma was never again permitted to dominate.

At the same time as Isaac Stone was attempting to control the growing numbers of Jewish tailoring workers in the East End, the AST was becoming increasingly concerned over the economic backwash from the never-ending stream of cheap and desperate immigrant labour. Until this time the Society's policy had been to refuse membership to any Jews who were not 'English born and employed in the West End or highest class East End workshops'.[26] But the effects of an expanding immigrant labour force prepared to work longer hours for less pay than any other class of workman persuaded the Society that the unionisation of the East End alien tailoring population, under the guidance and control of the AST, was the only practical solution to the problem of wage undercutting and deteriorating working conditions. Thus, in January 1884, the Jewish East End branch of the AST was opened at the Brown Bear public house in Leman Street with an inaugural membership of 150. Subscription charges were high, 12s. 0d. for full benefits and 6s 0d if sickness was excluded,[27] far more suited to the skilled artisan than the unskilled tailor. During the slack and times of depression, cost governed membership and, after the initial enthusiasm had died down and trade union support fell nationally, membership of the East End Jewish branch of the AST dropped to twenty, a figure that was not exceeded until after the successful conclusion of the Jewish tailors' strike in 1889 when it rose by a massive 2,000 per cent, from 11 to 216![28]

As previously illustrated, the alien Jewish tailoring work-force of the

West End of London was small. Accordingly the AST did not consider it necessary to open a Jewish West End branch until 1903.[29] The timing of the opening was correct, for, within a short while, membership stood at 200, a figure which represented almost 20 per cent of the total alien West End tailoring work-force,[30] and one which proves the strength of trade union support amongst the West End tailors, alien and English.

In the early 1880s there was a significant change in attitudes towards trade unions among the semi-skilled and unskilled. Traditionally the Liberal Party had supported the 'new model' unions; most working men who became Members of Parliament did so on the Liberal ticket. But they were educated artisans. By the penultimate decade of the nineteenth century there were those who had begun to look upon trade unionism for all as beneficial and, more importantly, as a controlling facet of working-class life, a conclusion the investigative journalist Henry Mayhew had reached as early as 1850.[31] Samuel Montagu, the Liverpool-born Jewish Liberal Member of Parliament for Whitechapel favoured the new Liberal ideology and supported the view put forward by the government's Factory Inspector, Lakeman, that combination would improve the material and mental condition of immigrant Jewry.[32] Montagu cannot have been immune to the concerns of his fellow members of the Cousinhood over the threat, or imagined threat, posed by the sudden flood of pauper alien immigrants following the assassination of Tsar Alexander II in Russia, to the so recently secured position of established Anglo-Jewry. From Montagu's point of view, unionisation of the unskilled labour force would accelerate their acculturation and Anglicisation and steer them away from attitudes and actions likely to inflame an increasingly anti-alien host society. To this end, in 1886, he provided the stimulus, financially and theoretically, for another form of East End tailoring trade union. His original intention was to create a society which would represent the joint interests of small employers and working tailors, a policy later put forward by Lewis Lyons and one which recurs throughout the years leading to the Second World War. It was a directive which did not find favour and Samuel Montagu had to content himself with the creation of a union which represented only the employed. In March 1886 the London Tailors' Machiners' Society was established.[33] Whilst under Montagu's patronage and financial control it was forced to follow a moderate path which excluded the use of strike action. This stipulation created discord between himself and his choice for Society secretary, the handsome, charismatic but erratic, socialist trade unionist, Lewis Lyons. As a result of his differences with Lyons, Montagu withdrew his support from the Society in 1887. The departure of the Liberal *éminence grise* enabled Lyons to adopt a radical and aggressive policy. But so long as the economy showed few signs of improvement there was little chance of success. Membership fell away and Lyons returned to his previous position as secretary of the East End branch of the AST.

The one individual whose name runs like a thread through the history of Jewish trade unionism in London from 1885 until 1912 is Lewis Lyons. Between 1885 and 1912 he led, or was involved in the running of, no fewer than nine different tailoring trade unions and a number of AST branches. He was alternately criticised and driven from trade union ranks and then implored to return. Tragically, due to the flaws in his character, London's tailoring trade unionists were denied the leadership and continuity provided by the more stable Joseph Finn and John Dyche, both of whom later exhibited their expertise to the benefit of the mantle-makers in London, Moses Sclare in Leeds and David Zeitlin in Manchester. Lyons's inability to manage financial matters, the union's and his own,[34] and his talent to create internal disquiet and conflict, were at odds with his obvious charisma which led to his being called back again and again to organise newly founded societies.

Lewis Lyons was born in England of German parents in 1862. By trade a tailor's machiner he was soon able to recognise the iniquities of the trade in which he found employment. The awakening of Lyons's socio-political conscience coincided with the arrival of socialism and its intellectual appeal as a means of ending the exploitation of labour. In 1885 Lyons joined Hyndman's Social Democractic Federation. Unlike the Leeds branch of the Socialist League, 'the active Leaguers of London were a poor bunch'[35] and it was left to the Social Democrats, who were later to become involved in the organisation of the match-girls, dockers and general labourers, to provide the intellectual and grass-roots stimulus. It was whilst attending one of the Federation's meetings in Dod Street, East London, that Lyons crossed swords with officialdom and was arrested for obstructing the police. From the reports of the proceedings it is clear that the arresting officer and the magistrate at the subsequent hearing were not only anti-socialist, but also anti-semitic, as Lyons received far harsher treatment than the others arrested at the same meeting. Following the policeman's per-jured evidence, magistrate Saunders sentenced Lyons to two months' hard labour plus a fine of 40s. Fortunately, William Morris, who had attended the court hearing, and was himself arrested for disorderly conduct following the pronouncement of sentence, succeeded in getting Lyons's sentence quashed.[36]

What must be regarded as Lyons's most successful trade union phase was the period during which he led the Jewish tailors of the East End in the first major strike of alien workers in the capital. By 1887 the economic impact of the decade's recession on casual and seasonal workers had reached crisis point. Throughout the year the numerous unemployment marches and meetings, virtually all organised by the SDF,[37] had been the subject of increasing police brutality. The culmination was the large-scale meeting held on 13 November 1887, the day that has gone down in the history books as 'Bloody Sunday'. The intention had been to march contigents of unemployed from all over the capital to an enormous protest meeting scheduled to be held in Trafalgar Square. For once there was unity of purpose between the SDF and the Socialist League. Tragically this unusual example of co-operation did not produce the hoped-for result. What should have been a good-humoured and meaningful rally ended in a violent struggle between police and demonstrators which culminated in seventy-five arrests, countless injuries and three fatalities. The failure of the march was greeted with rejoicing by the police and traditionalists, with an embarrassed silence by the Gladstonian Liberals and with the growing recognition by the socialists that revolution in England, as a means of overthrowing the status quo and improving the lot of the working man, was, at best, most unlikely.

In spite of Bloody Sunday and the gradual upswing in the economy, marches by the unemployed continued. The trickle-down effects of economic improvement which began early in 1888 took their time and by the spring of 1889 had not reached the Jewish immigrants of east London. Attempts to control labour unrest and ease the fears of the middle and upper classes had done little to ameliorate the condition of the sweated worker or the unemployed. The House of Lords Committee on Sweating, established in 1888, was still in session and a long way from presenting its findings and recommendations. Throughout this time Lewis Lyons remained active in the cause of the Jewish workforce. As joint secretary, together with the anarcho-socialist Philip Krantz,[38] of the Jewish Unemployed Committee he targeted the Chief Rabbi Herman Adler, spiritual leader of Anglo-Jewry. Lyons's plan was to marshal the unemployed and sweated Jewish workers of the

East End and march them in protest to the Great Synagogue, the cathedral of the Ashkenazi establishment, where they would confront the Chief Rabbi and demand 'work to buy bread, and the hours of labour to be 8 per day'. Action was timed to coincide with Adler's scheduled series of addresses to the Jewish working men and women. It was naïve to expect support and sympathy from a man who had responded to earlier pleas for help by saying that he too 'toiled from morning till night and probably had to work harder than any and was ill as a result of extreme overwork'.[39] Adler refused to sanction the proposed marches. Instead he publicly stated that the socialists' requests for an eight-hour day and legislation to control wage payments were 'absurd'. Almost as ridiculous in the eyes of this dedicated *laissez-faire* spiritual leader was the concept of relief, either for the poorly paid or the unemployed. His view was that 'A man endowed with health and ten fingers'[40] should not consider accepting benefit. It was fortunate for the unemployed and sick, Jew and Gentile, that future government legislation ignored the words of Herman Adler.

Throughout the long hot summer of 1889 tensions heightened as labour discontent grew. Workers throughout the country were showing their support for what was to become known as 'new unionism', the organisation of the semi-skilled and unskilled into industrial or general unions. In the capital, centre stage was held by the dockers, who successfully fought for, and won, their 'tanner'. It was not only the English working man who was fighting back. During the summer East End fur trade workers and cap-makers staged successful strikes against their Jewish employers, but these were small-scale and of short duration and did not catch the headlines as would the 'Great Strike of London Tailors' which began on 29 August 1889.

The 1889 East End Jewish tailors' strike has been referred to by one Anglo-Jewish historian as just another of the 'sporadic strikes' carried out by Jewish workers in the years between 1888 and 1890.[41] When viewed in the context of the climactic events of 1888 and 1889 it has to be argued that the Jewish tailors' strike was neither an isolated ethnic phenomenon nor a spontaneous event. As we know, by 1888 the socialists, both SDF and SL, had recognised that progress could not be made unless the unskilled and semi-skilled English and alien workforce were harnessed to their cause. Both James MacDonald and Lewis Lyons were members of the SDF and AST whilst Charles Mowbray, a tailor by trade, and William (Woolf) Wess, a compositor, were members of the Socialist League. These men provided the links that ensured that, at such an important juncture in labour history, the alien tailors of London did not operate in a vacuum.

The failure of the House of Lords Committee 'to reach a satisfactory conclusion as to the conditions of the sweated tailors' and the rejection of the East End Jewish Master Tailors' Association of a personally presented set of demands resulted in the Jewish working tailors taking what to them was the only alternative, strike action. The decision, and the subsequent strike, was masterminded by Lyons, who became chairman of the Strike Committee, and William Wess,[42] the multi-talented poet, journalist, compositor and Socialist Leaguer, who was appointed Committee secretary.

The resolution to call a strike was taken by the three unions active in the East End at the time, the Jewish branch of the AST, which had Lyons as its secretary, and two smaller machiners' and pressers' organisations. The Strike Committee was made up of seventeen unionists based at the unimposing White Hart public house in Green-field Street, the headquarters of the Jewish branch of the AST. Battle began. Lacking funds but fired with purpose and passion, the strike's organisers 'begged, borrowed or stole enough to print a few bills and hire a brass band', to lead the daily street processions needed to stimulate public support and encourage contributions to the strike fund. A manifesto to fellow workers, printed in Yiddish and English, clearly stated the striking tailors' demands. These were:

- Hours to be reduced to twelve, with an interval of one hour for dinner and half-an-hour for tea.
- All meals to be had off premises.
- Government contractors and sweaters to pay wages at trade union rates.
- Government contractors and sweaters not to give work home at night after working hours.

In less than three weeks the number on strike rose to 6,000. Support came from leading members of the English labour movement such as John Burns, Tom Mann and Ben Tillett, who joined the tailors' marches and shared the speakers' platforms. The unexpectedly large-scale support manifested by the alien work-force captured the imagina-tion of the local and national English press together with, of course, the Jewish and Yiddish papers, which gave blow-by-blow accounts of the events surrounding the strike. On 12 September, concerned about prospects for a return to work in time for the busy the Jewish Master Tailors' Assocation, led by Mark Moses, agreed to a joint meeting of employers and workers. The outcome was a tentative agreement on the following terms:

- Hours to be reduced to twelve a day, with an interval of one hour for dinner and half-an-hour for tea.
- All meals to be eaten off premises.
- Only four hours' overtime a week.
- Not more than two hours' overtime in any one day.
- The first two hours' overtime to be worked at the ordinary rate, the second two at time-and-a-half.

The settlement was due to be confirmed the following day, but at the eleventh hour, the employers refused to sign. Instead, they attempted to precipitate an early return to work by circulating a rumour that the strike was over. This devious act gave the strikers the will to fight on, even though they were completely without funds. The strike committee immediately printed a poster informing the working tailors that no agreement had been reached and that the masters had broken their pledge by refusing to sign. In an interview with a reporter from the *East London Observer*, Wess confirmed his intention to carry on the strike in spite of the hardship: 'Our people are not used to luxuries or even good living...so that we have no fear whatever of getting sufficient money to meet all the demands made upon us for relief.' The strike secretary, considered by the journalist to be a well-educated foreigner of remarkable intelligence, was confident of the successful outcome of the strike. The workers had the support of the manufacturers and wholesalers. If loss of work continued the sweaters would be forced by those at the top of the chain of production to reach a settlement. Wess was convinced that with victory would come the entry of 'every tailor and presser and machinist into one of the three societies...we shall thus have a Union which it will be impossible for the employers to resist.'[43] A Utopian ideal indeed.

The strike and the bitterness continued. An appeal was made to the English trade unions for money and moral support. Financial aid came in the form of £100 from the residue of the dockers' strike fund and smaller sums from the compositors and bootmakers. Instead of falling away support grew. It was at this point that the Anglo-Jewish establishment intervened. Lord Rothschild made it known that he was prepared to act as a mediator. At the same time Samuel Montagu declared

himself prepared to become directly involved and willing to put up the
£100 demanded from the masters before negotiations could be
resumed. On 29 September the strikers organised a mass demonstration in Hyde Park. Support for the Jewish working tailors was impressive, alien and Englishman uniting against what they saw as the forces
of exploitation. At a meeting chaired by Lewis Lyons on 30 September
at the Jewish Working Men's Club, James MacDonald, representing
the AST, made, what was for him, an unusually pro-alien speech. He
praised the Jewish workmen for their gallant stand, made not only for
themselves and their families, but in the interests of labour generally.
He continued by saying that,

> These same Jewish workers have struck the blow which the
> English mechanic ought to have struck years ago, therefore they
> would now stand together shoulder to shoulder, and they would
> not remain contented with a ten and one-half hour workday, an
> eight hour day would be their future aim.[44]

Even so, settlement seemed no nearer. The Anglo-Jewish establishment
became increasingly concerned about the image that the Jewish tailors
were projecting, one which appeared to fan the flames of socialism and
discontent. Montagu called a meeting with the master tailors at which
he made it clear that he and Lord Rothschild were determined to end
the strike. On 3 October an agreement was signed. All the working
tailors' demands were met, and an additional clause ensured that 'the
hour system (piece work) would not be introduced'. For their part the
workers agreed not to make any claims on the masters during the
following twelve months. However, with a labour pool which was
constantly refilled by newly arrived hungry greeners, success was
short-lived. According to Lyons, 'two weeks had not passed from the
signing of the agreement before some masters had broken it'.

The support manifested by the tailors and other Jewish trade
unionists during the summer and autumn of 1889 encouraged William
Wess to propose the creation of a 'Federation of (Jewish) East London
Labour Unions'. He later dropped the word Jewish from the title
although all the constituents were Jewish. Wess's object was to create a
federation which would 'assist in every possible way in the organisation of East London Labour' and which, as well as providing advice
and assistance, would 'bring the affiliated unions into close communi-
cation with each other, and with the labour organisation of this and
other countries'. The unionists invited to federate were, in addition to

the tailors, the cabinet-makers, stick- and cane-dressers, lasters, cap-makers and journeymen boot-finishers. The socialist element was represented by the Berner Street Club and the anarchist faction by the Knights of Liberty Group. The inauguaral meeting of the Federation took place on 1 December 1889[45] in the presence of John Burns, James MacDonald, Tom Mann and Charles Mowbray. The one name which does not appear in the list of those invited to attend is, significantly, that of Lewis Lyons.[46] Was this a demonstration of anarcho-socialist opposition to his dream of uniting working tailors and small masters? The Federation of East End Labour as an independent body had a short life. By 1892 it had disappeared from the labour scene.

Following his successsful chairmanship of the 1889 strike, Lyons left the AST and took up the appointment of president of the International Tailors', Machiners' and Pressers' Trade Union, the society formed in 1890 from the ashes of the independent unions that had participated in the 1889 strike. Initially all went well. Six months after its foundation the union's first strike was successfully led by its new president.[47] Lyons then embarked on action aimed at eliminating the role of the middle-man and master by persuading wholesalers to open indoor work-shops.[48] The infuriated masters counter-attacked by enforcing conditions which could only, as indeed they did, force strike action. But the strike collapsed owing to lack of funds, poor support and Lyons's determination to continue with the strike against the wishes of many of the union's members.[49] Lewis Lyons had not learnt the basic principles of strike action – adequate strike pay, support of the membership and practical, not radical, ambitions. It was something the Leeds Jewish trade unionists knew only too well. The International's membership, weakened by discord and disillusion, splintered at the end of 1891. In an account of the year's events published in the Socialist League's journal *Commonweal*, Lyons was castigated for his incompetence and dishonesty, thereby 'having caused great harm to the labour cause'. As a result, Jewish trade unionists, so eagerly praised two years previously, were now harangued for their weaknesses. *Commonweal* bemoaned: 'It is a pity that the Jewish workers of the East End are so trammeled by their religion, jealousy and suspicion as renders it almost impossible to organise themselves.'[50] The breakaway group formed the Independent Tailors', Machiners' and Pressers' Trade Union which by 1893 had attracted a membership of 272. The remainder renamed themselves the International Journeymen Tailors', Machiners' and Pressers' Trade Union. But internal division and the existence of a parallel union led to a drop in support until by 1899 there remained only fourteen members. In 1900 the two unions reunited and became the London Tailors', Machiners' and Pressers' Union. Its beginning, with an initial membership of 425, augured well but, by 1903, with trade unions everywhere under threat and the economy in the doldrums, it had disappeared. Mismanagement by Lyons over a decade earlier had fractured a union which, if successful, could have united all the men's tailors under one society umbrella.

With the exception of those unions mentioned above, the Jewish Branch of the AST, which barely kept in double figures, and the mantle-makers' union founded in 1892 (see below), trade union activity amongst the Jewish East End tailors in the first half of the 1890s was unimpressive. Whilst disillusionment amongst those who had been so actively supportive in 1889 was no doubt a factor, there was the additional, but ever constant, problem of the depressed economy and the harsh reality of unemployment. The latter was a problem which occupied the mind and the heart of Lewis Lyons and, as the economy slipped back into recession, he again turned his attention to the Jewish unemployed. On 7 November 1892 Lyons wrote to the Chief Rabbi, Herman Adler, asking for a meeting to discuss the level of distress being suffered by more than 10,000 Jews in London.[51] Adler agreed to meet with Lyons and his delegation but took the opportunity in his reply to say that he considered Lyons was overestimating the level of suffering. The meeting eventually took place on 14 November. Adler pointedly addressed the delegation as his 'fellow working men' in order to reinforce his belief that the plight of the sweated worker was no different from his and from that of many others who put in an 'honest hard day's work and toiled from morning until night'. During the meeting Adler expressed his total opposition to Lyons's proposal to lead a barefoot march of the Jewish unemployed through the streets of east London. The Chief Rabbi said that it would achieve nothing but ill-health and derision. The point obviously went home as Lyons cancelled the proposed march. The Chief Rabbi also vetoed the suggestion that a trade unionist, doubtless Lyons, be permitted to preach a 'labour sermon' from the pulpit of the Great Synagogue. Such an event was, in the eyes of the spiritual leader of Anglo-Jewry, atheistic; the place for labour rhetoric was Trafalgar Square and the working men's clubs. Though Adler still refused to support the eight-hour day movement he was ever mindful of the tensions between the host and immigrant work-force and, as though this part of his script had been written by the Anarchists, went out of his way to stress the need for 'working men' to maintain unity with Christian comrades, advocating that they should all 'work hand-in-hand.'[52] As the delegation departed the Chief Rabbi congratulated its members for trying to keep the Sabbath sacred. A year before, in an attempt to eradicate Saturday working, the International had begun what it called Sabbath agitation.[53] As a parting shot Lyons asked the Chief Rabbi how they were to succeed if 'rich synagogue members worked their men 18, 19 or 20 hours a day, often on the Sabbath'.

The need to feed their families and themselves frequently forced Jewish workers to overlook the tenets of their religion. Unlike the masters they could not afford the luxury of regular synagogue attendance. The more orthodox members of the work-force took positive action. In 1894 a small group of AST Jewish East End branch members broke away and formed a Sabbath Observance Branch which survived for several years though membership never exceeded fifty-five.[54] In 1899 the lax attitude towards the 'Day of Rest' manifested by employers and workers motivated the ultra-orthodox Machzikei Haddath to sponsor a Jewish National Tailors' Union whose main objective was to secure the acceptance of Saturday as a day of rest by Jewish employers.[55] Within four months the membership of the union had risen from an initial 500 to 639,[56] but religion was invariably subservient to work. Intolerant employers and workers concerned at possible job losses put pressure on the National's membership which, by the end of 1901, had fallen to zero.[57]

In the course of their correspondence Lewis Lyons tried to make the Chief Rabbi see that for many relaxation of Sabbath Observance was the result of economic necessity not lack of faith. In a letter to Adler he referred to the 'gulf that exists between rich and poor Jews... and the insults to which they are subjected.' Whilst the poorer immigrants had their *chevras* (small synagogues or rooms in which small services were held), the grand United Synagogue, with its high membership fees, was 'closed against us, the pulpits are denied us'.[58] The correspondence between Lyons and Adler on the subject of the plight of the unemployed continued for several years. Though unsympathetic and harsh, Adler's view, that only an upturn in the economy could really help the downtrodden workers, was perhaps the more realistic in an era when the provision of welfare and benefits for the unemployed was seen as a concession to weakness rather than an acceptance of social responsibility.

After the failures of the 1890s Lewis Lyons faded from the east London labour scene. For a while he and his family lived in Bristol where he ran a cigarette and cigar shop and his wife made and rolled cigars. Lyons returned to London at the turn of the century. In the following twelve years he accepted appeals to take on the position of secretary of a number of newly formed, specialist unions, which included those created for garment-workers and waistcoat-makers as well as various Jewish branches of the AST. A pattern developed whereby Lyons would take on the mantle of secretary then, after a brief interlude, when discord erupted, usually as a result of his financial mismanagement or because of his advocacy for the creation of a union composed of small masters and workers, he would resign or be dismissed. His concept of an association of small masters and workers remained a source of irritation to Jewish trade unionists and anarchists alike; the *Arbeiter Fraint* persistently attacked Lyons for what it saw as this capitalist trait.[59] The concept did have a practical dimension. So often, as William Morris had realised, were masters in the hands of the wholesalers and shop owners, that a union which combined small-scale employers and employees, if well structured, would have succeeded in putting the pressure and responsibility on those at the top of the chain of production.

By the close of the first decade of the twentieth century Lewis Lyons was a sick man and no longer able to continue as chairman of the London Tailors' Council, an organisation he established in 1909, the year of the passing of the Trade Boards Act.

The Council's objective was to increase trade union membership in the industry, strengthen existing unions and maintain agitation for an eight-hour day. In 1910 Clement Attlee chaired the Council's first major public meeting which was held at Toynbee Hall. In reality the Council was an east London labour federation with the radical element removed. All those who spoke at the meeting were representatives of Jewish tailoring unions. Their aim was to enlighten the work-force as to the benefits of the new Act and the need for active trade union membership. Lyons was selected to sit on the Tailoring Trade Board in 1911,[60] but ill-health forced him to retire from that and from his role as representative of several of the East End tailors' unions that were engaged in the preliminary amalgamation talks which had begun in 1910. Had Lewis Lyons enjoyed the provision of a full-time salary, as had Young and Sclare in Leeds, his contribution to the history of Jewish tailoring trade unionism in London might well have been of greater worth. Sadly he was denied the opportunity. The obituary published in the *Jewish Chronicle* following his death in July 1918 sums up some of the contradictions in his character:

> He caused discontent…fanned class hatred…he was one of the first Jews to champion the rights of the Jewish worker and led them in the fights and in the harsh and unconscionable dealings with their employers.[61]

As the previous chapter has already highlighted, mantle-making was a relatively new arrival on the sub-divisional tailoring scene. The higher level of skill required, and the economic buoyancy enjoyed by that sector of the industry during the 1890s may well have accounted for the durability of the mantle-makers' union during the decade. In January 1892 the United Ladies' Tailors' and Mantle Makers' Trade Union was founded.[62] With the exception of a short-lived Anarchist mantle union which surfaced briefly in Hanbury Street in 1891,[63] and a breakaway union, the Amalgamated Mantle Makers' Trade Union, which existed for a few months in the mid-1890s, the United Ladies' Tailors was the only representative of mantle-makers during the decade. The union, founded by one E. Guilanoff, expanded and prospered during the 1890s. Initially offering only trade benefit, by 1897 it was sufficiently secure to offer providential benefits as well.[64] This was clearly an attraction, as membership peaked at a figure of 550.[65] There is one major ingredient in the mantle-makers' union which cannot be overlooked and that is its leadership between 1895 and 1900. During those five years it lay in the capable and experienced hands of, first, Joseph Finn freshly returned from America and, subsequently, John Dyche, another who had cut his teeth in Leeds. Reportedly due to ill-health, Dyche relinquished his leadership of the mantle-makers' union in 1900. Shortly afterwards he left for New York where, revitalised, or perhaps encouraged by more positive attitudes than he found in the East End, he became prominent in the American trade union movement. Dyche was appointed General Secretary and Treasurer of the International Ladies' Garment Workers' Union in 1904, a position he held for ten years during which time he was able to visit London in his official capacity as a highly respected representative of the American labour movement.[66] Dyche's departure from the London mantle-makers' union, and the reduction in that union's membership, resulted in further fragmentation. According to Joseph Finn, there was no doubt as to the cause of the union's eventual collapse, it was, as he succinctly explained to the Royal Commission on Aliens three years later, due to 'a lack of efficient leaders and organisers'.[67]

The division between the men's and ladies' tailoring unions was bridged only once before 1905. In 1902 the chaotic state of organisa-tion in the East End tailoring trade, with only 600 alien workers out of a conservatively estimated total of 18,000 organised by 1899,[68] resulted in a brief marriage. Following a merger between the United Ladies' Tailors' Union and yet another, newly created, radical Mantle Makers' Union, the International, a fusion took place with the Independent Tailors' Union and the Military Tailors' Union. The result was the United Garment Workers' Union under the secretaryship of the ubiquitous Lewis Lyons. Separation took place after two weeks when the military tailors resigned, divorce followed two months later with the departure of the men's tailors.[69] Shortly afterwards, the United Garment Workers' Union collapsed. The residual mantle-makers reformed and became the London Ladies' Tailors Union. But the members' 'weak, feckless and unsupportive' attitude frustrated its general secretary Sam Ellstein, brother of the Leeds Anarchist trade unionist Louis,[70] who, shortly afterwards, resigned in despair.[71] Some-how the remnants of the union survived until 1905 when, as a result of external political, economic and social pressures, it followed the lead of a number of diverse men's tailoring unions[72] and took its 201 members into the Amalgamated Society of Tailors.[73]

The decision to take shelter under the umbrella of the AST was the result of the forces of anti-alienism, anti-trade union legislation and economic hardship. The unprecedented expansion of the eastern European Jewish immigrant community in the decade between 1881 and 1891 was reflected in the words and deeds of political activists and English trade unionists. Passions ran particularly high in the East End of London, the heartland of immigrant settlement. The frustrations, concerns and xenophobia of the local native community, at times exploding into violent attacks on local Jews, were harnessed into an orchestrated movement by Major William Eden Evans-Gordon, Member of Parliament for Stepney, who in 1901 founded the British Brothers' League.[74] Ten years earlier trade unionists had openly mani-fested their concerns over the unlimited entry of pauper aliens into Britain and their impact on the labour market. By 1895 these senti-ments had been co-ordinated into the passing of the anti-alien resolu-tion at the Cardiff Conference of the TUC. The AST had been attempting to control the effects of immigrant labour on the indigenous work-force since 1883 but, except in the period immediately following the strike of 1889, its East End Jewish branch had failed to attract members. In 1892 Charles Mowbray told the *Arbeiter Fraint* that the branch 'had some hundred Jewish members' but there were still 'thousands of Jewish tailors unorganised'.[75] If that was an attempt to stir up support, it failed, as by the end of the century membership had dropped to zero.[76]

Problems for Jewish trade unionists were not just related to ethnicity. The Taff Vale Judgement of 1901 had exposed the vulnerability of all unions, large or small, English or alien, though there is no doubt that anti-alienism acted as the catalyst in pushing a number of Jewish societies into the arms of their English equivalent. In the summer preceding the implementation of the Aliens Act the Jewish Cabinet Makers' Union affiliated to the Amalgamated Furnishing Trades Association and the Jewish Capmakers' Union to the United Cloth Hat and Cap Makers of Great Britain.[77] The amalgamation of Jewish and English unions was strongly supported in the columns of the *Arbeiter Fraint*. In his editorials Rudolf Rocker consistently stressed that only through direct co-operation between Jewish and English workers and trade unionists could the battle be won. The columns of the Yiddish Anarchist paper supported Jewish membership of the AST. Jewish tailors must ignore the words of the 'Jewish demagogues' who said that English workers were anti-alien, 'Jewish workers must unite with the Society (AST) that had thrown open its arms to the Jewish working class and fight the common enemy, the sweating system'.[78]

In its early stages the union of English and Jewish tailoring trade unionists was successful, producing a 'remarkable renaissance of trade union support amongst the Jewish tailoring workers of the East End'.[79] If the *Arbeiter Fraint*'s editor wished to believe that this was due to a new-found search for brotherhood and solidarity, he was mistaken. As was so often the case pragmatism, not ideology, was the root cause. Unrest between masters and hands had been festering throughout late 1905 and early 1906. When an East End master declared a lock-out in mid-June the workers reacted by calling an immediate strike. They were convinced that support from the AST would force the Jewish Master Tailors' Improvement Association to meet their demands. The *Arbeiter Fraint* explained the reason behind the growth of trade union support during 1906 in an article published some months after the strike had ended. 'A rumour went around about a general strike in the

East End, they [the workers] all flocked into the union to grab a chance of getting benefits by paying 4d.'[80] It was the same old story, the Jewish trade unionist, no different from his English counterpart employed in a seasonal trade, disliked paying dues; short-term membership for strike benefit was economically very appealing.

It was the AST's traditional method of settling strikes that weakened the relationship between the alien trade unionists of the East End and the English craft society. The London executive of the AST did not have the authority to sanction a strike called by one of its branches or a group of their members. All disputes had to be referred to Manchester head office in order that the action could be approved as constitutional; if it were not then a return to work had to be enforced in order to avoid a general lock-out. The hot-blooded Jewish tailors in the East End were not prepared to stick by the rules and, without waiting for approval from headquarters, within days called twenty-five workshops out on strike. Discontent grew when the East End branch office refused to hand out strike pay; it was more than likely that it did not have the funds. Whilst the Manchester executive deliberated the rights and wrongs of strike action, the East End Jewish tailors held impassioned meetings which were regularly concluded with cries of 'long live the strike' and the singing of the Marseillaise.[81] Within the week the AST, keen to uphold the idea of collective bargaining, reached a settlement with the masters. This was immediately deemed 'a defeat' by the Jewish workers.[82] The *Arbeiter Fraint* attempted to take the heat out of the situation by terming the outcome a 'compromise'.[83] However the settlement included certain clauses which ensured the abolition of piece-work and the taking of meals off the premises. To many tailors, this meant nothing more than a reduction in take-home pay. At the heart of the issue was the continuing debate over piece-work and the preparedness of some to disregard working environment in favour of higher wages.

The bitterness and disappointment engendered by the settlement of the 1906 strike was reflected in the departure of certain Jewish members of the London branches of the AST and the subsequent anti-semitic statements issued by AST officials in London and Manchester. The battle was fought in the colums of the AST Journals and the *Jewish Chronicle*. Guerney Rowlerson, general secretary of the AST, lost little time in attacking the discontented Jewish workers. Through the society's journal he told them that 'if Jewish members are not happy they should leave the AST, it will survive'.[84] The departure of Jewish men's tailors and mantle-makers from the society continued throughout the year. Months later Rowlerson and his London chief officer, Mike Daly, lashed out at the Jewish workers and their trade unions. Rowlerson criticised the Jewish branch secretaries, one of whom was Lewis Lyons, for their inefficiency and financial mismanagement. Daly fanned the flames of anti-alienism still further by stating that 'it was a matter for regret that the uniform branch of the tailoring trade was in the hands of the Jews'.[85] The *Jewish Chronicle*, traditionally the champion of integration, reported both statements and questioned the validity of Jewish membership of the AST.[86] The *Arbeiter Fraint* was reluctant to support departure from the AST. Even so, Rocker was forced to condemn certain aspects of the society's organisation and its executive officers' behaviour. In spite of this, the paper continued to stress the value of organisation beneath the AST's umbrella. New unions, such as those for pressers, machiners, plain machiners and under-pressers, were told that instead of manifesting division they should unite with the English society and bring a 'new spirit of unity into the AST'.[87]

In an attempt to keep the tailoring work-force united in its fight against the employers the *Arbeiter Fraint* published a list of key points which it suggested should be forwarded to AST headquarters in Manchester by the Jewish tailors. The items highlight not only the divisions between the alien members in east London and the Manchester executive but, in addition, some of those that, as we will see below, forced the artisan-based West End bespoke branch to break away in 1905. The points were as follows:

1. There should be direct communications with the Executive Council and all letters to be dealt with within four days.
2. Demands for wage increases should be supported regardless.
3. If the Executive deemed an appeal or case illegal then an explanation be given so that those involved could 'learn their trade unionism'.
4. Support be given for the abolition of workshop sub-contracting, and for all workers to be employed directly by the masters in order to 'prevent intrigues between the workers'.[88]

No records exist of a response. The proposals were either ignored or rejected out of hand and the vitriolic exchanges continued. Within three years nearly all the AST's Jewish members who, in 1905, had 'thrown in their lot with the AST',[89] had departed the English society. In

1908 the newly created (Jewish) London Ladies' Tailors' Union criticised the craft society for its outmoded and highly centralised organisation. Guerney Rowlerson's response, which was aimed directly at the alien nature of the Jewish tailoring work-force, appeared in the *AST Journal*. He was reported as saying that 'most of the ladies' tailors are foreigners...the AST represents trade unionism in England'.[90] Those words precipitated a rapid departure by the majority of the Jewish ladies' tailors who had retained their membership of the AST. Within a year membership of the London Ladies' Tailors' Union had risen from its initial 304 to 500.[91]

With the possible exception of the second point the list drawn up and published in the *Arbeiter Fraint* was pragmatic and, if it had been taken up by the AST executive, or even used as a basis for negotiation, could have resulted in unity of purpose and deed. As it was, the majority of the society's Jewish membership returned to the pattern of small-time unionism which characterised trade unionism in the capital. When we come to examine the dispute between the Manchester executive and the West End branch it will be seen that there were faults on both sides. So far as the divisions between the Jewish tailors and Manchester head office are concerned, though the tailors' volatility and unreliability were frustrating to the point of exasperation, the anti-alien sentiments, so much in keeping with the times, did little to narrow the divide. It was not until 1912 that those employed in the London tailoring trade took truly united action and crossed the geographic and racial demarcation lines. Previously, even the large-scale strikes of 1889 and 1906 had been of a purely alien and local nature. Similarly, action taken by English craftsmen in the West End, which though occasionally supported by a refusal of East End tailors to complete West End work, never resulted in a universal laying down of tools. The tailors' strike of 1912 changed all of this. It involved the handicraft tailor of the West End and the under-presser in the grimy workshop of the East End. In order to fully appreciate the events of 1912, which took place during the 'second forward march of labour', and the trade union allegiances that followed, we must first examine the organisation of the English tailors of London.

ORGANISING THE ENGLISH TAILORS OF LONDON

It has already been described how, in 1870, the three-year-old Amalgamated Society of Tailors entered the capital and opened two branches, one in the West End, the centre of high-class bespoke tailoring, and one in the City, wherein lay the power of finance and commerce. It was not an imposing entry, as the total inaugural membership amounted to only 199, less than one per cent of the capital's tailoring work-force.[92] Within six years the AST had opened three further branches in the West End and could boast a membership of 1,027. To the east of the capital there were two East End branches, one in Leman Street specifically for German tailors and one in Minories reserved for skilled workers employed in, or close to, the City of London. The paucity of support beyond the boundaries of the West End and the society's refusal to admit eastern European semi-skilled and unskilled tailors is highlighted by the inability of the society to recruit more than sixty-three members in both branches.[93] As ever, the strength and reputation of the AST in London lay with the bespoke and craft tailors of the West End.

The two main West End branches, known as West End and Dragon, were located in the heart of the bespoke quarter. They weathered the depressions of the late 1870s and early 1880s without loss of membership.[94] In fact the West End branches of the AST actually expanded during the period and by 1884 accounted for 1,250 of the AST's total membership of 1,995. The tremors of 'new unionism' were hardly felt by those whose roots lay in an artisan heritage. Of far more significance was the agreement in 1890 reached between James MacDonald on behalf of the AST and the London Master Tailors' Association, for a uniform log rate. Following the announcement of the newly agreed 6d. log hour rate the West End membership rose by 75 per cent, from 705 to 1,200 and that of the Dragon branch by 50 per cent, from 500 to 750.[95]

Another name which recurs throughout the history of the tailoring unions of London is that of the socialist tailor James MacDonald, born in Edinburgh in 1857, who arrived in London at the end of the 1870s. MacDonald, 'a charming and entertaining personality',[96] was cast in the mould of the radical, intellectual tailors of the first half of the nineteenth century. As early as 1879 he was exploring socialist principles with Charles Booth,[97] and later provided Booth with several chapters on tailoring for inclusion in the London Life and Labour volumes. His socialist convictions led to his taking a seat on the executive of the (Social) Democratic Federation in 1883[98] and to his standing as an (unsuccessful) ILP parliamentary candidate for Dundee in 1892 and 1898. It has been suggested that the politician James

Ramsay MacDonald owed some of his popularity in the capital in the early years of his political career to the fact that he was mistaken for his tailoring namesake.[99]

Parallel with his socialist activities was MacDonald's role as a trade unionist. He was secretary of the London Trades Council for seventeen years, at some time a member of the AST and subsequently secretary of the breakaway London Society of Tailors and Tailoresses. As district secretary of the London sector of the AST, and an active member of its West End branch, MacDonald was conscious of the overall decline in membership. For while the West End retained an aggregate membership in excess of one thousand in the years between 1891 and 1905, other branches suffered severe fluctuations. In order to overcome these weaknesses MacDonald argued for a lowering of craft barriers; for the admission of female members (a change not conceded by the national executive until 1900) and factory workers. He was also determined to acquire autonomy for the powerful West End branch which increasingly resented being controlled by a head office 200 miles north. These differences led to disagreement and to MacDonald's being expelled from the AST executive in 1892. It was a sore that never healed even though he remained a society member until 1905. Relations between Manchester and London deteriorated in 1901 when the West End branch refused to pay a levy imposed by head office or to permit its officers to collect funds from all the London branches. What James MacDonald called 'the wrangling of 20 years' finally came to a head in 1905 when the AST's West End branch refused to pay its outstanding debts or to accept a head office reorganisation scheme.[100] At heart was the battle for autonomy and a movement away from the ideal of the large-scale, centralised craft union which controlled its members and branches from afar. (It has to be said, however, that by entering into the amalgamation of 1914 the LST&T was once again a West End branch controlled by a head office 200 miles north.) In May 1905 discussions between the AST and the LST&T had reached an impasse. On the twenty-fourth of the month the majority of the West End branch executive of the AST, including James MacDonald, Charles Collcutt, J. Blythe and William Rines, seceded from the AST and formed a new union, the London Society of Tailors and Tailoresses with an inaugural membership of 787, all previously members of the old-established craft society. In spite of considerable rank-and-file support the breakaway did not go down well with the established labour movement; the LST&T was refused membership by the TUC, the GFTU and the Labour Party.[101]

Although isolated from the institutions of labour the newly created society of West End tailors enjoyed a healthy period of growth. Its predominantly male membership consisted of a 'large numer of foreign members on the same footing as the English'.[102] By 1910 the LST&T's membership had risen to 1,304; in the same period the residual West End branch of the AST never rose above 400.[103] In 1909, the LST&T's secretary Blythe was able to boast that 'probably we are the only trade union which can show an increased membership...when most unions are being drained through the great amount of unemployment'.[104] In spite of this outward show of confidence life for the newly created craft society was lonely and towards the end of 1911, in common with other craft societies, attempts were made at a merger. The AST *Journal* reported that the LST&T had requested a meeting to discuss a fusion.[105] No satisfactory agreement was reached and, as history tells us, three years later the young society sacrificed its autonomy to become part of the newly created United Garment Workers' Trade Union.

At the same time as London was swept by the burst of 'new unionism', a singular example of the old-style 'new model' emerged amongst craft tailors. In 1889, 'at the instigation of Messrs. T. Whately, A.J. Middleton and G. Taylor', the London Clothiers' Cutters' Trade Union was founded for the purpose of 'regulating apprenticeship, maintaining fair wages, regular and uniform hours and fair log conditions and the supervision of all matters relating to cutting'. Membership was open to 'all cutters connected with clothing, trimming, waterproof, army and other contract departments, wholesale or retail'.[106] At a time when the trade union world was developing industrial and general unions to accommodate the unskilled and the semi-skilled, the cutters of London went against the trend by creating a protective craft society. As part of its policy the LCCTU instituted efficiency tests for new members. However, this proved counterproductive as it deterred would-be members and did little to maintain the skill level of new entrants to the trade. Exclusivity was eventually sacrificed to expansion when Tom Whately, secretary of the union, announced the opening of a machiners' branch in order to 'attract the less-skilled elements of the trade',[107] a euphemism for the alien tailor. By 1905 the ratio of alien machiners to English cutters was 1:5 out of a total membership of 350.[108]

Why did the cutters' union change direction? Though established as a craft union, by the close of the nineteenth century the LCCTU was looking to expand or amalgamate, motivated by a need for security at a time when unions were coming under increasing pressure from employers and the state. In 1899 discussions for a proposed merger with the AST failed.[109] But the feeling of insecurity remained and the decision was taken to open up to that group which posed the largest threat in terms of labour and wages, the alien workers in the East End; though few, if any, of the eastern Europeans were actually cutters. Even after the opening of its new branch the LCCTU was unable to equal its inaugural membership of 684.[110] As the years passed the need to merge subsided. In 1904 the LCCTU rejected the opportunity to become the London branch of AUCO and, in 1908, turned down an approach from the AST.[111] Merger with an established union which would retain control and its original form was clearly not acceptable, whilst participation in a fusion which created a new union, even if provincially based, was.

Though James MacDonald had argued for the admission of women to the AST in the early 1890s their organisational fervour in London was disappointing. We have seen how in Leeds the Tailoresses' Union was instrumental in encouraging male organisation. In London, in 1888, the match-girls' strike action and subsequent trade union formation was an example to the unskilled of both genders, but not one followed by women in the tailoring trade. Most attempts made to encourage female combination in London proved unsuccessful. In the early 1880s the Women's Protective and Provident League was active in the East End and, in 1881, founded a Tailoresses' Union. Though not essentially a Jewish union, the bulk of the membership was composed of unmarried Jewish tailoresses[112] attracted by the idea of protection and benefit. There was little incentive for the majority of tailoresses to organise as their employment was casual and, in many instances, home-based in isolated circumstances. Even where there was large-scale and regular employment attempts at organisation failed. In the 1880s Lewis Lyons had tried, without success, to persuade women working in the factories of Lottery and Schnieder to combine. The male contingent of the labour movement was no friend of female trade unionism. As Tom Mann explained, the employment and organisation of females 'has nearly always a prejudicial effect on the wages of the male worker'.[113] Even after the AST opened its doors to women in 1900 and changed its title to the Amalgamated Society of Tailors and Tailoresses, female membership was small and unreliable. The structure of London industry, so different to that in Leeds, did little to further the cause. Small-scale units of production did not facilitate organisation amongst the male work-force, so why should it succeed amongst the females who had little or no job security and who were even more scared of incurring the wrath of their employers than were their menfolk?

Once again it was welfare legislation in the name of sickness benefit that provided the stimulus for female trade union membership. National Insurance was available only to direct members of trade unions and societies, not to dependents. Women wishing to claim sickness pay were compelled to join societies in their own right. Without statistics, and none are available, it is impossible to analyse fluctuations in the female membership of London's tailoring unions, but the non-appearance, before 1911, of an independent and enduring tailoresses' union suggests that organisation amongst women workers in the clothing industry was motivated by material benefit not by the ethic of combination and the ideal of sisterhood.

A GENERAL TAILORS' STRIKE

In 1911, as conditions of trade and employment improved, the workers of England set forth on the 'second forward march of labour'.[114] In common with the period 1888–9, the end of the first decade of the twentieth century saw a movement out of recession into growth. But this is not the sole explanation for the wave of strikes that followed in the years leading up to the outbreak of the First World War, and though comparisons can be made, the backdrop was somewhat different. During the 1900s, as prices inflated, workers suffered a fall in real wages. As the bad times turned to good, opportunities for labour action grew – particularly amongst transport, building, mine and tailoring workers. If the 1880s was the decade of the socialists then, in terms of radical movements, the 1900s was the decade of the Anarchists and Syndicalists. Although the latter were greatly feared by contemporary commentators,[115] trade union historians such as Clegg and Laybourn suggest that in real terms their impact lacked the power earlier writers have suggested. Syndicalism arrived in England in three forms: that advocated by Daniel de Leon in America which allowed for a parliamentary path to the overthrow of capitalism, that supported by the Oxford group which emphasised the education of the workers and that which gained the support of Tom Mann in 1910. This last was French in origin and tied its flag to the mast of the General Strike; it was best known as Industrial Syndicalism. And it was the latter which can be detected in the London Tailors' Strike which took place in 1912.

The idea of a General Strike that would lead to the destruction of existing organisations and the removal of power from the capitalists appealed to the Anarchists.[116] Charles Mowbray made a speech in favour of Syndicalism as early as 1905,[117] whilst Rudolf Rocker believed in the concept of co-ordinated industrial action and later wrote books on that theme.[118] But the only union which overtly followed the radical path was the Jewish Syndicalist Tailors' Union founded in the East End of London in November 1908.[119] The *Jewish Chronicle*'s announcement of the creation of the union was its only entry into the public arena; it is never heard of again. There had been opposition to the concept of a 'French' union in the East End as early as 1907. The *Arbeiter Fraint* reported that the East End tailors 'have enough with the Garment Workers' Union and Lewis Lyons at the top'.[120] Shades of the 1870s. Forty years on the Jewish tailors still had no time for untried and extreme political philosophies, their priority remained bread today. This was something Rudolf Rocker understood, as he understood the need to challenge the 'detested sweating system' and the need for unity of Jew and Gentile working in the same trade.[121]

Nineteen-eleven was a year of 'organisation' strikes.[122] Mine workers and transport workers, dockers and seamen had demonstrated their discontent and refusal to accept falling wages and harsh conditions. One by one employers gave in and, together with representatives of the work-force, reached conciliated settlements. Agreements were invariably followed by a rapid increase in trade union membership, though this cannot be taken as the only stimulus, for 1911 was also the year in which the Trade Boards became operative and Parts One and Two of the National Insurance Act were passed. With the successes of the previous year as a precedent, in April 1912 1,500 West End tailors put in a demand for an increase in wages and improved conditions. Their demand was immediately upheld by the LST&T. As in 1906, the strike was not sanctioned by the Manchester headquarters of the AST or its London West End branch, even though its members were amongst the dissatisfied. When the tailoring masters rejected the demands out of hand the West End tailors issued an immediate strike call. Here was the opportunity Rudolf Rocker needed to demonstrate labour unity and, equally as important, a chance to remove the stigma of the strike-breaking Jewish worker.

Following an editorial in the *Arbeiter Fraint*, Rocker and Philip Kaplan, secretary of the London Ladies' Tailors' Union, organised a meeting in the Mile End Assembly Hall for 9 May. The 8,000 workers that attended voted unanimously for a general tailors' strike in support of their West End brothers. Irrespective of race, creed, skill or nationality, all downed tools. At the same time the East End tailors took the opportunity of putting forward their own demands to their employers. Two days later over 13,000 East End tailors had stopped work, the majority non-union members. English, Jewish, Italian, French and Czech men's tailors and mantle-makers in the bespoke, ready-made, high-quality and slop sectors of the industry had, for the first time, taken joint action in an attempt to increase wages and improve conditions in an industry renowned for its low pay and unhygienic workshops. Fraternal feeling extended far beyond the perimeter of the tailoring trade. The Jewish unions levied their members for contributions for the strike fund and individuals gave food and cigarettes. It was now May and the London dockers were on strike in protest at their employers' refusal to honour the Port of London Authority agreement of the previous year. This time it was the aliens' turn to help their striking brothers, and Jewish families undertook to care for undernourished and ragged dockers' children in their own homes. And as in 1889, so again in 1912, joint dock workers' and tailors' strike meetings were held on Mile End Waste and Tower Hill. [123]

After three weeks the West End workers and the men's civil and military tailoring unions reached separate agreements with their employers and returned to work. The mantle-makers were left to fight on alone. Once again the cleavage between east and west, between mantle-maker and men's tailor, was highlighted. Left alone, with no funds, the mantle-makers faced a tough choice. In his autobiography Rudolf Rocker describes the charged atmosphere at the meeting in the Pavilion Theatre where the decision whether to continue or give up was to be made. In front of thousands of 'pale, pinched, hungry faces'[124] he carefully explained what the options were. There was only one decision that could be made, to continue the strike. By now the masters' association was under pressure from wholesalers and retailers anxious for completion of garments ordered for the London Season. Within a day they had capitulated. The strike's organisers and the rank and file of the mantle-makers' union were triumphant. They had weakened the hold of the employers and proved their worth as members of the labour movement. Rocker was euphoric. Writing in the *Arbeiter Fraint* he said that the 'iron determination and solidarity' the mantle-makers had shown in their fight had made a 'deep impression on the entire Jewish workers' world and had given a lead to the whole trade union world'. He did add a warning, that if the mantle-making trade unionists did not hold on to their gains they would eventually lose everything.[125] He also, mistakenly, believed that the strike had dealt the 'death-blow to the sweatshop system'. Conditions at the end of the twentieth century have shown that forecast to be misguided. His successful leadership of the strike entered Rudolf Rocker into the mythology of the East End. He was the Gentile who had taken up the cause of the Jewish workers, urging them to stand firm and fight for victory. As one elderly Jew said to him, 'May God bless you... You are not a Jew, but you are a man!'[126]

Was that strike different from other strikes? The answer must be 'yes' as, for once, factors had mitigated in favour of the oppressed. Their co-ordinated action was facilitated by the progress of the assimilation and Anglicisation process and also by the integration of all but the very highest levels of production, which had resulted in a narrowing of the lacuna between East End and West End. Timing was of the essence. May was the height of the busy season, when the employers' and wholesalers' dependence was greatest. But the prime factor was leadership, as manifested by Philip Kaplan and Rudolf Rocker. Without their guidance, support and tenacity the mantle-makers would never have persevered to total victory. The strike's legacy was an impressive rise in membership of both the mantle-makers' branch of the AST and the London Ladies' Tailors' Trade Union. The latter rose by 340 per cent in the years between 1912 and 1914, from 700 to 3,000.[127] Some joined the unions because of the strike's success, some because of recent legislation and some, like Charlie Bromberg, a thirteen-year-old under-presser in 1912, 'weren't really sure what unions were about' but joined the mantle-makers' union because he 'just knew they were good for the workers'.[128]

The key points in the foundation and duration of the tailoring trade unions of London can be summed up as follows: the unique nature of London's industrial structure, its seasonal and cyclical economic peaks and troughs, the interaction between native and alien labour activists, the quality of their leadership, the influence of the Anglo-Jewish elite and the complex nature of the alien community. All but the last two points apply both to the tailoring industry, and to other small-scale

London industries in general, the final two relate to the eastern European Jewish community alone.

The complex infrastructure of the London tailoring industry, with its locational and craft divisions, bred small units which enervated attempts at combination. Evidence from other industries, other countries and other periods of history confirms that in the case of small-scale units of production, where there is enforced personal contact between employer and employee, trade union support was, and continues to be, difficult to encourage and hard to retain. This was true in the boot and shoe industry in the latter years of the nineteenth century,[129] the early stages of organisation amongst the print workers of New Delhi[130] and today, at the end of the twentieth century, in the small immigrant tailoring sweatshops that are still a part of east London.

The busy and the slack created further problems for those seeking to ensure the survival of young and fragile unions. Dovetailing was a feature of seasonal trades. The springtime tailor was so often the summer baker, a change of season necessitating a change of trade. What value the specialist union then? For all but the most highly skilled hands seasonal re-employment was not guaranteed, thus there was little incentive to invest money in membership dues when there was no job security. The Annual Reports of the AST illustrate clearly the fluctuations in London branch membership. During the busy, the second and fourth quarters of the year, membership expanded impressively. No other tailoring union, London or provincial, has left records which demonstrate so clearly the impact of seasonality. Age and size enabled the AST to withstand the departures and debts that accompanied the slack. The emphemeral London Jewish unions could not bear the strain.

The autocratic, anti-alien, provincially conceived AST did little to retain fraternity in spite of the opportunities available. It was the rift between the AST and its West End branch that proved such a stumbling-block to amalgamation. The antagonisms that existed between English and alien workers stemmed from a mutual concern for economic welfare plus, undeniably, a degree of covert anti-semitism. In spite, or because, of this members of the English labour movement supported alien workers in times of industrial strife and encouraged their combination even within their own societies. Their actions were not altruistic. Organisation of the alien work-force was seen as the only means of securing wage rates and conditions acceptable to the English working man. The alien worker had to be made to realise that it was to his advantage to unite with his English counterpart. It was for these reasons that Jewish tailoring trade unionism in the capital cannot be said to have taken place in isolation. It was very much part of the two forward marches of labour, reflecting local and national patterns of organisation and responding to contemporary political and economic conditions.

As has been proven by their actions, pragmatic, socially and economically aware leaders were vital ingredients in the recipe for trade union success. Men such as MacDonald, Rocker, Kaplan, Wess and Finn understood their members' immediate and long-term needs as well as the necessity to run trade unions on a businesslike day-to-day basis. Lewis Lyons had compassion and charisma, but what he lacked was the stability to ensure his unions' and his own financial survival. Nor did he truly appreciate when to subjugate the ideal to the reality.

The proximity of the established Anglo-Jewish community did not stifle Jewish trade unionism in the capital but it did inhibit its effectiveness, if the latter can be measured by strike action. By the time the discussions for amalgamation were under way the divisions within the East End Jewish community, so prominent in the 1870s and early 1880s, had largely been resolved; Litvaks, Galicians, Romanians, and Choots (Jews of Dutch origin) had overcome their differences for the common cause. Many were now first-generation Englishmen fighting to provide a better life for themselves and their children.

By the end of the first decade of the twentieth century some of the problems of the previous thirty years had been resolved, others had been reduced to a point where it was possible to think in terms of 'the few' as opposed to 'the many' tailoring trade unions of London. In 1910 discussions for an amalgamation of clothing unions were initated on a national scale. Two years later the London tailors' strike successfully demonstrated that co-ordinated action was a possibility. In the years that followed, the strengths and weaknesses of London's tailoring trade unions were once again highlighted as the talks and debates became more intense. As we shall see, a truly amalgamated clothing workers' union did not arrive until 1939.

NOTES

1. Cole, op. cit., p.2.
2. In 1911, of the capital's 112,302 engineers recorded in the decennial census, only 9,432 were recorded as members in the 61st (1911) *Annual Report* of the ASE.
3. *Decennial Census 1911*, op. cit.
4. *AST Annual Reports 1914–1915* and *Ballot for the Amalgamation 1914*, op. cit.
5. For obvious reasons the statistics relate to those unions or branches which were specifically Jewish, and it is impossible to include those more Anglicised members of the Jewish religion who might have been members of the 'English' unions.
6. That is, 5,634 were Jewish and 2,676 English.
7. See Appendix, Table 13, for breakdown of membership of London unions at the time of the amalgamation in 1915.
8. For details of the split in the AST *see below*, p.150.
9. A.R. Rollin, 'Russo-Jewish Immigrants in England Before 1881', *Transactions of the Jewish Historical Society of England*, Vol.XXI, 1968.
10. *Poilishe Yidel*, 8 Aug. 1884.
11. Ibid., 8 Aug. and 15 Aug. 1884.
12. For a detailed account of Lieberman and the Hebrew Socialist Union *see* Fishman, op. cit., pp.103–24.
13. Ibid., p.105.
14. *Jewish Chronicle*, 23 June 1876.
15. *Poilishe Yidel*, 22 Aug. 1884.
16. Notes of Aaron Rollin, Rollin Collection, loc.cit.
17. *Poilishe Yidel*, 22 Aug. 1884.
18. *Poilishe Yidel*, 22 Aug. 1884.
19. Fishman, op. cit., p.124.
20. Ibid., p.131.
21. *Poilishe Yidel*, 29 Aug. 1884.
22. *Arbeiter Fraint*, 15 July 1885.
23. Gartner, op. cit., p.106.
24. *Poilishe Yidel*, 29 Aug. 1884.
25. *See below*, p.154.
26. *Royal Commission on Alien Immigration 1903*, op. cit., qq 14061.
27. *AST Annual Report*, 1884.
28. *AST Annual Reports*, 1885–9.
29. *AST Annual Report*, 1903.
30. *Arbeiter Fraint*, 16 March 1906.
31. *See* Kershen, 'Henry Mayhew and Charles Booth', op. cit., pp.97–8.
32. *Jewish Chronicle*, 25 April 1884.
33. *Jewish Chronicle*, 12 March 1886.
34. Information about Lyons's family background supplied by his daughter Lily, in conversation with the author on 23 July 1983.
35. Thompson, op. cit., p.533.
36. The account of Lyons's arrest and the court hearing are recounted in Thompson's biography of Morris, op. cit., pp.394–9.
37. *See* Thompson, op. cit., pp.482–503.
38. By 1890 Krantz had left the London labour scene to settle in New York.
39. *Jewish Chronicle*, 22 Feb. 1889.
40. Ibid.
41. Gartner, op. cit., p.122.
42. William Wess was born in Kovno in 1861 and emigrated to England at the age of 20. On arrival he met Morris Winchevesky who introduced him to socialism.

Wess then became a member of the Socialist League, worked on the *Arbeiter Fraint* and was founder and secretary of the International Working Men's Education Club in Berner Street where he met Kropotkin, Stepniak, William Morris, John Burns and many other anarchists and socialists. A pioneer and builder of the Jewish trade union movement he gave up his active involvement in the early 1900s. After a period as a bookkeeper in a tobacco factory he became a dealer in tobacco and snuff. He died in 1945.

43. *East London Observer*, 21 Sept. 1889.
44. *The Jewish World*, 4 Oct. 1889.
45. Within two years all reference to the Federation had disappeared.
46. Handwritten notes of William (Woolf) Wess, Rollin Collection, loc. cit.
47. *Commonweal*, 24 May 1890.
48. *Arbeiter Fraint*, 29 May 1891.
49. Ibid., 19 June 1891.
50. *Commonweal*, 12 Dec. 1891.
51. Letter from Lyons to Adler dated 5 Nov. 1892.
52. *Daily Telegraph*, 14 Nov. 1892.
53. *Arbeiter Fraint*, 3 April 1891.
54. *AST Annual Reports*, 1894–9
55. *Jewish Chronicle*, 6 Oct. 1899.
56. Ibid., 15 Feb. 1901.
57. Ibid., 22 Nov. 1902.
58. Letter from Lyons to the Chief Rabbi, dated 30 Nov. 1892.
59. See *Arbeiter Fraint*, 13 March 1891, 29 March 1907 and 16 Aug. 1912.
60. *Jewish Chronicle*, 21 April 1911.
61. Ibid., 26 July 1918.
62. *Report of Trade Unions and Friendly Societies 1895*, PP 1896, LXXVIII.
63. It is not surprising that during the politically explosive years between 1889 and 1891 such a union would emerge, however its membership of 240 soon disintegrated. See *Arbeiter Fraint*, 20 Feb. 1891.
64. Weschler, op. cit., p.258.
65. Ibid.
66. Levine, op. cit., p.583.
67. *Royal Commission on Alien Immigration 1903*, op. cit., qq 20271.
68. *Jewish Chronicle*, 17 Feb. 1899.
69. Ibid., 26 Sept. and 26 Nov. 1902.
70. See Buckman, op. cit.
71. *Jewish Chronicle*, 13 March 1903
72. In the years before 1906 Jewish tailoring workers founded separate unions for tailors, machiners, pressers, waistcoat-makers, military tailors and trouser-makers. In addition the divisions created by workshop sub-contracting led to the foundation of an Under-pressers', Plain Machinists' and Plain Hands' Union in 1902 and an Anti-sub-contracting Union in 1904. None of these outlived 1904. (See *Commonweal*, 7 Sept. 1889, *Arbeiter Fraint*, 20 Feb. 1891, 20 Oct. 1891, 23 and 9 Aug. 1912. *Annual Reports of AST 1890–1915*, *Jewish Chronicle*, 29 April 1902 and 14 Oct. 1904).
73. *AST Annual Report*, 1905.
74. For the background to the emergence of the League and its activities in east London see Holmes, op. cit., pp.89–97.
75. *Arbeiter Fraint*, 17 Oct. 1892.
76. *AST Annual Report*, 1898.
77. *Jewish Chronicle*, 13 Oct. 1905.
78. *Arbeiter Fraint*, 18 March 1905.

79. Ibid., 16 March 1906.
80. Ibid., 7 Dec. 1906.
81. Ibid., 15 June 1906.
82. *Jewish Chronicle*, 13 July 1906.
83. *Arbeiter Fraint*, 29 June 1906.
84. *AST Journal*, Aug. 1906.
85. Ibid., July 1907.
86. *Jewish Chronicle*, 9 Aug. 1907.
87. *Arbeiter Fraint*, 1 March 1907.
88. Ibid., 20 Sept. 1907.
89. *AST Journal*, March 1905.
90. Ibid., Aug. 1909.
91. *Report on Trade Unions 1908–1910*, PP 1912, XLVII.
92. *AST Annual Report*, 1870 and *Decennial Census 1871*, op. cit.
93. *AST Annual Report*, 1876.
94. Ibid., 1884.
95. Ibid., 1890 and 1891.
96. Rollin Collection, loc. cit.
97. *See* Kershen, 'Henry Mayhew and Charles Booth', op. cit., p.104.
98. *See Justice*, 11 July 1896.
99. *History of London Trades Council* (1950), p.59.
100. *AST Journal*, 1905.
101. *The Journeyman*, (journal of the LST&T) July 1909.
102. *Tailor and Cutter*, 4 Dec. 1915.
103. *Report of Trade Unions 1908–1910*, PP 1912–13, XLVII and *AST Annual Reports*, 1905–10.
104. *Journeyman*, Aug. 1909.
105. *AST Journal*, Oct. 1911.
106. *Tailor and Cutter*, 15 April 1915.
107. Evidence of T. Whately to *Royal Commission on Aliens 1903*, op. cit.
108. *Report of the Chief Registrar of Trade Unions 1906*, PP 1907, LXXIX.
109. *AST Journal*, May 1899.
110. *Report of Chief Labour Correspondent on Trade Unions 1893*, PP 1895, CVII.
111. *AST Journal*, April 1908.
112. *Jewish Chronicle*, 9 Dec. 1881.
113. Quoted in Lewis, op. cit., p.174.
114. Trade union membership rose from 2,477,000 in 1909 to 4,145,000 in 1914. *See* Laybourn, op. cit., p.106.
115. Laybourn, op. cit., p.99.
116. *See* J. Quail, *The Slow Burning Fuse*, Ch.13 for its effect on the Anarchist movement in England.
117. *Jewish Chronicle*, 27 Oct. 1905.
118. *Die Prinzipieens des Syndikalismus* and, later, *Anarcho-Syndicalism* (1938).
119. *Jewish Chronicle* 10 Nov. 1908.
120. *Arbeiter Fraint*, 19 March 1907.
121. Rocker, op. cit., p.219.
122. *See* Clegg, op. cit., pp.37–56.
123. For a detailed account of the Jewish tailors' strike *see* Rocker, op. cit., pp.217–25 and Fishman op. cit., 294–301.
124. Rocker, op. cit., p.223.
125. *Arbeiter Fraint*, 16 Aug. 1912.
126. Rocker, op. cit., p.224.
127. *Report on Trade Unions 1908–1910*, op. cit and *SOTTA Ballot for the Amal-*

gamation 1914, op. cit.
128. Charlie Bromberg, conversations with the author, Aug. 1982.
129. A. Fox, *A History of the National Union of Boot and Shoe Operatives* (1958), pp.27 and 15.
130. F. Munson, *Indian Trade Unions* (1970), p.36.

6 Uniting the Tailors

> What we want... is unity of purpose and unity of action; and this can only be attained by the workers in their respective industries being joined together in one solid organisation which shall represent their collective interests.[1]

The amalgamation which created the United Garment Workers' Trade Union in 1915 was the first of four which, in the twentieth century, bonded together the diverse unions which represented the clothing workers of Great Britain. It is the creation of the UGWTU which is of paramount significance as it represents the fusion of those who previously had been considered irreconcilable. Even so, there were those, Jew and Gentile, craftsman and unskilled sub-divisional tailor, who chose to remain outside the newly established union for reasons which embraced ethnicity, economics and independence. Here we explore the background to the amalgamations which took place in the years between 1914 and 1939, a period which began in the dying embers of Edwardian England and drew to its close as a second world war became inevitable. The socio-economic changes which took place in those years were some of the most dramatic since the 1880s. War on a global scale had taken British menfolk out of the factories and on to the battlefields of northern France. In their place one and a half million women entered the work-force and discovered the financial and social independence and pleasure a job and a wage packet could bring. War affected fashion as well as the domestic and industrial scene. Hemlines rose above the ankle, in some instances almost to knee level, as evidenced by the uniforms designed for women tram and bus conductors. There was no turning back. In the post-war years, the women's wholesale clothing industry expanded impressively and, with the introduction of brand advertising, mantle and dress manufacturing companies became household names. Disillusion followed the euphoria of victory. The harsh economic climate which characterised the 1920s and the 1930s brought with it wage reductions, the National

Minority Movement, the General Strike and Mondism. In their different ways each acted as a stimulus for amalgamation, as did the gathering clouds of Fascism and Nazism which, in the mid-1930s, brought home to the Jewish ladies' tailors of London the fact that independent union was a luxury they could no longer afford.

AMALGAMATION: PART ONE

But first, back to 1907 and the belief of Mike Daly, organising secretary of the denuded West End Branch of the AST&T,[2] (quoted above) in the worth of 'one solid organisation'; one which, as far as he and his Manchester-based executive were concerned, was viable only if the dominant governing body and rules were those of the AST&T.

From the second half of the first decade of the twentieth century the push for amalgamation was on. It came from two points on the labour compass, the extreme radical left and the traditional trade union institutions. As Professor Clegg points out, amalgamation was seen by the large unions as a 'way of pushing forward' and by the smaller unions as a way of 'getting into the race'.[3] The Syndicalists saw the creation of large-scale single unions as a positive and offensive move and, in addition, as a means of taking the craft unions out of the 'new model' school and into the industrialist scene. The policy and its progress was considered of sufficient import to warrant an 'Amalgamation News Page' in the magazine *Industrial Syndicalist*.[4] There were two other forces for fusion. First was the Parliamentary Committee of the TUC, whose efforts were not always successful or well received. One minority group's reaction to merger was that it was no more than their 'absorption and extinction by another body which depends for its boasted superior strength on a horde of persons...who are not trade unionist at all, but simply joined as insured persons'.[5] The second was the GFTU. In the September 1910 issue of its *Quarterly Report*, the chairman of the GFTU stressed the importance of consolidation. He considered that there were too many trade unions in some industries and not enough trade unionists. As he explained, 'lack of solidarity has indeed been the curse of the Labour Movement'.[6] In keeping with this theme the GFTU's December *Report* for the same year announced its 'eagerness to promote the amalgamation of trade unions catering for similar occupations'.[7] It is at this stage that the bitterness, divisions and jealousies that coloured the clothing trade unions in the first decades of the twentieth century become manifest. In keeping with the move towards strength through unity, in February 1910 Robert Girvan, general secretary of the Scottish operative Tailors' and Tailoresses' Association (SOTTA), invited all the unions that represented workers in the clothing industry to send delegates to a conference scheduled for August that year. The intention was to promote 'Federation amongst the various Societies in the Tailoring Trade in Great Britain'. Significantly the conference was to be held in Manchester, headquarters of the AST&T. SOTTA and the AST&T had long been rivals for the same membership north of the border and though the latter had captured the support of one Emanuel Shinwell, who was secretary of the Glasgow branch of the AST&T in 1909,[8] it was the former that attracted local members. Of the unions invited to the conference, nine sent delegates. In addition to SOTTA, there were delegates from the AUCO, LCCTU, AJTMP, LST&T, plus four of the small London Jewish tailoring unions, two of which were jointly represented by Lewis Lyons. The ULTTU's delegation, unable to attend due to 'unforeseen circumstances', proclaimed its wholehearted support for the conference and its objectives in a letter which Girvan read to the conference in its opening session.

The AST&T refused to attend the conference for reasons its pragmatic general secretary, Terence Flynn, son-in-law of the Society's founder, Peter Shorrocks, made quite clear. His letter to Girvan read as follows:

Dear Sir,

In answer to your invitation to attend this conference, to be held in Manchester on Tuesday August 16. I am instructed by my executive Council to inform you that the above Society [AST&T] is affiliated to the Trades Union Congress, the General Federation of Trade Unions and the Labour Party, the joint board of which has declared that the London Society of Tailors and Tailoresses is not a bona-fide trades union and refuses them affiliation and has also advised affiliated societies not to recognise them. Further a large proportion of the societies in the list forwarded to us are societies that have broken away from existing unions and, as the policy of the United Labour Party is in the direction of assimilation in national unions of these unnecessary societies, we have no option, as part and parcel of this policy, but to refuse your invitation.

Yours truly,
Terence A Flynn, Secretary[9]

Hell hath no fury like a trade society scorned!

The conference survived without the presence of the long-established craft society. In the opening session the objectives were clearly spelt out. They were to create a 'CLOTHING TRADES FEDERATION' which would effect:

> closer union of the different Societies in the Clothing Industry, in order to render mutual aid in various ways; a system of education in the principles of Federation being organised; combined action taken when necessary; and an effort to make the several Societies as strong as possible in numbers and principles.'[10]

It was the first step on the path to amalgamation.

Less than a year later the Journal of the AST&T revealed that the management of the GFTU were making significant efforts to bring about an amalgamation of unions representing 'the same industry'. The society gave this its full support, for, after all was not 'sectional organisation an effective barrier to unity of aim and concentration of purpose'? The rhetoric continued in the April 1911 issue of the Journal, 'sectionalisation spelt weakness, disunity and disorganisation amongst workers...the best form of organisation was expressed in the word "amalgamation".'[11] But, as the article went on to make quite clear, the management committee of the society saw amalgamation as a condition whereby all workers in the clothing industry would become members of the AST&T. They believed that the current leader, AUCO, was a trade union that had mushroomed in the excitement of the late 1880s and early 1890s and where failure was long overdue. In their committee room in Manchester the leaders of the 'Mal (the abbreviation for Amalgamated Society of Tailors and Tailoresses) believed that nothing could force them to sacrifice their superiority.

No doubt because of their perceived immortality the executive of the AST&T agreed to attend a conference to discuss the amalgamation of all clothing unions sponsored by the GFTU in 1912. In fact the AST&T's attendance had been endorsed at a public meeting which passed the following resolution:

> This meeting heartily endorses the action of the Management Committee of the Federation of Trade Unions in the efforts they are making to bring about an amalgamation of unions represent-

ing the same industry. The meeting urges the men and women engaged in our industry to join the AST&T.[12]

The Resolution was passed in March 1912; the second forward march of labour was under way but the strike of London tailors had not yet taken place. Unaware of the divisions that would surface the next month, the Tailors' Amalgamation Conference held on 28 March was 'a great success'. However, shadows of the future can be detected in the Minutes of the Conference. The chairman reported that the 'chief obstacles to amalgamation were personal', but there were also others which related to the 'fear of technical difficulties and differential rates of contribution and benefits'.[13] In spite of the bitterness of the 1912 strike and the division between the LST&T and the AST&T discussions continued throughout the following year. Perhaps the words of the general secretary of the GFTU, W.A. Appleton, which promised that the scheme outlined by his Federation would secure greater efficiency, economy and, the most potent message, 'far greater influence with employers' which would lead to the acceptance of 'every just and reasonable demand', struck a chord with unions which were just beginning to see the way ahead after years of economic recession. At that point it even seemed possible that the clothing workers would, as Appleton recommended, 'be prepared to organise an army and not officer a mob'.[14] But the seeds of dissension had not withered, and though it continued to attend subsequent amalgamation meetings, the AST&T was not prepared to forgive what had been its old West End Branch for breaking away and taking with it membership contributions which 'were rightly ours'.[15]

It is clear from the records available that economic hardship and inflation were powerful forces in keeping the talks going. There was a need to concert attempts to improve the clothing workers' standard of living as the cost of rents, taxation and food continued to rise. All the clothing unions agreed that 'better organisation and stronger combination' were what was needed. The evil of piece-work had not been eradicated and tailors were being forced to work longer and harder hours in order just to keep pace with inflation. But it was not only a fusion of organised bodies that was necessary. In spite of the successful London strike of spring 1912, and the forward march of labour, it was estimated that only 30,000 of the one million workers employed in the clothing industry belonged to a trade union.[16] Strength and solidarity would, it was hoped, act as a magnet for the unorganised as they had in 1889. Perhaps it was that hope, and the fact that the AST&T still believed that, in the event of an amalgamation, it could, with a membership of almost 12,000 retain control, that encouraged members to voice their full support for the speedy finalisation of the plans under discussion.

The spirit which existed to 'carry the amalgamation through as quickly as possible' prevailed into the winter of 1914. Then the cracks began to appear. Not unexpectedly it was the AST&T which departed first. The Society's executive had disagreed with the management committee of the GFTU over its policy of encouraging small trade unions to affiliate independently for insurance purposes, rather than become branches of the AST&T. In February 1914 the Society withdrew from the discussions. If by doing this Flynn and Rowlerson believed they would wreck the discussions and subsequently take-over as the major union in the industry they were mistaken. The amalgamation would go ahead. However, other more disturbing factors were on the horizon which resulted in that first fusion, intended as the saviour of the exploited sub-divisional worker, craft tailor and factory operative, being a weaker and far less powerful body than originally intended.

In its 15 July 1915 issue the *Yorkshire Factory Times* announced that the amalgamation of clothing unions which was to be known as the United Garment Workers' Trade Union 'was a fact'. But the earlier forecast of a union with 'A probable 40,000 members throughout the country'[17] was out by almost 50 per cent. The inaugural figure was 21,457.[18] Two of the major parties to the amalgamation had pulled out at the last minute, the first as a result of war, the second in the cause of ethnicity. Throughout the discussions SOTTA had favoured the proposed amalgamation, indeed it had been Robert Girvan who had called the original conference to discuss federation. But, in spite of SOTTA's membership voting by a majority in favour of the amalgamation in the ballot held in September 1914, the outbreak of war and its repercussions on finance and manpower made consummation impossible. In its end of year report for 1914 SOTTA highlighted the problems created by the depression in the tailoring trade, which had followed the declaration of war, and the departure of members to join the armed forces or wartime industry. No one had foreseen, in August 1914, that war would last more than a few months, no one had dreamt it would continue for four years. The executive of SOTTA decided that fusion with the newly created union would simply have to be deferred for a short while. Robert Girvan cautioned that matters should be delayed until spring 1915. In a letter written to his fellow members in September 1914 he clearly identified the problems faced by his, and no doubt many other unions, in those first, unnerving months of the First World War:

> It is quite evident that the war is having a very serious effect on our Society, as large numbers of our members are away on service with the military, naval and territorial forces, and trade is also very bad. This will have the effect of depleting our income, and if we were to go forward with Amalgamation at the present time and meet our other obligations we would require to levy for the necessary money, and that we consider out of the question... We believe that the course suggested by us ['the whole question be postponed until the Spring of next year'] is the only possible way to bring about a successful Amalgamation, and we hope that what has been accomplished to further the Cause may not be damaged or destroyed through any hasty action in attempting to press forward to a conclusion when it is obvious that the forces intending to combine are not quite ready for it.
>
> Robert Girvan
> Gen. Secretary SOTTA[19]

Girvan was absolutely correct in stating that there were those who were 'not quite ready'. The initial ballot held by the AJTMP Leeds branch favoured a rejection of the amalgamation. As the historian and trade union organiser Aaron Rollin recalled, at the last hour, Moses Sclare had 'wanted out'.[20] However, Rollin and others persuaded him otherwise and, on 29 May 1915, the branch held a meeting at which a unanimous resolution was passed to the effect that, 'this meeting expresses itself in favour of amalgamation and requests committee to take a further ballot with a view to securing a proper majority'.[21] Sclare's reasons for 'wanting out' are unclear. They may have been financial, as in the case of the Scottish Association, as each society was required to levy 2s. 6d. for each male member and 1s. 6d. for each female member for payment into the new union before amalgamation could take effect. With the fluctuations in membership and trade difficulties, as SOTTA understood, this could present problems. Perhaps the second ballot reflected the financial optimism which accompanied the industrial upturn that began in the spring of 1915. Or Sclare's cold feet may have been a manifestation of the reluctance of some of his members to sacrifice ethnicity for labour unity. This latter consideration was a constant in the case of the United Ladies' Tailors' Trade Union.

Although the ULTTU had participated in some of the early amalgamation discussions they did not respond to the ballot vote in 1914 and thus were eliminated from those who fused to create the UGWTU. The union which, as we know, had grown strong after the 1912 strike, had a membership of 3,000 by 1914. Many members still clung to their *stetl* origins, and would continue to do so. Their headquarters, in what was part of an old coaching inn in Black Lion Yard, Whitechapel, recreated an atmosphere of eastern Europe which the description below so vividly illustrates.

> Climbing the rickety wooden steps members would congregate in the loft, eating black bread, pickled herrings and onions and whiling away the time with interminable games of dominoes as they waited for work. Their domino teams were in the championship class. An employer would enter the yard and shout the number and kind of worker he wanted. A mad stampede down the stairs would bring a jostling crowd of members into the yard surrounding the employer and begging to be taken on. He would often savour his power by humming and hawing, appearing to make up his mind and then changing it, and then make some new proviso which shaved a few pence off the prospective earnings. The unsuccessful would return to the loft and new games of dominoes until the next employer was pleased to present himself and repeat the degrading performance.[22]

It was a performance that, even after the union's offices moved to Great Garden (now Greatorex) Street, was repeated time and time again until the outbreak of the Second World War. Performers such as Moishe Pickled Herring and The Hoicke (hump) were reluctant to sacrifice their Jewish union and identity for a place in the new faceless, centralised body that was to be the United Garment Workers' Trade Union. In the eyes of the ULTTU no vote was no go.

AMALGAMATION: PART TWO

The outbreak of war in 1914 resulted in a complete standstill in the production of clothes, and some masters even turned to the production of blankets in order to survive. After three months a reversal took place, as the need for military uniforms grew. Needles were rethreaded, treadles pumped and sewing machines started up, even if some that had only handled suit materials had to be exchanged for those that could make up the heavier khaki. As in so many other industries, so in the clothing factories, women replaced their male counterparts in the job boom that followed. Trade union membership increased for a variety of reasons. Generally the standing of trade unionists rose as their leaders participated in planning the war effort with employers and government. In the clothing industry the respectable face of organisation encouraged new recruits to join a union. Factory workers had the option of the UGWTU or the AST&T, which had adopted a reprisal policy of capturing operatives where it could. Support for organisation further increased after the Stoker Award, which followed a dispute in Leeds in May 1917 between members of the UGWTU and the manufacturing companies of Hipps Ltd. and Lyons Ltd. The disagreement, based on inadequate wage rises since the outbreak of war, went to arbitration under W.H. Stoker, who awarded increases of 20 per cent for female piece-workers and ten per cent for male piece-workers, with the wages of all those on time-work increased to the same level.[23] What was openly acknowledged as an award duly related to 'the existence of abnormal conditions now prevailing in consequence of war' resulted in the influx of a considerable number of new members into the union.

A further stimulus for union membership came with peace and the extension of the Trade Boards to cover all sections of the clothing industry. The old Tailoring Board was dissolved and replaced by two new Boards, a Retail Bespoke Tailoring Board in December 1919 and a Ready-Made and Wholesale Bespoke Board in February 1920. At the same time new minimum rates were laid down at 7d. per hour for women working piece-rates and 28s. per week time-rate and 1s. 0d. for men working piece-rates and £2. 8s. per week time-rate. This was a one hundred per cent increase on the Trade Board Rates in operation in 1913. By 1919 the UGWTU, which now operated 96 branches, had 89,332 members, of which 74,463 were female. It could be truly said, as the Report of the UGWTU did in June 1920, that the union was making splendid progress in organising and increasing trade unionism in the garment-making industry.

With peace came a resumption of amalgamation negotiations. Once again the AST&T participated, as did SOTTA and two smaller unions.[24] At this stage no attempt was made to renew talks with the ULTTU or to encourage the Manchester Waterproof Garment

Workers' Union, which had resigned from the original amalgamation shortly after it had taken place, to join in. The joint report of the negotiations held with the AST&T and SOTTA was a clear case of *déjà vu*. Once again the 'Mal is heard expressing its support for an amalgamation with the UGWTU, particularly as there was 'a degree of overlap between the two'. Discussions even reached the point at which Gurney Rowlerson announced his Society's agreement to an amalgamation, subject to a ballot being held within three months of that agreement. The ballot was never carried out. In 1914 the AST&T had withdrawn from negotiations, supposedly because of 'unfortunate circumstances of a financial character'; this time the reason given was that it was not happy with the rules which would result from the merger.[25] However, nothing stood in the way of SOTTA and on 1 July 1920 the second amalgamation of clothing unions took place. The result was the creation of the Tailors' and Garment Workers' Trade Union (TGWU) with an initial membership of 101,481.[26]

AMALGAMATION: PART THREE

Within five months membership of the newly created union had dropped by almost 20 per cent, to 86,761, as a result of the 'unexpected slump in trade'.[27] The boom created by orders for 'demob' suits for soldiers returning from the war was quickly followed by the downturn in trade and the onset of recession. As jobs became scarce and wages fell trade union membership, which had peaked nationally in 1920, plummeted.[28] By 1923 membership of the TGWU stood at 45,000. It had lost 9,000 male members and 48,000 female members, many of the latter returning to their pre-war roles as housewives and mothers. The 1920s were tough years for all, clothing workers and their representative unions providing no exceptions. The harshest factor for those in employment was the continuing drop in wage rates. In the clothing industry there was a downward spiral from 1921 to 1925. For the remainder of the decade wages did not rise above their mid-1922 level.

Whilst economic problems and reduction of trade union numbers acted as an incentive to amalgamation, they also opened the door to militant, radical trade unionism which, in the form of the National Minority Movement (NMM), founded in 1924, set out to mobilise workers 'for the overthrow of capitalism'.[29] A weapon in the hands of the communist-inspired and led NMM was the further deskilling of the clothing industry. This was evident in London as well as Leeds where the introduction of the conveyor-belt system was augmented by the rationalisation of hand-cutting. Both encouraged employment of female and juvenile labour at lower wage rates than male workers. Amongst its London membership there was a grass-roots feeling that the TGWU was not defending their best interests. As so often in the past, distant provincial control was a thorn in the side of the London organisers, one of whom, Sam Elsbury (himself originally from Leeds), was a founder member of the NMM. It was Sam Elsbury who was to take the lead in a dispute at the Rego clothing factory which brought about the creation of a breakaway, communist-inspired clothing trade union, which in its early stages attracted a large proportion of the membership of the TGWU.

The story of the United Clothing Workers' Union has been told in fine detail by Shirley Lerner in her thesis and in her book *Breakaway Unions and The Small Trade Unions*.[30] There is no need for its retelling here. What is relevant for the purposes of this brief study of the amalgamations which took place in the inter-war years is the realisation that when, in July 1929, the TUC promoted negotiations between the AST&T, the ULTTU and the Waterproof Garment Workers' Union, with a view to creating a simple 'great Union catering for the tailoring and garment industry' it was in a climate shaken by the parallel existence of an active and disruptive militant union. The United Clothing Workers' Union was founded on 7 March 1929, following TGWU Head Office refusal to sanction a strike at the Rego factory called over a dispute about the closed shop. At that time Sam Elsbury was London Organiser of the TGWU. When Andrew Conley refused to support him, subsequently dismissing him and forcibly taking his office keys, the result was the UCWU. It was only to be expected that by the end of the 1920s Conley and Elsbury would have become politically distanced. The former was in favour of the Mond–Turner talks which were aimed at involving trade unions, through the TUC, in economic policy, a priority of which was 'the substitution of modern plant and techniques for existing machinery and methods'.[31] As a member of the NMM Elsbury was opposed to the Mond–Turner talks, and as representative of workers who were suffering as a result of the introduction of 'modern plant and techniques' he was doubly opposed. Whatever working relationship had existed between the blunt, feisty Catholic who stood, unsuccessfully, as a parliamentary candidate for the Labour Party in 1918 and 1922, and the passionate, militant Russian-born Jewish member of the Communist Party, whose oratorical skills were renowned, it was now doomed.

In its nascent stages the communist clothing workers' union attracted members in large numbers from the capital and, in smaller numbers, from Leeds and Glasgow. This at a time when there was no sign of an improvement in the tailoring trade and when the membership of the TGWU, at 40,180, was still under the figure registered in 1923. The industry was suffering severely from the combined effects of the global depression and the changes in production methods which, by use of even further extremes of sub-division and up-to-date machinery had increased usage of the low paid at the expense of the craftsman and craftswoman. As Gurney Rowlerson explained, 'once a girl or youth reaches an age at which they would be legally entitled to the higher rates determined by the Trade Board they are discharged, thrown on the scrap-heap, and replaced by younger workers who can be obtained at the cheaper rates'.[32] It was not only in the wholesale sector of the trade that conditions were worsening. In retail bespoke tailoring the handicraft worker was being ousted by persistent use of the 'cheapest methods of production'. The outcome was parental reluctance to apprentice their sons to the trade and a shortage of skilled labour. In London these factors were compounded by the closure of commercial workshops and, as in Leeds decades earlier, the mushrooming of domestic workshops. The outlook for growth of trade union membership, particularly amongst skilled workers, was bleak.[33]

The ULTTU was also suffering. In his General Review of 1929 Secretary Jacob Fine referred to the year just past as one of the most difficult periods ever experienced by his union. In its specially built Greatorex Street headquarters, funded through the generosity of its members and supporters who had purchased bricks at £3 a time, it had survived a 'sinister plot to disorganise our members' and an all-time high level of unemployment. Surprisingly, Fine viewed the year ahead with admirable optimism. His perspective was coloured perhaps by the prospect of amalgamation in conditions which, he believed, were 'more favourable than at any time in the past'.[34] Russian-born Fine had spent his early years working as a tailor's machiner in a workshop in Bethnal Green and acquiring his political education in Rudolf Rocker's Jubilee Street Club.[35] As a youthful member of the ULTTU at the time of the Great Tailors' Strike of 1912 he knew only too well the vagaries of the mantle trade and the problems of organising its labour force. He was appointed secretary of the ULTTU in 1918 and brought to it all his literary skills and Yiddish oratory. One of his great talents was his ability to negotiate with employers and members in fluent Yiddish. If he was lacking in any skill it was in organising at the factory gate or workshop door. By the time of the third set of amalgamation discussions Fine was thoroughly convinced of the importance of fusion with the national union – 'better be the tail of a lion than the head of a fox'. Unfortunately, there were too many members of his union who did not agree. It was to take another ten years, and the arrival of the young Mick Mindel on the scene, to persuade them to change their views.

The discussions for amalgamation which began in 1929 went to a ballot in 1931. There had been little or no improvement in the economy and the incentive for the AST&T to fuse was strong. On the political front, the threat posed by the UCWU had subsided by 1930. Elsbury had fallen out with the Communist Party after they failed to provide the promised strike pay for his members. As so often in the past, without strike funds a gradual return to work began. Rego and Poliakoff, the latter a victim of the second strike called by the UCWU, agreed to take back striking workers provided they did not join a union that was not affiliated to the TUC. The Trade Union Congress had been constant in its opposition to the communist-inspired union, and pressure from both the Wholesale Clothiers' Federation[36] and the TGWU finally ensured that no employer would tolerate UCWU members.

In the case of the AST&T it was third time lucky. The ballot for a national tailoring union was impressive, over 80 per cent of the two main unions' members participated and gave the proposal their overwhelming affirmation. The AST&T produced an 80 per cent vote in favour of amalgamation and the TGWU a 93 per cent vote in favour.[37] As the new executive board proudly announced in the *Tailor and Garment Worker*, 'No amalgamation could have had a more auspicious beginning or a more enthusiastic send-off.'[38] The negotiations had been protracted but it is clear that, at last, past differences had been set aside. The new union was to be called the National Union of Tailors and Garment Workers. For the first time 'National' was used in conjunction with the organisation of clothing workers. The NUTGW's scope was to embrace 'all workers employed in wholesale and retail establishments employed in the manufacture of male and female clothing and attire'.[39] Its objects were:

> The protection and furtherance of the interests of its members, the improvement of the conditions of employment in the whole

clothing industry, the moral and social elevation of its members, the regulation of the relations between workmen and employers and between member and member, and to eliminate all unfair exploitation of Labour by Capital.

To provide financial assistance in times of unemployment, sickness, accident, old age, distress or death, and to render legal assistance to members in cases arising out of their employment.[40]

The photograph of the new executive board shows Conley and Rowlerson, respectively general secretary and general president, seated together in the front row with the indefatigable original female organiser Edith Machin and Edith Maycock of the executive board on either side.

The General Council of the TUC had asked the three unions involved in the amalgamation discussions (the Waterproof Garment Workers' Union did not take up the 1929 invitation) to forward the essential points they considered necessary for inclusion in the basis of a scheme for amalgamation. Between 1929 and 1931 these 'essential points' were considered by the joint conferences held by the three unions. The ULTTU's essential points appeared in its Annual Report for 1929. They were:

1. That the amalgamation embrace all clothing workers.
2. That the Ladies' Tailors (factory and sub-divisional Workers) shall form a separate District Branch for London, and that all such workers who, at the time of amalgamation may be members of either the TGWU or the AST&T shall be transferred to that branch.
3. That a special strike fund shall be provided by the central body, which shall be at the disposal of the London District Branch of the Ladies' Tailors, and that the branch committee shall have power to decide upon and call a local strike.
4. That all customs, concessions, and privileges which now obtain in our Union shall be retained and maintained by the new London branch of the Ladies' Tailors, with the support of the National Executive.[41]

Items 2,3 and 4 would clearly not have met with general approval, biased as they were in favour of the ULTTU and its membership. Though talking and writing amalgamation the union had not yet reached the point where independent identity and autonomy were

14 Officials of the Tailors' and Garment Workers' Trade Union, 1926: A. Conley, J. Young, M. Sclare and Miss A. Loughlin (*The Garment Worker*)

15 The first Executive Board of the United Garment Workers, 1915 (Henry Rollin)

16 Seventeen years later, the Executive Board of the newly amalgamated Society of Tailors and Tailoresses and the Tailors' and Garment Workers' Union, 1932

17 Mick Mindel reliving the ballot of 1938 (London Museum of Jewish Life)

NATIONAL UNION OF TAILORS AND GARMENT WORKERS

LONDON SUB-DIVISIONAL & MANTLEMAKERS BRANCH

48, New Road, E.1

Tel.: BIS. 3809

A CALL TO THE LONDON CLOTHING WORKERS

Events of great importance to the Workers in our Industry have recently taken place. The separate Unions which existed in our trade, acting independently, and often in opposition to each other, are now no more.

The membership of the United Clothing Workers Union and of the Old Trouser Makers Union have now merged into the above branch of the great National Organisation catering for all Sections of the Industry.

The policy of the united forces in our branch is to forget the past differences, to bring back into our Union the thousands of old members, and the many thousands of young workers who grew up in our Industry, without any knowledge of Trade Unionism whatsoever.

During the past years of apathy and division in our ranks the conditions in the trade have grown worse. Men workers have been replaced by women at low wages, and adult Women are replaced by young girls just leaving school at sweated low wage rates.

These conditions must, and can. be abolished if only the Workers are united under the leadershp of one strong organisation the—

National Union of Tailors and Garment Workers

Mr. A. R. Rollin. the London Area Organiser of the Union is the Acting Secretary of this branch and attends personally to the members' complaints and grievances.

Join the Union to protect and improve your conditions, and safeguard your livelihood

18 A call for stronger Union membership in the Depression years

PROPOSED   AMALGAMATION

of

The United Ladies' Tailors Trade Union

with the

National Union of Tailors and
Garment Workers

BALLOT PAPER

Place a **X** in this column opposite the opinion you desire to express.

FOR Amalgamation	
AGAINST Amalgamation	

This Ballot Paper must be completed and returned to the Head Office, 12, Greatorex Street, London, E.1. as early as possible, but certainly **not later than SEPTEMBER 24th, 1938.**

WILDBLOOD & WARD, LEEDS (T.U.)

19 Voting for – or against – the proposed amalgamation of the United Ladies' Tailors with the National Union of Tailors and Garment Workers, 1938

easily sacrificed. From remarks made later it is clear that Jacob Fine was totally in favour of an early fusion with the national union, as he explained, 'I fought from within and without a lonely battle...'.[42] In 1931 it was a battle he lost.

The National Union of Tailors and Garment Workers came into existence in January 1932 with a membership of 15,754 males and 34,330 females, a total of 50,084. Depression and radicalism had combined to convince the two giants of the tailoring trade union world that whatever the difficulties it was better to fight the decade ahead together and achieve their potential strength than fight each other and lose the support of present and future members.

AMALGAMATION: PART FOUR

The report which followed the 1935 NUTGW conference, the first since the amalgamation, portrayed an industry in the depths of recession, an industry still beset by the continuing replacement of skilled labour by machinery, by high unemployment and insecurity. Whilst in Leeds conditions were stabilising and union membership increasing, in London gent's and ladies' tailors were finding it harder than ever to get work. The ULTTU's Report for 1935 also made depressing reading, the slack periods were lengthening and it was becoming increasingly difficult to find jobs for unemployed members.

With the benefit of hindsight it can be argued that 1935 was a turning-point in the history of independent Jewish tailoring trade unionism. On the political and organisational fronts the climate was changing. The decision by Oswald Mosley to focus his Fascist attacks on the East End and its Jewish community after 1934 brought the darkening clouds of Nazism and Fascism to the doorsteps of tailoring workers in Whitechapel, Stepney and Bethnal Green. Younger men such as Mick Mindel, who in 1938 was to become Chairman of the ULTTU during the last few months of independent existence, took the Communist Party route. Older men clung to their Anarchist and Bundist views, whilst the more moderate, including Jacob Fine, followed the Labour Party. By 1935 Fine had become a Labour Councillor in Stepney. As Mindel discovered in the years between 1936 and 1939, those who constantly opposed amalgamation on the grounds that the national union 'won't understand our Jewish ways' were finally forced to give way as economic hardship and the revelations of the treatment of Jews in Germany became more widely known and the mantle-makers' isolation from the national union more anachronistic. It should be noted that for those who pleaded ignorance of events taking place in central Europe, the *Tailor and Garment Worker* was publishing details of Nazi atrocities from the early 1930s onwards.[43] Some of the details, even for that time, are quite shocking, but it is hard to say how much of the information was actually digested when priorities in the East End of London remained bread and work.

By 1934 the communist UCWU was disintegrating, though not without damage to the NUTGW London District which suffered internal disruption and the loss of thousands of members.[44] The executive knew that a firm and capable hand was needed to restructure the London division and encourage new membership. They persuaded Russian-born Aaron Rollin to move from Leeds to London and take on the challenging role of Area Organiser. Rollin, a socialist, who had arrived in England in 1905 as a political refugee, had a similar background to Moses Sclare, having trained as an engineer in Russia. Like Sclare he began his active trade union life in Glasgow. He moved to Leeds during the First World War as an organiser for the AJTMP. Rollin was not a passionate orator or a charismatic character in the mould of Elsbury or Lyons. However, the perceptive Conley knew that, as a quiet but firm leader, he was the right man to repair the damage in London. Rollin[45] took over his job in the capital in August 1934. His calm, intellectual and compassionate approach was combined with an innovative and pragmatic method of recruitment; he was the first to use the loudspeaker as a recruiting device. Aaron Rollin was the man who restored confidence in the NUTGW and the ethos of organisation in the minds and hearts of the tailors of London.

Rollin's London No. 2 Branch catered for sub-divisional tailors and male mantle-makers. As such it provided one of the largest contingents in the October 1935 anti-Nazi demonstration, a clear indication of the NUTGW's commitment to anti-Fascism. Encouraged by Rollin's recruitment methods, his active involvement in Jewish communal and labour affairs and his acknowledged trade union management, in March 1936 the London Trouser Makers' Union, a small Jewish union which had not participated in the two earlier series of amalgamation discussions, gave up its independence to be absorbed into the NUTGW.[46] No doubt its members and others of the branch, together with those from the ULTTU, were amongst the thousands who fought the Battle of Cable Street on 4 October 1936 and prevented Oswald

Mosley and his blackshirts marching through the streets of the East End and making them 'their own'. Yet again, as they had in 1889 and 1912, Jew and Gentile, tailor and docker, stood side by side in the face of victimisation and iniquity. By the end of the year Aaron Rollin was able to report marked progress in the rehabilitation of his branch, the membership having doubled since his arrival.[47] Surely the ULTTU must have read the signals that were going out from the national union which, in the November, had invited the executive of the Ladies' Tailors to discuss once again an amalgamation. If further evidence of the NUTGW's influence was needed it came the following April and June when a new national agreement was successfully negotiated, under the auspices of the Trade Boards, for wage increases for workers in the clothing industry. These ranged from two to eight shillings a month. Four months later, in October, the NUTGW and the ULTTU took joint, and successful, action against the master tailors.

For the ladies' tailors' union this was a complete reversal of tactics as, after the breakdown of discussions in 1931, Fine had developed a different tack. Following in the wake of Lewis Lyons he initiated discussions with the Master Ladies' Tailors' Association. This began in the form of a wage agreement and developed into discussions for a possible federation between the two.[48] By 1935 the gulf between the masters' association and the ladies' tailors' union, instead of narrowing, had widened. The former wanted it all their own way, demanding that the workers call a general strike whenever the masters needed their unqualifed support against the manufacturers. In return the ULTTU would only get its requirements 'if and when the masters' demands were successful'.[49] Jacob Fine foresaw a situation in which a general strike would become inevitable. Concerned at what he termed the masters' ultra-revolutionary policies he demanded the setting up of a special reserve fund for general strike purposes. This, and his justifiable request to be kept fully informed of developments, were rejected by the master tailors. A year later the ULTTU announced the abandonment of any plans to federate with the master tailors. There was but one option now, amalgamation with the NUTGW. This in fact was what Mick Mindel had urged all along, but although he and Jacob Fine were to work together towards amalgamation their relationship was not always harmonious. Fine did not approve of Mindel's Communist Party affiliation nor his continued preference, throughout the negotiations with the masters, for amalgamation with the NUTGW. In keeping with those who had opposed Lyons, Mindel believed the federation to be an unnatural alliance between employer and employee.

Mick Mindel was born in London in 1910, the son of a bookbinder and founder member of the Workers' Circle. He was trained as a cutter, and was the only cutter to be a member of the ULTTU. In 1931 he joined the Communist Party, seeing it as the only alternative to the inertia of mainstream politics and the emergence of Fascism. It is not surprising that, as a result of their political differences – Fine was on the right side of the Labour Party – for a short while in 1936 Mindel was expelled from the ULTTU due to his radical stance on amalgamation; for him it was the only way forward. Mindel was the organiser, the young man dedicated to amalgamation and to the recruitment of women into the ULTTU. The union's traditional Jewish membership discouraged female affiliates. It was Mindel that persuaded his members not only to actively encourage female affiliation but to appoint Sarah Wesker (Arnold's aunt) as a full-time women's organiser in 1937. Wesker had been an original member of the UCWU and had found it almost impossible to get employment in the years following the communist union's failure. It was only as a result of the amalgamation of 1939 that she was readmitted to the NUTGW.[50] Mindel, together with his supporters, including the extremely able Hymie Kantor, a craft ladies' tailor who took over Mindel's job as vice-chairman of the ULTTU in 1938, began a crusade to persuade the older members, who were a majority of the union, that fusion was the only way foward.

Once Conley had approached the ULTTU Mindel took over the negotiations. In spite of his Communist Party membership, the general secretary took to the pragmatic, articulate and intelligent organiser. In fact, following the amalgamation in 1939, Mindel and Hymie Kantor became the only two card-carrying members of the Communist Party to serve on the executive of the NUTGW. As Mindel recalls, there was no problem negotiating with the national union; his problem was in persuading those ladies' tailors who clung to their *stetl* ways of the benefits of fusion. However, certain events on the industrial canvas took a hand. In September 1937 the Master Ladies' Tailors' Association announced a closure of factories and workshops in protest at what they considered excessive demands by the manufacturers. Jointly the ULTTU and the executive of the NUTGW's London No. 2 (Rollin's) Branch worked out a strategy which they delivered to their members at the People's Palace in Mile End on 23 September. At a packed meeting

Rollin, Fine and Mindel called upon those still in employment to stay at their jobs and not to give in to the master tailors' recommendations. The only real solution was an end to piece-work, the elimination of small masters, the establishment of a five-day week and legislation which would eliminate sweating.[51] The recommendations met with unanimous support and, as Rollin later reported, 'all references to unity between the two Trade Unions were received with thunderous applause'.[52] With such powerful organised opposition the masters had little alternative. An agreement was reached with the manufacturers within hours. In the week that followed membership of the London No. 2 Branch of the NUTGW rose by over 350 new members.

The ballot for the fourth attempt at an amalgamation of the national clothing workers' union and the ULTTU was issued on 24 September 1938. It should have been a *fait accompli*, but was not so; there was a final hurdle. It was decided to hold an open meeting at which a past president of the ULTTU, Lew Colton, an ex-Communist Party member and an opponent of amalgamation, and Mick Mindel would be given three-quarters of an hour each to put forward their arguments to the union membership. The debate would be followed by the actual ballot. Two boxes marked YES and NO stood at the ready. Mindel was determined that, after all his hard work in persuading his members that they could no longer go it alone, the decision should be made demo-cratically. The meeting was held at the Mile End Baths on 24 September 1938. The outcome was the 'annihilation' of those opposed to the amalgamation. There was a 95 per cent vote, five to one in support of fusion with the National Garment Workers' Union.[53] The team of Jacob Fine and Mick Mindel had won the day. In reality, under the terms of the subsequent amalgamation agreement very little changed on a day-to-day basis. The ULTTU became the central branch for the mantle and costume trade in London, taking over complete control of the ladies' tailoring trade in the capital. Jacob Fine was appointed branch secretary and Mick Mindel, branch chairman.

In the April 1939 issue of the *Tailor and Garment Worker*, Andrew Conley announced the 'beginning of the one big Union for all sections of workers in the tailoring and garment-making trades'. It was '... A new chapter in the history of Trade Unionism in the garment-making industry'.[54] Making his first appearance in the national union's journal two months later, Jacob Fine expressed his delight and pride at the amalgamation and at the lifting of the 'veil of prejudice and mistrust which had obscured the light from the Mantle Makers'.[55] His reference to his 'lonely battle' and his happiness that his labours had not been in vain, present a somewhat biased account as they omit the major contribution made by his *aide-de-camp*, Mindel, who had fought so valiantly to bring the negotiations to a successful conclusion. The omission is suggestive of the unspoken fear Fine had that Mindel, the organiser, might prove a threat to his position in the national union. It was a fear that in the years ahead proved to be totally unfounded. It was not until Fine retired in 1948 that Mindel took over his position as Branch Secretary.

What is clear is the eventual recognition by the membership of the ULTTU, young and old, English-born and alien, that there was only one decision they could make. It is not within the bounds of this book to discuss the motivations and debates that finally induced the Waterproof Workers to rejoin the national union but what is undeniable is that the arrival of Aaron Rollin on the London scene was a decisive factor. Not only did he demonstrate his ability to recruit new members at an impressive rate, thus posing a threat to the ULTTU, but he also projected a sympathetic, intelligent, compassionate, Jewish image, with an eastern European background, to those older ladies' tailors who had interpreted the NUTGW as an alien, cold and unfriendly body. Rollin disposed of that view. He was in the vanguard of those protesting in the face of Fascism. The shock waves of Mosley's attempted march through the East End on 4 October 1936 cannot be underestimated. Edith Ramsay recalled quite clearly the terror in the eyes of an elderly Jewish woman on that Sunday afternoon in Whitechapel when the BUF were turned back from Cable Street.[56] Had the pogroms of the Pale reached the Whitechapel ghetto? Rollin was a member of the NUTGW who understood the alien, the mantle-maker, the sub-divisional worker, and his union got results. The vision of Rollin, Fine and Mindel working together toward the common good was the ideal commercial for amalgamation.

It had taken more than 50 years for all the unions in the clothing industry to amalgamate, to overcome the vast divisions which separated skill, gender and ethnicity. It had been a long and exhausting learning process which encompassed the broadening of the skill spectrum, changing and enlarging patterns of consumption, the continued introduction of innovative technology, climates of peace and war, the increased demand for female labour and a flood of arrivals from eastern Europe carrying in their pathetic baggage a heritage of tailoring. Different sectors and different conditions spawned different unions. Some fell by the way, some survived by the skin of their teeth, some were meant to come out on top. How and why provides the conclusion to this story.

NOTES

1. Mike Daly in *The Tailors' Journal* (magazine of the AST&T), Sept. 1907.
2. Following the admission of women to the AST in 1900 the society became known as the Amalgamated Society of Tailors and Tailoresses (AST&T).
3. Clegg, Vol.II, op. cit., p.105.
4. Ibid., p.106.
5. Ibid., p.108.
6. *Quarterly Report of the GFTU*, Sept. 1910, Archives of the GFTU, London.
7. Ibid., Dec. 1910.
8. *AST&T Annual Report*, 1909.
9. *AST&T Journal*, Feb. 1910.
10. *REPORT OF CONFERENCE held in Caxton Hall, Chapel Street, Manchester, 16 August 1910, for the purpose of promoting Federation amongst the various Societies in the Tailoring Trade in Great Britain.*
11. *Journal of the AST&T*, April 1911.
12. *Report of the GFTU*, March 1911, Archives of the GFTU, London.
13. GFTU Minutes of the Management Committee Meeting held on 28 March 1912.
14. Ibid.
15. *Journal of the AST*, May 1912.
16. *Report of the Scottish Operative Tailors and Tailoresses*, July–Dec. 1912, Library of the TUC, loc. cit.
17. *Yorkshire Factory Times*, 3 July 1913.
18. The composition of the original membership of the UGWTU was as follows: of the 21,457, 7,913 were males, 13,094 females, 450 youths (*1st Annual Report of the United Garment Workers' Trade Union, June 1915–December 1916*).
19. Result of Ballot Vote Re Amalgamation, with Accompanying Statement, despatched to all members of SOTTA, on 24 Sept. 1914, TUC Library, loc. cit.
20. Aaron Rollin's personal recollections, Rollin Collection, loc. cit.
21. *Yorkshire Factory Times*, 3 June 1915.
22. Stewart and Hunter, op. cit., pp.177–8.
23. Notes of A.R. Rollin, Rollin Collection, loc. cit.
24. These were the Belfast Shirt and Collar Society and the Clothing Workers Union.
25. *Report and Balance Sheet of the United Garment Workers' Trade Union, January–June 1920*, Rollin Collection, loc. cit.
26. *First Half-Yearly Report and Balance Sheet of the Tailors' and Garment Workers' Trade Union, July–December 1920.*
27. Ibid.
28. In 1920 membership of trade unions reached its highest inter-war figure at eight million.
29. For the history of the National Minority Movement *see* R. Martin, *Communism and the British Trade Unions, 1924–1933* (1969).
30. Op. cit.
31. Clegg, op. cit., p.468.
32. *Tailor and Garment Worker*, May 1932, p.3.

33. Ibid.
34. *Annual Report of the ULTTU 1929*, Rollin Collection, loc. cit.
35. Information from Professor W.J. Fishman. For the details of Rocker's Jubilee Street Club *see* Fishman, op. cit.
36. The Federation was founded in 1909 when the provisions of the Trade Board Act made an employers' organisation a necessity.
37. *Tailor and Garment Worker*, February 1932, p.4.
38. Ibid., p.2.
39. Proposed Scheme of Amalgamation, 1931, Rollin Collection, loc. cit.
40. Ibid.
41. *LLTU Annual Report 1929*, loc. cit.
42. *Tailor and Garment Worker*, June 1939, p.6.
43. In its February 1935 issue the *Tailor and Garment Worker* (p.7) reproduced an account of the experience of one Herr Kantor who had witnessed an horrific demonstration of brutality at the Sonnenburg Concentration Camp. It was a sombre warning of what was to come.
44. *Tailor and Garment Worker*, Aug. 1934, Vol. III, No. 8 p.12.
45. Aaron Rollin was also an earnest amateur historian who not only wrote and lectured in his spare time but also amassed a superb and diverse collection of trade and labour documents which are now housed at the Modern Record Centre at the University of Warwick. The author had the privilege of being given sight of the collection at the home of Aaron Rollin's son, Dr Henry Rollin, at Warwick.
46. *Tailor and Garment Worker*, March 1936, Vol. V, No. 3, p.2.
47. Ibid., Dec. 1936, Vol. V, No. 11, p.8.
48. Information from a meeting between the author and Mick Mindel, 19 May 1981.
49. *ULTTU Report, 1935*, Rollin Collection, loc. cit.
50. Information provided by Mick Mindel in discussion with the author, 13 Jan. 1994.
51. *Tailor and Garment Worker*, Oct. 1937, Vol. VI, No. 10, p.18.
52. Ibid.
53. Author's meeting with Mick Mindel, 27 July 1981.
54. *Tailor and Garment Worker*, Vol. VIII, No. 4 p.1.
55. Ibid., Vol. VIII, No. 6, p.6.
56. Taken from a scene in the 1968 television documentary, *Yesterday's Witness: The Battle of Cable Street*. Edith Ramsay arrived in the East End, from middle-class Highgate, in 1920 as a teacher. She never left until her death in 1983. Her work as a teacher, pioneer of education for working women and her activities as a superb but 'unofficial' social worker are commemorated in B. Sokoloff, *Edith and Stepney* (1987).

Conclusion

The final amalgamation of tailoring unions that took place in 1939, equally as neglected by contemporary commentators and recent historians as that which took place in 1915, was a rewarding conclusion to a movement which had begun almost thirty years before. Trade unions in an industry renowned for its reliance on unskilled female and immigrant labour, bedevilled by the destabilising effects of seasonality and divided by craft jealousies had demonstrated their ability to survive the pressures of war and depression. In addition, they had proved that ethnic pride and craft jealousy could be subjugated to common purpose. The ghosts had finally been laid. The ethos of separatism had been rejected in favour of equality within one union. The ideal had been promoted by the Jewish trade unionist, later Labour Minister, Emanuel Shinwell in the early 1900s. Shinwell had been opposed to the concept of independent Jewish unions or even Jewish branches of English unions. He saw no future in them as he had no faith in the ability of Jewish workers independently to ameliorate their position and maintain effective organisational bodies. It was only when, he maintained, 'the hand of fellowship' was genuinely extended 'that Jew and Gentile may be able to work together for the emancipation of the human race'.[1] Although his thinking was pragmatic and the ideal eventually achieved, Shinwell was unjust in his estimate of the Jewish trade unionists' inability to succeed. Jewish unions were not futile or doomed to failure. Given the right conditions and circumstances they could, as indeed they did, come through.

What then were the factors that enabled the Jewish and English tailoring unions of London and Leeds to override the general and particular industrial, economic and demographic problems that beset them in the years between 1870 and 1939 and go on to achieve the goal of amalgamation? As Chapter 5 illustrates, the strengths and weaknesses of the tailoring trade unions resulted from a combination of factors, some weighing more heavily than others. These can be summed up as: industrial structure; the composition of the work-force and the relationships that existed between and within different ethnic groups and skills; gender and politics and, finally, leadership.

The structure of the Leeds clothing industry, with its dimension of separation yet interdependence and its concentration on wholesale consumer markets, developed from the formula set down by Barran and Friend, encouraged the continuing use of medium- to large-scale production units, an acknowledged asset in the formation and survival of trade unions. As we know it was not only the factories which expanded. Jewish workshops followed the trend, some moving into vacant flax mills, thus enabling masters to become virtual wholesale clothiers at a cost that was half that of the London equivalent. The large-scale Leeds clothing factory achieved its most impressive form in 1925 when Montague Burton, founder of the 'largest clothing manu-facturing concern in the world' opened his Hudson Road factory which occupied 100 square acres and employed 8,000 clothing workers.[2] As one of the six largest employers of labour in Britain, Burton, a sombre and retiring man, had a paternalistic and pragmatic approach to labour organisation which he recognised as just and reasonable. Working on the Barran ethos that a happy and contented work-force was a reliable production unit Burton was amongst the earliest to provide welfare facilities for his staff. He also insisted that all labour disputes be submitted to compulsory arbitration. In the inter-war years only two strikes, one unofficial, took place in Hudson Road.[3]

In the years leading to the amalgamation of 1915 the London tailoring trade, with its complex industrial infrastructure and craft and market separations, was dominated by small-scale units of production operating in areas of high rental. In many ways the inhibiting economic and spatial limitations of London industry provided the basis for its continuing viability. As rental costs in the capital were prohibitive there was little incentive for unit expansion. Indeed, by the end of the first decade of the twentieth century, many previously overcrowded tenements were, according to the Journal of the AST&T, 'devoid of tenants'.[4] Those clothing manufacturers that wished to expand and run larger factories moved to the industrialising suburbs of Edmonton, Tottenham and Hackney.

Large-scale production units facilitated trade union creation and survival. The reasons for this were several. First, as illustrated in the case of the male clothing operatives of Leeds, it was far easier to propagandise and assemble workers employed in one large factory or workshop than gather together small groups who were spatially dispersed. The sole surviving Minute Book of the AJTMP (for the year 1907) illustrates clearly that membership was most secure in the larger workshops whilst the founder members of the LWCOU confirm the debt their union's origin owed to the large clothing factory. This point is further confirmed when trade union membership and employer/employee relations are examined in the context of Burtons. The company's welfare policy, in common with others, spawned choral societies, amateur dramatic societies, football clubs and other leisure activities which, whilst investing a company identity into the social life of the employee, reinforced the bonding and homogeneity found on the shop floor. A fraternity that was reflected in organisational strength and survival. There was a twofold effect as trade unions and employers such as Burton and the NUTGW secured a mutually beneficial working relationship built on trust and respect.

If big was, in trade union terms, beautiful, small was not. Spatial factors were indeed debilitating but there was another condition which, particularly in the case of the alien Jewish tailor, made the creation and duration of trade unions in the years preceding the First World War a challenge to all those who saw organisation as the only way forward. In both cities class division and exploitation within the confines of the ghetto ignited protest and encouraged the formation of trade unions. All too often these were of but a few months' duration. In the small Jewish workshop the nexus of kinship and religion, the experience of working at the same bench as the master, enervated the forces of protest. In his evidence to the Royal Commission on Aliens Joseph Finn explained that 'intimacy between masters and men' had weakened tailoring trade unionism in London's East End.[5] An Orthodox Rabbi, Dayan Dr Maurice Lew, who lived and worked in the East End during the 1930s, recalled how frequently the workshop master and his hands would sit side-by-side in prayer, whilst at other times, he reluctantly acknowledged, they gambled and drank together.[6] It was not only the Jewish worker who bowed to the ties of religion. Though the Gentile working class were reputedly poor churchgoers, in instances where employer and employee attended the same chapel, the nexus of religion again blurred the labour/capital divide. As factories and workshops expanded, as the suburbs blossomed and transport links improved, employers moved away from the smoke and grime and the tenement buildings where they had lived cheek by jowl with their workers. The boss became a remote individual living and worshipping in another world, his office far removed from the production line. In some cases mutual concern remained, but other examples demonstrate that, with the emotional links geographically severed, membership of an organisation which was at times in conflict with management, was far easier to sustain.

Seasonality and style rode tandem with size and space. As the economic problems of those sectors of the clothing trade governed by the vagaries of fashion highlight, the Leeds industry developed with less dependence on the making-up of orders than on the travellers who sold garments from a predetermined range. Barran's policy was the basis of the wholesale clothing trade and one which reduced the insecurity of seasonality. The benefits of regularised production are reflected in the survival of both the AUCO and AJTMP following their formation in the early 1890s. The London tailoring trade sent out no missionaries to explore and develop new territories. It was home-based, largely dependent on individual customer orders. That dependence, with its accompanying insecurity, was transmitted to the sub-divisional workers in the capital's multitude of workshops. What price trade union membership when next week's work was an unknown factor and the slack, for so much of the late nineteenth and early twentieth centuries, seemed to last longer and longer?

As has already been underlined, the tailoring trade was beset by craft differences and skills. It is understandable that at the height of 'new model unionism' those skills would have been jealously guarded and their unions defensive of newcomers and new technology. Whilst the AST took a back seat in Leeds, only waking up to the threat of AUCO at the end of the nineteenth century, in London it dominated. But its organisational and administrative heart was in Manchester and it was the geographic divide, articulated anti-alienist bias and inability to appreciate the march of progress that weakened the Society's hold on its membership and forced the sacrifice of identity. An alternative approach, a cognisance of the various needs of its membership might have enabled the AST&T to absorb other unions and metamorphose into *the* national tailoring trade union.

In an industry which grew strong on the backs of an unskilled female work-force, the organisation of women began slowly and was viewed with apprehension by many who fought for the creation of male unions. The threat of wage-cutting posed by the female operatives and tailoresses acted as a disincentive to their organisation. Male chauvinists saw the female role as that of housewife, manager and mother. If she did work it was only until marriage removed her from the labour market. If she returned it was either to supplement the household budget or to compensate for the absence of a male provider. In neither case was female trade unionism on the agenda of the average working man, or indeed woman. There were a minority who thought otherwise, but it was not until the welfare legislation of the Liberal government in 1911 introduced the concept of sickness benefit that female membership of the tailoring unions expanded but, even then, women viewed union dues with caution.

Throughout the years covered in this study politics remained a central factor in the birth, growth and, in certain instances, death of tailoring trade unions. From the 1870s onwards it was the political ideologues who sought to organise the exploited tailors. In the 1880s it was the Social Democrats and Socialist Leaguers who recognised that in order to fulfil their political ambitions they had to harness the frustrated and dissatisfied workers of Britain. Some had learnt the lesson of the earlier decade and appreciated the need to combine dreams with reality, food and wages with political philosophy. Politics could not combat the ravages of economic recession and hardship. There were those intellectuals who seemed unable to grasp the reasons behind the ephemerality of those organisations they had worked so hard to create. Even in the 1930s radical politics could not sustain the survival of a breakaway clothing union without financial reinforcements. Yet again ideology alone could not support the exploited and downtrodden.

It is a direct line from the role of politics in the formation and duration of the tailoring trade unions to the final determining factor, leadership. After all it is men, and women, who make history. In the formative years of the last decades of the nineteenth century it was activists such as Joseph Finn, James Sweeney, John Dyche, Tom Maguire, Sam Freedman,[7] William Wess, Rudolf Rocker, John Burns, Tom Mann, Clara Collet, Isabella Ford and yes, even at times Lewis Lyons, who built the bridges between Jew and Gentile. They recognised the need to overcome the antagonisms that existed between English and alien workers which stemmed from a mutual concern and fear for their economic welfare plus that degree of anti-semitism that is to be found beneath the surface of all levels of English society. In spite, or because, of this, members of the English labour movement supported Jewish workers in times of industrial strife and encouraged their combination even within their own societies. Organisation of the resident alien work-force was imperative. Alien and native differences had to be overcome in the cause of fraternity. In the twentieth century that goal was finally achieved. Full-time salaried general secretaries, such as MacDonald, Young, Conley, Sclare and Hillman, experienced in trade union administration and the needs of the work-force, under the threat and the reality of war, led their members to amalgamation. In Leeds, Young and Sclare developed a working relationship which enjoyed the support and respect of their members and of each other. In each case leadership demonstrated efficiency and stability. In the years which followed the First World War, as Guerney Rowlerson and Terence Flynn of the AST&T became increasingly aware of the isolation of their union, there was only one decision to make. It was the same one as was made by J.L. Fine and Mick Mindel in the 1930s when the rise of Fascism and Nazism highlighted the vulnerability of their members and the need to achieve, as they did just months before the outbreak of war, equality within one union.

POSTSCRIPT

The story of amalgamations does not quite end with 1939. The 1980s were traumatic years for the trade union movement. As legislation undermined their powers and membership fell in a recessed economy, a re-examination of structure, role and direction was called for. The route favoured was once again that of fusion. By 1992 the National Union of Tailors and Garment Workers had ceased to exist, it had been absorbed into that monolith, the GMB, as the clothing workers' section. On 30 August 1993 the Wages Council, descendant of the Trade Boards, was dissolved. So what does the future hold for the clothing workers of Britain at the end of the twentieth century? Their current leader, Anne Spencer, looks to the future with optimism.[8] Women now make up 92 per cent of the work-force. Over 50 per cent of their number are members of the union. At factory level working conditions are good and wage negotiations are going ahead satisfactorily. However, the evil of sweated labour has yet to be eradicated from the immigrant landscapes of east London and provincial cities such as Bradford. There the conditions of the 1880s and 1890s are replayed one hundred years on. There is a need for organisers with the perception and compassion of Rocker and Sclare, of the tenacity of Sarah Wesker and the flair of the female organiser of the 1930s, Annie

Loughlin – later General Secretary of the NUTGW. There is a need for men and women who recognise the needs of a new generation of immigrant workers and who can work together with the national organisers as did the trade unionists of eighty years ago. Only by co-ordinated and rational negotiation can the iniquities of the clothing trade be overcome.

NOTES

1. *Journal of the AST&T*, Sept. 1909.
2. Redmayne, op. cit., p.85.
3. E. Sigsworth, *Montague Burton The Tailor of Taste*, (1990), p.128.
4. *Journal of the AST&T*, Sept. 1909.
5. *Royal Commission on Alien Immigration*, op. cit., qq 20271.
6. Author in conversation with (the late) Dr Lew, 24 Aug. 1982.
7. We must show some tolerance for his misdemeanour and commemorate his ability.
8. In conversation with the author, 24 Jan. 1994.

APPENDIX: Tables

TABLE 1

NUMBER OF WHOLESALE CLOTHING COMPANIES
IN LEEDS, 1881–1911

Year	No. of Companies Listed
1881	21
1891	65
1901	104
1911	145

(Sources: *Kelly's Leeds Directory*, 1881; *Salter's Directory Manchester*, 1891; *Robinson's Directory Leeds*, 1901 and 1911.)

TABLE 2

NUMBER OF TAILORS AND TAILORESSES IN LEEDS, 1851–1911

Year	Male	Female	Total
1851	935	29	964
1861	951	87	1,038
1871	1,523	483	2,006
1881	2,148	2,740	4,888
1891	4,773	10,919	15,692
1901	5,792	14,021	19,813
1911	7,625	15,917	23,542

(Source: *Decennial Census*, 1851–1911.)

APPENDIX

TABLE 3
WAGES PAID TO FEMALE EMPLOYEES IN WHOLESALE CLOTHING FACTORIES FOR A 52½-HOUR WEEK IN 1891

Machinists	10s.0d. to 18s.0d.
Binders	15s.0d. to 30s.0d.
Buttonholers	£1.5s.0d.
Pressers	8s.0d. to 9s.0d.
Suit Finishers	2s.0d. to £1.3s.0d.
	(average 10s.4d.)
Trouser Finisher	3s.0d. to 16s.0d.
	(average 9s.11d.)
Buttonhole Finisher	6s.0d. to £1.3s.0d.
	(average 13s.4d.)
Buttoners	3s.6d. to 10s.0d.
	(average 6s.3d.)

(*Source*: The above table was compiled by Clara Collet and appeared in her article in the *Economic Journal* published in 1891.)

TABLE 4
WAGES PAID TO FEMALE EMPLOYEES IN JEWISH WORKSHOPS*

	Master's Statement	Men's Statement
Machinists	5s.0d. to 6s.0d. daily	5s.0d. to 5s.2d. daily
Fellers	2s.0d. to 3s.0d. daily	1s.9d. to 2s.3d. daily
Buttonholers	5d. to 6d. per doz (up to 4s.0d. to 5s.0d. daily)	

* Length of week not stated.

(*Source*: *Report to the Board of Trade on the Sweating System in Leeds*, 1888, op. cit., p.561.)

TABLE 5

ANALYSIS OF JOBS CARRIED OUT BY 839 TAILORESSES IN
52 WORKSHOPS IN LEEDS, 1888

	Jewish	Non-Jewish
Buttonholers	257	42
Fellers	238	64
Finishers	15	109
Machinists	1	113

(*Source*:   John Burnett, *Report to the Board of Trade on the Sweating System in Leeds*, op. cit.)

TABLE 6

ESTIMATED NUMBER OF MALE CLOTHING OPERATIVES EMPLOYED IN
THE LEEDS CLOTHING FACTORIES, 1881–1911

Year	Number
1881	1,196
1891	2,240
1901	2,500
1911	3,500

(*Source*: See explanation in Chapter 2, note 150.)

TABLE 7

DEPLOYMENT OF 926 MEN AND BOYS IN LEEDS JEWISH TAILORING
WORKSHOPS, 1894

Workshop Size	Average Number Employed	Tailors	Pressers	Fixers	Machiners
40+	58	180	107	19	268
25–40	33	67	43	8	114
10–25	18	40	24	2	54

(*Source*:   *Board of Trade Report into Volume and Effects of Recent Immigration from Eastern Europe into the United Kingdom*, 1894, op. cit.)

TABLE 8
WAGE RATES OF MEN EMPLOYED IN LEEDS JEWISH TAILORING WORKSHOPS IN 1888 (PER DAY)

Job	Wage (Men's Evidence)	Wage (Master's Evidence)
Fixer	6s.0d. to 6s.2d.	7s.0d. to 7s.6d.
Machiner	6s.0d. to 6s.8d.	6s.0d. to 7s.6d.
Presser	4s.0d. to 6s.0d.	5s.6d. to 7s.0d.
Basters (out)	2s.6d. to 4s.0d.	3s.0d. to 5s.0d.
Basters (under)	4s.8d. to 5s.6d.	4s.6d. to 6s.6d.

(*Source*: J. Burnett, *Report to the House of Lords on Sweating System in Leeds*, 1888.)

TABLE 9
NUMBER OF TAILORS AND TAILORESSES IN LONDON, 1851–1911

Year	Tailors	Tailoresses	Total
1851	22,249	8,294	30,543
1861	22,301	12,377	34,678
1871	23,516	14,780	38,296
1881	22,744	18,477	41,221
1891	27,474	24,872	52,346
1901	31,389	33,114	64,503
1911	33,275	31,718	64,993

(*Source*: *Decennial Census*, 1851–1911, op. cit.)

TABLE 10

NUMBER OF TAILORS AND TAILORESSES IN THE WEST END OF
LONDON, 1871–1911

Year	Tailors	Tailoresses	Total
1871	9,135	13,895	23,030
1881	*	*	*
1891	11,352	6,740	18,092
1901	4,215	2,145	6,360
1911	3,436	2,946	6,382

* No figures available.

(*Source*: *Decennial Census* 1871–1911, op. cit.)

TABLE 11

NUMBER OF TAILORS AND TAILORESSES IN THE EAST END OF
LONDON, 1871–1911

Year	Tailors	Tailoresses	Total
1871	11,412	14,905	26,317
1881	6,247	9,427	15,674
1891	9,030	12,836	21,856
1901	12,964	8,024	20,988
1911	15,721	11,441	27,162

(*Source*: *Decennial Census* 1871–1911, op. cit.)

TABLE 12
BEATRICE POTTER'S TABLE OF CLASS OF WORK AND WAGES (1888)

Class of Work	Wages per Day	Hours per Day	Rate per Hour
Best Bespoke			
Tailor	7s. to 9s.	13–14	6d. to 8d.
Presser	7s. to 10s.	13–14	6d. to 9d.
Tailoresses	4s. to 6s.	12	4d. to 6d.
Bespoke and Stock			
General Tailor	7s. 6d. to 8s. 6d.	13–14	6½d.–7½d.
General Tailor			
(lower grade)	6s.0d. to 6s.6d.	13–14	5½d. to 6d.
Machiner	7s.0d. to 7s.6d.	13–14	6½d. to 7d.
Plain Machiner	5s.0d.	13–14	4½d.
Presser	7s.6d. to 8s.6d.	13–14	6½d. to 7½d.
General Hand	5s.0d.	13–14	4½d.
Stock and Common			
Machiner	6s.0d. to 7s.0d.	13–14	5d. to 6½d.
Plain Machiner	3s.0d. to 4s.0d.	Indefinite	2d. to 3d.
Baster	4s.0d. to 5s.6d.	13–14	3¾d. to 5d.
Presser	6s.0d.	13–14	5d.
Very Common			
Machiner	6s.0d.	13–14	5d.
Plain Machiner	3s.0d.	Indefinite	1d. to 2½d.
Presser	6s.0d.	13–14	5d.

(*Source*: Booth, op. cit., Vol. IV, pp. 37–68.)

TABLE 13
ENGLISH AND JEWISH TAILORING TRADE UNIONS IN LONDON, 1914–1915

English Trade Union		Jewish Trade Union	
Union	Membership	Union	Membership
London Clothiers'		International	
Cutters	400	Mantle Maker (AST)	591
London Society of Tailors		London Ladies'	
and Tailoresses	1,600	Tailors	3,000
AST (London, Gentile)	676	London Jewish	
		Tailors	1,800
		Men's Tailors (AST)	243
Total	2,676		5,634

TABLE 14

DISTRIBUTION OF ORGANISED TAILORING WORKERS IN LEEDS,
1913–1914

AUCO (Leeds Branch, 1913)	3,000
AJTMP (Leeds Branch, 1914)	1,500
AST (Leeds Branch, 1914)	111
Total Leeds Tailoring Trade Unionists	4,611

(*Sources*: *Yorkshire Factory Times*, 30 Jan. 1913, *AJTMP Annual Report 1915*, *AST Annual Report 1915*.)

TABLE 15

DISTRIBUTION OF ORGANISED TAILORING WORKERS
IN LONDON, 1914

London Society of Tailors and Tailoresses	1,600
London and Provincial Clothiers' Cutters	400
London Jewish Tailors' Trade Union	1,800
London Ladies' Tailors' Trade Union	3,000
AST London branches	1,510
Total	8,310

(*Source*: *AST Reports 1914–1915, SOTTA Ballot for Amalgamation 1914*.)

TABLE 16

MEMBERSHIP OF LONDON JEWISH TAILORING TRADE UNIONS FOR WORKERS IN THE 'GENTS' TAILORING SECTION, 1890–1903

	1890	1891	1892	1893	1894	1895	1896	1897	1898	1899	1900	1901	1902	1903
International Tailors', Machiners' and Pressers' Trade Union	Founded 1890, dissolved 1891													
International Journeymen Tailors' Machiners' and Pressers Trade Union														
Independent Tailors', Machiners' Pressers' Trade Union			107	155	118	87	559	70	30	14)Became London Tailors',)Machiners' and Pressers')Trade Union, 1901				
Jewish Military Uniform Tailors' Tailoresses Trade Union				272	124	492	504	269	468	115				
London Tailors', Machiners' and Pressers' Trade Union							130	180	150	80	121	60		
Pressers' Trade Union													425	297
London Garmet Workers' Machinists' Society												1901–1903, no membership figures available		
Independent Tailors' Union												1901–1903, amalgamated with United Garmet Workers' Trade Union, 1902–3		
East London Waistcoat Makers' Trade Union												Founded 1901, dissolved by 1904		
United Garment Workers' Trade Union														
Jewish National Tailors', Machiners' and Pressers' Trade Union											507	639	818	171
London Men's Tailors', Machiners' and Pressers' Trade Union												Formed from remains of Independent Tailors' Union of 1901		
Anti-Sub-Contracting Trade Union												Existed for several months during 1904		

Note: In 1904 all London Jewish tailoring trade unions abandoned their independence and became affiliated to the AST. By 1906 dissension had set in and gradually the Jewish branches seceded and resumed independent existence. By 1908 only four Jewish branches remained. For independent unions 1906–1915 see *Table 17*.

TABLE 17

MEMBERSHIP OF LONDON JEWISH TAILORING TRADE UNIONS FOR WORKERS IN THE 'GENTS' TAILORING SECTION, 1906–1915

	1906	1907	1908	1909	1910	1911	1912	1913	1914	1915
Independent Tailors' Union	456	Became Garment Workers' Union in 1907								
Garment Workers' Union		250	Dissolved 1908							
West London Jewish Tailors' Trade Union			67	100	98					
East London Waistcoat Makers' Trade Union				72	102					
Jewish Garment Workers' Trade Union				40	100					
Military & Uniforms Tailors', Machiners' and Pressers' Trade Union				112	Dissolved 1910					
International Tailors' & Tailoresses' Trade Union				189	Joined London Society of Tailors and Tailoresses, 1910					
London Tailors' Trade Union		Founded 1908, no membership figures available until 1915								1800
Syndicalist Tailors' Union		Founded 1908, no further details available								

TABLE 18

MEMBERSHIP OF LONDON JEWISH TAILORING TRADE UNIONS, MANTLE-MAKING SECTION, 1891–1904

	1891	1892	1893	1894	1895	1896	1897	1898	1899	1900	1901	1902	1903	1904
Mantle Cutters' and Pressers' Trade Union (Anarchist)	61													
United Ladies' Tailors and Mantle Makers' Trade Union			250	450	392	375	459	550	461	351	316	325	*	**
Amalgamated Mantle Makers' Trade Union					84	89								
International Mantle Makers' Trade Union											180	*	**	
London Mantle Makers' Trade Union													750	250
Underpressers', Plain Machinists' and Plain Hands' Trade Union												48	200	

* Merged with United Garment Workers
** Subsequently became London Mantle Makers' Trade Union

Note: By the end of 1904 all trade unionists in the mantle-making section had affiliated to the mantle-making branches of the AST. Whilst some retained their allegiance to the Society, others turned their backs on trade unionism completely. Those that wished to maintain trade union affiliation but with an independent Jewish union founded the London Ladies' Tailors', Machiners' and Pressers' Trade Union in 1908 – that union retained its independence until 1938. See Table 19.

TABLE 19

MEMBERSHIP OF LONDON LADIES' TAILORS', MACHINERS' AND
PRESSERS' TRADE UNION, 1908–1915

1908	1909	1910	1911	1912	1913	1914	1915
304	500	251	328	700	*	*	3,000

* No figures available.

TABLE 20

JEWISH TAILORING TRADE UNIONS IN LONDON, 1872–1915

Men's Tailoring Trade Unions Name of Union	Period of Existence
Lithuanian Tailors' Union	1872
Jewish Tailors' Union	1876
Jewish Tailors' Union	1883
London Jewish Tailors' Machinists' Society	1886–1887
Pressers' Union	1887–1889
Machiners' Union	1887–1889
International Tailors' Machiners' and Pressers' Union	1890–1892
International Journeymen Tailors' Machiners' and Pressers	1892–1900
Independent Tailors' Machiners' and Pressers' Union	1893–1900
Jewish Military Uniform Tailors' Union	1896–1901
London Tailors' Machiners' and Pressers' Union	1901–1902
Pressers' Trade Union	1901–1903
London Garment Workers' Machinists' Society	1901–1903
Independent Tailors' Union	1901–1903
United Garment Workers' Union	1902–1903
Jewish National Tailors' Union	1899–1900
East London Waistcoat Makers' Union	1901–1904
London Men's Tailors' Union	1901–1904
Anti-sub-contracting Union	1904
Independent Tailors' Union	1906–1907
Garment Workers' Union	1907–1908
West London Jewish Tailors' Union	1908–1910
East London Waistcoat Makers' Union	1909–1910
Jewish Garment Workers' Union	1909–1910
Military and Uniform Tailors' Union	1909–1910
International Tailors' Union	1909–1910
London Tailors' Union	1908–1915
Syndicalist Tailors' Union	1908

Table 20 cont.

	Mantle-Making Trade Unions	
Name of Union		Period of Existence
Mantle Cutters' and Pressers' Union		1891
United Ladies' Tailors & Mantle Makers' Union		1892–1901
Amalgamated Mantle Makers' Union		1895–1896
International Mantle Makers' Union		1901
London Mantle Makers' Union		1903–1904
Underpressers' Plain Machinists' and Plain Hands Union		1902–1903
London Ladies' Tailors' Trade Union		1908–1938

London Jewish Branches of the Amalgamated Society of Tailors

Year	No.
1881–1902	1 (East End)
1903	3 (opening of West End branch)
1904	3
1905	9
1906	16
1906	11
1907	4
1908	2
1909	4
1910	3
1911	3
1912	4
1913	2
1914–1915	3

TABLE 21

AMALGAMATED UNION OF CLOTHING OPERATIVES:
MEMBERSHIP AND NUMBER OF BRANCHES, 1894–1915

Year	Male	Membership Female	Total	No. of Branches
1894	506		506	4
1895	503		503	6
1896	827		827	*
1897	1,042		1,042	10
1898	990		990	11
1899	1,245	63	1,308	12
1900	1,400	109	1,509	14
1901	1,222	63	1,285	*
1902	1,421	27	1,448	18
1903	1,460	154	1,614	20
1904	1,427	44	1,471	*
1905	1,482	78	1,560	*
1906	1,682	140	1,822	18
1907	1,988	592	2,580	18
1908	1,919	619	2,538	*
1909	1,780	636	2,416	*
1910	1,844	1,488	3,332	*
1911	+	+	4,200	*
1912	+	+	6,700	22
1913	+	+	8,000	*
1914	+	+	10,000	29
1915	4,000	8,000	12,000	36

* Details not available.

+ Separate figures not available.

(*Sources*: *Yorkshire Factory Times*, 28 Dec. 1894, 19 Aug. 1898, 21 Nov. 1902, 6 March 1903, 25 Aug. 1905, 23 March 1906, 15 Aug. 1912, 2 July 1914. Amalgamated Union of Clothing Operatives' *Monthly Gazette*, Dec. 1897, April 1899, February 1900, loc. cit. Tawney, op. cit., p. 93. *Report on Trade Unions*, 1898, PP 1899, XCII; ibid., *1902–1904*, PP 1906, CXIII; ibid., *1907*, PP 1909, LXXXIX; ibid., *1910*, PP 1912, XLVII. *The Garment Worker*, December 1965; Dobbs, op. cit., p. 132.)

APPENDIX

TABLE 22
AMALGAMATED UNION OF CLOTHING OPERATIVES: LOCATION OF BRANCHES, 1915

Barnsley	Liverpool
Basingstoke	London
Belfast	Manchester
Birmingham	Middlesbrough
Blackburn	Nantwich
Bristol	Newark
Chatham	Newcastle-on-Tyne
Colchester	Newcastle-under-Lyme
Cork	Norwich
Crewe	Nuneaton
Derby	Peterborough
Dublin	Reading
Glasgow	Stroud
Haverhill	Swindon
Hebden Bridge	Todmordon
Huddersfield	Walsall
Leeds	Wigan
Leicester	Yarmouth

(*Source*: United Garment Workers' Trade Union, *First Annual Report, 8 June 1915–31 December 1916*, Archives NUTGW, London.)

TABLE 23

AMALGAMATED JEWISH TAILORS', MACHINERS' AND PRESSERS'
TRADE UNION: MEMBERSHIP, 1894–1915

Year	Male	Female
1894	152	
1895	510	
1896	1,205	
1897	1,210	
1898	1,055	
1899	*	
1900	1,500	
1901	1,600	
1902	*	
1903	920	
1904	700	
1905	610	
1906	900	
1907	960	
1908	700	50
1909+	730	20
1910	970	
1911	*	
1912	1,810	
1913	2,465	
1914	4,465	
1915	4,465	

*   Figures not available.

+   After 1909 no further figures appear for female membership.

(*Sources*: *Trade Union Reports 1895*, PP 1896, LXXVIII; *1896*, PP 1897, LXXXII; *1897*, PP 1898, LXXXVII; *1898*, PP 1899, XCI; *1902–1904*, PP 1906, CXIII; *1905–1907*, PP 1909, LXXXIX; *1908–1910*, PP 1912–1913, XLVII; *Annual Report of General Federation of Trade Unions*, 1912; *Jewish Chronicle*, 1 May 1914, 7 May 1915.)

APPENDIX

TABLE 24
AMALGAMATED JEWISH TAILORS', MACHINERS' AND PRESSERS' TRADE UNION: LOCATION OF BRANCHES, 1915

Bradford	Liverpool
Edinburgh	Manchester
Glasgow	Newcastle-on-Tyne
Hanley	Nottingham
Hull	Sheffield
Leeds	Stockport
Leeds Tailoresses	West Hartlepool

(*Source*: United Garment Workers' Trade Union, *First Annual Report, 8 June 1915–31 December 1916*, Archives of NUTGW, London.)

TABLE 25
LONDON AND PROVINCIAL CLOTHIERS' CUTTERS' TRADE UNION: MEMBERSHIP, 1890–1914

Year	Number
1890	684
1891	550
1892	500
1893	520
1894–9	*
1900	385
1901–5	*
1906	240
1907	236
1908	288
1909	348
1910	364
1911–13	*
1914	400

* Figures not available.

(*Sources*: 1890–1893, *Chief Labour Correspondent on Trade Unions, 1893*, PP 1895, CVII; *Report of Chief Registrar on Trade Unions 1900*, PP 1901, LXII; *Report of Chief Registrar on Trade Unions 1906*, PP 1907, LXXIX; 1907–1910, *Report on Trade Unions 1908–1910*, PP 1912–1913, XLVII; *SOTTA Ballot for Amalgamation 1914*, loc. cit.)

TABLE 26

LONDON SOCIETY OF TAILORS AND TAILORESSES: MEMBERSHIP,
1906–1914

	Male	Female
1906	862	40
1907	872	76
1908	935	82
1909	1,020	86
1910	1,204	100
1914	1,600	(overall total, individual figures not available)

(*Sources*: 1906–1910, *Trade Union Reports 1908–1910*, PP 1912–1913, XLVII;
SOTTA Ballot for Amalgamation 1914, loc. cit.)

TABLE 27

AMALGAMATED SOCIETY OF TAILORS AND TAILORESSES, JEWISH
LONDON BRANCH: MEMBERSHIP, 1884–1915

Year	No. of Branches	Area	Total Membership
1884	1	East End	150
1885	1	East End	20
1886	1	East End	21
1887	1	East End	0
1888	1	East End	18
1889	1	East End	216*
1890	1	East End	61
1891	1	East End	27
1892	1	East End	60
1893	1	East End	60
1894	1	East End	23
1895	1	East End	43
1896	1	East End	26
1897	1	East End	15
1898	1	East End	11
1899	1	East End	0
1900	1	East End	0
1901	0		0
1902	0		0
1903	1	West End	113
1904	3	East and West End	151
1905	9	East and West End	2,242
1906	16	East and West End	3,090
1907	11	East and West End	942
1908	4	East and West End	168
1909	2	East and West End	106
1910	4	East and West End	259
1911	3	East and West End	305
1912	4	East and West End	1,387
1913	2	East and West End	255
1914	3	East and West End	668
1915	3	East and West End	947

* After strike.

(Sources: Derived from information contained in Annual Reports of Amalgamated Society of Tailors.)

TABLE 28
WORKSHOPS VISITED BY BEATRICE POTTER, 1888

	Whitechapel	Whitechapel Section Part St. Georges	Part Mile End Town	Total
No. of Workshops	703	173	139	1,015
Coats and General Shops				901
Vests				10
Juvenile Clothing				7
Trousers				97
				1,015

	Remainder of District							
	Part St. Georges	Part Mile End Old Town	Stepney	Poplar	Bethnal Green	Shoreditch	Hackney	Total
No. of Workshops	26	55	17	54	31	52	21	257
Coats and General Shops								57
Vests								1
Juvenile Clothing								65
Trousers								61
								184
Unclassified								73
								257

Note: The figures and addition in this table are as produced by Beatrice Potter for Charles Booth's survey.
(Source: Booth, op. cit., p. 67.)

TABLE 29
NUMBERS OF WORKERS IN WORKSHOPS VISITED BY BEATRICE POTTER, 1888

	25+	10–25	Under 10	Total
Whitechapel Section				
Coats and General	15	201	685	901
Vests, Trousers and Juvenile	6	35	73	114
	21	236	758	1,015
Remainder of District				
Coats and General	6	4	47	57
Vests, Trousers and Juvenile	15	25	87	127
	21	29	134	184

Overall Total = 1,199

Note: The figures and addition in this table are as produced by Beatrice Potter for Charles Booth's survey.

(*Source*: Booth, op. cit., p. 67.)

Bibliography

PRIMARY SOURCES

Amalgamated Branch of the Tailors' and Garment Workers' Trade Union 7th Annual Report April 1923. Archives of the National Union of Tailors and Garment Workers.

Amalgamated Jewish Tailors', Machiners' and Pressers' Trade Union Minute Book, 1905–1907. Archives of the National Union of Tailors and Garment Workers.

Amalgamated Jewish Tailors', Machiners' and Pressers' Trade Union 22nd Annual Report. Rollin Collection. Modern Records Centre, University of Warwick.

Amalgamated Society of Engineers Annual Reports: 1868, 1871, 1881, 1891, 1901, 1911, 1914 and 1915. Modern Records Centre, University of Warwick.

Amalgamated Society of Tailors Annual Reports, 1870–1915. Archives of the National Union of Tailors and Garment Workers.

Amalgamated Society of Tailors Journal, 1896–1915. Archives of the National Union of Tailors and Garment Workers.

Amalgamated Union of Clothing Operatives Monthly Gazette, 1898–1899. Modern Records Centre, University of Warwick.

John Barran & Co. Balance Sheet 1911. Leeds City Archives.

John Barran & Co. Minute Books, 1895–1912. Leeds City Archives.

John Barran No. 1 Briggate Stock Book. Leeds City Archives.

John Barran Staff Selection Book, 1873–1895. Leeds City Archives.

John Barran Story. Undated Pamphlet. Leeds City Archives.

W. Blackburn & Co. Undated Brochure. Leeds City Archives.

General Federation of Trade Unions Annual Reports, 1912–1915. Archives of the GFTU.

General Federation of Trade Unions Quarterly Reports, 1908–1915. Archives of the GFTU.

Leeds Trades Council Annual Reports, 1881–1915. Leeds City Archives.

Leeds Trades Council Meeting Minutes, 1884–1900. Leeds City Archives.

The Rollin Collection, Modern Records Centre, University of Warwick.

Scottish Operative Tailors' and Tailoresses' Association Ballot re Amalgama-

tion, 1914. Archives of the National Union of Tailors and Garment Workers.

Scottish Operative Tailors' and Tailoresses' Association Report July–December 1914. Archives of National Union of Tailors and Garment Workers.

Scottish Operative Tailors' and Tailoresses' Association Report on Meeting to Discuss Federation of Tailors' Unions. Nottingham, March 1910. Archives of the National Union of Tailors and Garment Workers.

Speech to the Leeds Branch of the Tailors' and Garment Workers' Trade Union by M. Sclare 1923. Rollin Collection. Modern Records Centre, University of Warwick.

Trade Union Congress Annual Reports, 1890–1915. Archives of the TUC, Congress House, London.

United Garment Workers' Trade Union 1st Annual Report, 8 June 1915–31 December 1916. Rollin Collection, Modern Records Centre, University of Warwick.

Webb Trade Union Collection, LSE Library; Coll E. Sec. BC VI.

GOVERNMENT PAPERS

Annual Report of Chief Inspector of Factories and Workshops, 1878. PP 1878–1879. XVI.

Annual Report of Chief Inspector of Factories and Workshops, 1883. PP 1884. XVIII.

Annual Report of Chief Inspector of Factories and Workshops, 1888. PP 1888. XXVI.

Annual Report of Chief Inspector of Factories and Workshops, 1889. PP 1889. XVIII.

Annual Report of Chief Inspector of Factories and Workshops, 1890. PP 1890–1891. XIX.

Annual Report of Chief Inspector of Factories and Workshops, 1895. PP 1896. XIX.

Annual Report of Chief Inspector of Factories and Workshops, 1898. PP 1899. XII.

Annual Report of Chief Inspector of Factories and Workshops, 1905. PP 1907. X.

Annual Report of Chief Inspector of Factories and Workshops, 1910. PP 1911. XIII.

Annual Report of Chief Inspector of Factories and Workshops, 1914–1916. PP 1914–1916. XXI.

Board of Trade Report into Earnings and Hours of Labour in the Clothing Trades, 1906. PP 1909: LXXX.

Board of Trade Report on Cost of Living, 1913. PP 1913: LXVI.

Board of Trade Report on Volume and Effects of Recent Immigration from Eastern Europe into the United Kingdom, 1894. PP 1894: LXVII.

Children's Employment Commission 1864, 2nd Report: PP 1864: XXII.

Children's Employment Commission 1864, 4th Report: PP 1865: XX.

Decennial Census, 1801. PP 1801: VI.

Decennial Census, 1851. PP 1852: LXXVII.

Decennial Census, 1861. PP 1863: LIII.

Decennial Census, 1871. PP 1983: LXXII.

Decennial Census, 1881. PP 1883: LXXX.

Decennial Census, 1891. PP 1893–1894: CVI.

Decennial Census, 1901. PP 1904: CVII.

Decennial Census, 1911. PP 1913: LXXVII.

House of Lords Select Commission on the Sweating System, 1st Report, 1888. PP 1888: XX.

House of Lords Select Commission on the Sweating System, 2nd Report, 1889. PP 1889: XIV.

House of Lords Select Commission on the Sweating System, 5th Report, 1890. PP 1890: XVII.

Report of the Board of Trade on the Sweating System at the East End of London 1887. PP 1887: LXXXIX.

Report of the Board of Trade on the Sweating System in Leeds 1888. PP 1888: LXXXXVI.

Report of Chief Labour Correspondent on Trade Unions, 1893. PP 1894: LXXIX.

Report of Chief Registrar of Friendly Societies and Trade Unions, 1876. PP 1877: LXXCII.

Report of Chief Registrar of Friendly Societies and Trade Unions, 1880. PP 1883: LXVII.

Report of Chief Registrar of Friendly Societies and Trade Unions, 1883. PP 1884: LXXVI.

Report of Chief Registrar on Trade Unions, 1906. PP 1907: LXXIX.

Report of Chief Registrar on Trade Unions, 1907. PP 1908: XCVIII.

Report on Strikes & Lockouts, 1895. PP 1986: LXXX.

Report on Strikes & Lockouts, 1896. PP 1897: LXXXIV.

Report on Strikes & Lockouts, 1897. PP 1898: LXXXVIII.

Report on Strikes & Lockouts, 1898. PP 1899: XCII.

Report on Strikes & Lockouts, 1902. PP 1903: LXVI.

Report on Strikes & Lockouts, 1907. PP 1908: XCVIII.

Report on Strikes & Lockouts, 1912. PP 1914: XLVIII.

Report on Strikes & Lockouts, 1913. PP 1914–1916: XXXCI.

Report on Trade Unions and Friendly Societies, 1895. PP 1896: LXXVIII.

Report on Trade Unions and Friendly Societies, 1896. PP 1897: LXXXII.

Report on Trade Unions and Friendly Societies, 1900. PP 1901: LXXIV.

Report on Trade Unions and Friendly Societies, 1902–1904. PP 1906: CXIII.

BIBLIOGRAPHY

Report on Trade Unions and Friendly Societies, 1905–1907. PP 1909: LXXXIX.
Report on Trade Unions and Friendly Societies, 1908–1910. PP 1912: XLVII.
Report of the Truck Committee, 1906. PP 1908: LIX.
Royal Commission on Aliens, 1903. PP 1903: X.
Royal Commission on Labour, 1892. PP 1892: XXXVI and XXXV.
Royal Commission on Labour, 1892. PP 1893–1894: XXXVIII.
Select Committee on Homework, 1906. PP 1907: VI.

UNPUBLISHED SOURCES

Buckman, J., 'The Economic and Social History of Alien Immigration to Leeds 1880–1914', Ph.D. Thesis, University of Strathclyde, 1968.
Hamish Fraser, W., 'Trades Councils in England and Scotland', Ph.D. Thesis, University of Sussex, 1967.
Hendricks, H.J., 'The Leeds Gas Riots: Causes and Consequences 1889–1892', M.A. Thesis, University of Warwick, 1970.
Hendricks, June, 'The Tailoresses in the Ready-Made Clothing Industry in Leeds 1889–1899', M.A. Thesis, University of Warwick, 1970.
Lerner, S., 'The History of the United Clothing Workers' Union', Ph.D. Thesis, University of London, 1956.
Sokolic, L., 'Changes and Transitions in a Religious Immigrant Group in the East End of London 1891–1940', Ph.D. Thesis, University of London, 1984.
Weschler, R., 'The Jewish Garment Trade in East London 1875–1914', Ph.D. Thesis, Columbia University, 1979.

NEWSPAPERS AND JOURNALS

Anti-Sweater
Arbeiter Fraint
Clothiers' and Outfitters' World
Commonweal
East London Observer
Economic Journal
Economist
Fortnightly Review
Freedom
The Garment Worker
Jewish Chronicle
The Journeyman

Justice
Labour Chronicle
Labour Gazette
The Lancet
Leeds Daily News
Leeds Evening Express
Leeds Express
Leeds Mercury
Leeds Weekly Express
Men's Wear
Mercantile Age
Poilishe Yidel
Tailor and Cutter
Tailor and Garment Worker
The Tailors' Journal
The Times
The Trade Unionist
Yorkshire Evening News
Yorkshire Factory Times
Yorkshire Post

SECONDARY SOURCES

Adburgham, A., *Shops and Shopping 1800–1914* (London, 1989).
Alderman, G., The *Jewish Community in British Politics* (London, 1983).
—— and Holmes, C., *Outsiders and Outcasts* (London, 1993).
Allen, V.L., *Trade Union Leadership* (London, 1957).
—— *Trade Union and Government* (London, 1961).
Bacon's Pocket Maps and Plans: Leeds (Leeds, 1901).
Bain, G.S., *Social Stratification and Trade Unionism* (London, 1947).
—— *Bibliography of British Industrial Relations* (Cambridge, 1979).
Barclay, J.F., *The Story of Arthur & Co.* (Glasgow, 1953).
Baru, N.I., *British Trade Unionism* (London, 1947).
Bellamy, J., *A Dictionary of Labour History* (London, 1972–77).
Benson, J. (ed.), *The Working Class in England 1873–1914* (London, 1985).
Bermant, C. *The Cousinhood* (London, 1971).
Black, C., and Meyer, C., *Makers of Our Clothes* (London, 1909).
Black, E., *Victorian Culture and Society* (London, 1973).
Booth, C., *Life and Labour of the People of London*, First Series, Vol.IV (London, 1890–92).
Braverman, H., *Labour and Monopoly Capital* (New York, 1974).
Briggs, A., *Victorian People* (London, 1954).
—— *Victorian Cities* (London, 1963).

—— 'The Language of Class', in R. Neale (ed.), *History and Class* (Oxford, 1983).

—— and Saville, J. (eds), *Essays in Labour History*, (London, 1960).

—— *Essays in Labour History*, Vol. 2 (London, 1971).

Buckman, J., *Immigrants and the Class Struggle* (Manchester, 1983).

Burgess, J., *Will Lloyd George Supplant Ramsay MacDonald?* (Ilford, 1926).

Burman, R., 'The Jewish Woman as Breadwinner', *Journal of the Oral History Society*, Vol. 10, No. 2 (London, 1982).

Bythell, D., *The Sweated Trades* (London, 1978).

Cesarani, D. (ed.), *The Making of Anglo-Jewry* (Oxford, 1990).

Clapham, J., *An Economic History of Modern Britain* (Cambridge, 1950).

Clegg, H., *History of British Trade Unionism* (Oxford, 1964)

—— *History of British Trade Unionism, Vol. II, 1911–1933* (Oxford, 1985).

Cole, G.D.H., *An Introduction to Trade Unionism* (London, 1918)

—— *British Trade Unionism Today* (London, 1938).

—— *A Short History of the Working Class Movement* (London, 1948).

Collett, C., 'Women's Work In Leeds', *Economic Journal*, Vol. I (London, 1891).

Dobbs, S.B., *The Clothing Workers of England* (London, 1928).

Dobson, C., *Masters and Journeymen* (London, 1980).

Dubnow, S., *History of the Jews*, Vol. 5 (Philadelphia, 1973 edn).

Dyche, J., 'A Jewish Workman', *Contemporary Review* (London, 1898).

Dyos, H.J., and Wolff, M. (eds), *The Victorian City*, Vols. I and 2 (London, 1973).

Elman, P., 'The Beginning of the Jewish Trade Union Movement', *Transactions of the Jewish Historical Society*, Vol. XVII (London, 1951–2).

Englander, D. (ed.) *The Jewish Enigma* (London, 1992).

Epstein, M., *Profiles of the Eleven* (Detroit, 1965).

Ewing, E., *History of Twentieth Century Fashion* (London, 1975).

Fishman, W.J., *East End Jewish Radicals 1870–1914* (London, 1975).

—— *East End 1888* (London, 1990).

Flinn M.W., and Smout T.C. (eds), *Essays in Social History* (Oxford, 1974).

Floud, R., and McClosky D. (eds), *The Economic History of Britain Since 1700, Vol. 2, 1860–1970* (Cambridge, 1981).

Fox, F.A., *A History of the National Union of Boot and Shoe Operatives* (Oxford, 1958).

Fraser, D. (ed.), *A History of Modern Leeds* (Manchester, 1980).

Fraser, W.H., *The Coming of the Mass Market* (London, 1981).

Gainer, B., *The Alien Invasion* (London, 1972).

Galton, F.W., *Selected Documents: The Tailoring Trade* (London, 1896).

Garrard, J.A., *The English and Immigration 1880–1910* (Oxford, 1971).

Gartner, L., *The Jewish Immigrant in England 1870–1914* (London, 1960).

George, M.D., *London Life in the Eighteenth Century* (London, 1930).

Hall, P., *The Industries of London Since 1861* (London, 1962).

Harrison, R.J., *Before the Socialists* (London, 1965).
Henry Poole (pamphlet) (London, 1983).
Hinton, J., *The First Shop Stewards Movement* (London, 1973).
History of London Trades Council (London, 1950).
Hobsbawm, E.J., *Industry and Empire* (London, 1968).
—— *Worlds of Labour* (London, 1984).
—— *Labouring Men* (London, 1979).
Holmes, C., *Anti-Semitism in British Society 1876–1939* (London, 1979).
—— *John Bull's Island* (London, 1988).
Hunt, E.H., *British Labour History 1815–1914* (London, 1981).
Hunter, L., and Stewart, M., *The Needle is Threaded* (London, 1964).
Hutchins, B., *Women in Modern History* (London, 1915).
—— and Harrison, A., *A History of Factory Legislation* (London, 1926).
Hutt, A., *British Trade Unionism* (London, 1975).
Infield, H.F., *Essays in Jewish Sociology, Labour and Cooperation* (London, 1962).
Jacobs, J., *Out of the Ghetto* (London, 1978).
Jeffreys, J.B., *Retail Trading in Britain 1850–1950* (Cambridge, 1954).
Jones, G.S., *Outcast London* (London, 1984 edn).
—— *Language of Class* (Cambridge, 1985).
Kelly's Leeds Directory for 1881, 1901, 1903, 1911, 1914 and 1915 (London).
Kelly's London Postal Directory for 1872, 1876, 1881 and 1890 (London).
Kendall, W., *The Revolutionary Movement in Britain 1900–1921* (London, 1969).
Kershen, A.J., *Off-The-Peg* (London, 1988).
—— 'Trade Unionism amongst the Jewish Tailoring Workers of London and Leeds', in Cesarani, D. (ed.), *The Making of Modern Anglo-Jewry* (Oxford, 1990).
—— 'Henry Mayhew and Charles Booth', in Alderman, G., and Holmes, C. (eds), *Outsiders and Outcasts* (London, 1993).
Kingsley, C., *Alton Locke* (London, 1881 edn).
Klugman, J., *The History of the Communist Party* (London, 1968).
Knyaston, D., *King Labour* (London, 1976).
Krausz, E., *Leeds Jewry* (Cambridge, 1965).
Kropotkin, P., *Memoirs of a Revolutionary* (London, 1899).
Kuzmack, L., *Woman's Cause* (Ohio, 1990).
Lansbury, G., *Looking Backwards – Looking Forwards* (London, 1935).
Laybourn, K., *A History of British Trade Unionism 1770–1990* (Stroud, 1992).
Lees, L. H., *Exiles of Erin* (Manchester, 1979).
Lerner, S., *Breakaway Unions and Small Trade Unions* (London, 1961).
—— 'The Impact of Jewish Immigration on the London Clothing Industry and Trade Unions', *Society for the Study of Labour History Bulletin*, XII (Manchester, Summer 1966).

218

Levin, N., *Jewish Socialist Movements 1871–1917* (London, 1978).
Levine, L., *The Women's Garment Workers* (New York, 1924).
Lewis, J., *Women in England* (Brighton, 1984).
Lipman, V.D., *A Social History of the Jews in England 1850–1950* (London, 1954).
—— *A History of the Jews in Britain Since 1858* (Leicester, 1990).
Lunn, K., *Hosts, Minorities and Immigrants* (Folkestone, 1980).
Mackenzie, N. and J., *The First Fabians* (London, 1979).
—— *The Diary of Beatrice Webb*, Vol. 1 (London, 1982).
—— *The Diary of Beatrice Webb*, Vol. 2 (London, 1983).
—— *The Diary of Beatrice Webb*, Vol. 3 (London, 1984).
Martin, R., *TUC, The Growth of a Pressure Group* (Oxford, 1980).
Mayhew, H., *London Labour and the London Poor*, Vols. 1–4 (New York, 1968 edn)
—— *Labour and the Poor* (London, pamphlet, 1850).
Mayor, S., *The Churches and the Labour Movement* (London, 1967).
McCleod, H., *Class and Religion in Late Victorian London* (London, 1973).
—— *Religion and the People in Western Europe* (Oxford, 1981).
McCorqudales Directory of Leeds (Leeds, 1878).
Mendelsohn, E., *Class Struggle in the Pale* (Cambridge, 1970).
Middlemass, K., *Politics in Industrial Society* (London, 1979).
Mitchell, B.R., and Deane, P., *An Abstract of British Historical Statistics* (Cambridge, 1962).
Morris, J., *Women Workers and the Sweated Trades* (Aldershot, 1986).
Mowat, C.L., *Britain Between the Wars* (London, 1984 edn).
Munby, A., *Industry and Planning in Stepney* (London, 1951).
Munson, F., *Indian Trade Unions* (Michigan, 1970).
Neale, R., (ed.), *History and Class* (Oxford, 1983).
Newman, A., (ed.), *The Jewish East End 1840–1939* (London, 1981).
Oliver, H., *The International Anarchist Movement in Late Victorian London* (London, 1983).
Pelling, H., *The Origins of the Labour Party* (London, 1965).
—— *A History of British Trade Unionism* (London, 1972 edn).
Phelps Brown, E.H., *Growth of British Industrial Relations* (London, 1959).
Picciotto, J., *Sketches of Anglo-Jewish History* (London, 1875).
Pimlott, B., and Cook, D. (eds), *Trade Unions in British Politics* (London, 1982).
Pollins, H., *Economic History of the Jews in England* (London, 1983).
Postgate, R., *The History of the British Working Class* (Tillicoutney, 1943).
Pugh, M., *The Making of Modern British Politics* (Oxford, 1982).
Quail, J., *The Slow Burning Fuse* (London, 1978).
Rabinowicz, H., *A Guide to Hassidim* (London, 1960).
Redmayne, R., *Ideals in Industry* (Leeds, 1951).
Roberts, B.C., *The Trade Union Congress* (London, 1958).

Robinson's Directory for Leeds 1911 (Leeds, 1911).

Rocker, R., *Anarcho-Syndicalism (London, 1938)*.

—— *The London Years* (London, 1956).

—— *Alexander Palace Internment Camp, World War One* (London, 1918).

Rollin, A.R. 'Russo-Jewish Immigration into England before 1881', *Transactions of the Jewish Historical Society*, Vol. XXI (London, 1968).

—— 'The Jewish Contribution to the British Textile Industry', *Transactions of the Jewish Historical Society*, Vol. XVII (London, 1951–2).

Roth, C., *A History of the Jews in England* (Oxford, 1978 edn).

—— *The Rise of Provincial Jewry* (London, 1950).

Russell, C., and Lewis, H., *The Jew in London* (London, 1900).

Ryot, D., *J. Barran of Leeds 1851–1951* (Leeds, 1951).

Sacher, H.M., *The Course of Modern Jewish History* (New York, 1982).

Saipe, L., *A History of the Jews of Leeds* (Leeds, 1958).

—— *A History of the Jewish Welfare Board in Leeds* (Leeds, undated).

Salter's Directory (London, 1891).

Samuel, R., *People's History and Socialist Theory* (London, 1981).

Schmiechen, J.A., *Sweated Industries and Sweated Labour* (London, 1984).

Schneer, J., *Ben Tillet* (London, 1982).

Selitrenny, L., 'The Jewish Working Woman in the East End', *Social Democrat*, Vol. II (London, 1896)

Sigsworth, E., *Montague Burton Tailor of Taste* (Manchester, 1990).

Simey, T.S. and M.B., *Charles Booth Social Scientist* (Oxford, 1960)

Smith, H. Llewellyn, *New Survey of London Life and Labour* (London, 1930–5).

Soldon, A., *Women in Trade Unions* (Dublin, 1978).

Steele, E.D., 'Leeds and Victorian Politics', *University of Leeds Review*, Vol. 17, No. 2 (Leeds, 1974).

Tawney, R.H., *Establishment of Minimum Rates in the Tailoring Industry* (London, 1915).

Thomas, J. A., 'History of the Leeds Clothing Industry', *Yorkshire Bulletin*, January 1955 (Hull, 1955).

Thompson, E.P., 'A Homage to Tom Maguire', in A. Briggs and J. Saville (eds), *Essays in Labour History* Vol. 2 (London, 1971).

—— *William Morris* (London, 1970).

—— *The Making of the English Working Class* (London, 1971 edn).

—— and Yeo, E., *The Unknown Mayhew* (London, 1971).

Thompson, P., *Socialists, Liberals and Labour* (London, 1967).

Thorne, W., *My Life's Battles* (London, 1925).

Tillet, B., *A Brief History of the Dock Strike* (London, 1889).

—— *Memories and Reflections* (London, 1930).

Torr, D., *Tom Mann and His Times* (London, 1956).

Tsuzuki, C., *H.M. Hyndman and British Socialism* (Oxford, 1961).

Walkowitz, J., *Prostitution and Victorian Society* (Cambridge, 1991 edn).

BIBLIOGRAPHY

Webb, B., *My Apprenticeship* (London, 1926).
Webb, S. and B., *Industrial Democracy* (London, 1902 edn)
—— *History of British Trade Unionism* (London, 1920 edn).
White, J., *Rothschild Buildings* (London, 1980).
Wilkins, W.H., *The Immigration of Destitute Foreigners* (London, 1891).
Williams, B., *The Making of Manchester Jewry* (Manchester, 1976).
—— 'The Beginnings of Jewish Trade Unionism In Manchester', in K. Lunn,
   (ed.), *Hosts, Minorities and Immigrants* (Folkestone, 1980).
Winchevsky, M., *Yehi Or* [Let There be Light!] (London, 1884).
Wirth, L., *The Ghetto* (Chicago, 1928).
Wischnitzer, M., *A History of Jewish Crafts and Guilds* (New York, 1965 edn)
Woodcote, T., 'The Working Class', in D. Fraser (ed.), *A History of Modern
   Leeds* (Manchester, 1980).
Young, M., and Wilmott, P., *Family and Kinship in East London* (London,
   1972 edn).
Zangwill, I., *Children of the Ghetto* (London, 1892).

Index

Adler, H., 134–5, 140–1
Alexander II, Tsar, 9, 132
Alexon, 104
Alien Immigration, Royal Commission
  on, 87, 102–3, 144, 187
Aliens Act (1905), 19, 145
Amalgamated Furnishing Trades
  Association, 145
Amalgamated Jewish Tailors',
  Machiners' and Pressers' Trade
  Union (AJTMP) (Leeds), 2, 11, 20,
  41, 42, 51, 60–1, 79, 81–91, 165,
  168, 179, 187–8
Amalgamated Mantle Makers' Trade
  Union, 143
Amalgamated Society of Engineers (ASE),
  17, 62, 88, 126
Amalgamated Society of Tailors (AST)
  (and Tailoresses) (AST&T), 11, 17–
  18, 61, 83–4, 91, 118, 126–7, 131–2,
  135–58, 164–8, 170–1, 173–6, 188,
  190
Amalgamated Union of Clothing
  Operatives (AUCO), 2, 18, 20, 42,
  45, 49, 74, 80–4, 152, 165–8, 188
Amalgamation Act (1917), 1
anarchists, 78–9, 90, 107, 127, 139, 141,
  143, 153–4, 177
Ancient Order of Foresters, 62
anti-alienism, 66, 85–6, 88, 103, 144–5,
  147, 189
Anti-Sweating League, 120
Appleton, W.A., 167
Aquascutum, 102
Arthur & Co., 31–3, 44, 73–4, 82–3
Attlee, C., 142
Australia, 31, 33

Babbage, C., 50

Bainbridge & Co., 73
Baines, E., 20
bandknife, 27–8, 43
Barnardo, Dr T., 104
Barran, John, 4, 8, 12, 13, 25–35, 43–5,
  55(n),186, 188
Barran, Rowland, 28
Barran & Co., 48–9, 54(n), 73
Batley, 27
Belgrave Street Synagogue (Leeds), 37,
  65–6
Bentalls, 101
Berner Street Club, 139
Besant, Annie, 46
Besant, Walter, 108
Black, Clementina, 72, 114, 119
Blackburn, W. & Co., 29
Bloody Sunday (13 Nov. 1887), 134
Blythe, J., 150–1
Board of Trade, 90, 99
Board of Trade Report into Incomes &
  Earnings (1906), 49
Board of Trade Report into Volume and
  Effects of Recent Immigration
  (1894), 42, 50
Booth, Charles, 40, 52, 105, 108, 115,
  118, 149
Bradford, 8, 190
Braverman, H., 44
Brighty, S., 20
Bristol Clothing Operatives' Trade
  Union, 80
British Brothers' League, 103, 144
Bromberg, C., 156
Broughton Wholesale Clothiers, 83
Buckle, Alderman, 88
Buckley, W., 32, 73
Burgess, J., 32, 87
Burnett, J., 40, 47, 99, 109–10, 115
Burns, J., 136, 139, 189

Burton, Montague, 25, 29, 33, 186–7

Cadbury, G., 120
Cambridge, 16
Camrass, S., 35
Caplan, J., 78–9
Chartism, 26
Clegg, H., 3, 85, 153, 164
Cockayne, W., 77
Cohen, M., 102–4, 109, 111
Collcutt, C., 150
Collet, C., 13, 40, 44–8, 67, 189
Colton, L., 181
Communist Party, 174–5, 177, 179–81
Conley, A., 84, 173, 179–82, 190
Cook & Son, 99
Co-operative Wholesale Society, 32

Daly, M., 147, 164
de Leon, D., 153
Dewsbury, 27
Dickins & Jones, 101–2
Disraeli, B., 117
Dobbs, C., 121
Dock, Wharf, Riverside and General
    Labourers' Trade Union, 78
Dreen, S., 113
Dublin, 16, 84, 143
Dundee, 149
Dyche, J., 70, 78, 133, 189

Edinburgh, 16, 149
Ellis & Goldstein, 104
Ellstein, L., 144
Ellstein, S., 144
Elsbury, S., 173, 175, 179
Evans-Gordon, Major W., 103–4, 144

Fabians, 63
Fair Wages Resolution (1891), 120
Fascism, 164, 177, 182, 190
Federation of Jewish East London Labour
    Unions, 138–9
Fine, J., 174, 177, 179–82, 190
Finn, J., 11, 38–40, 51–2, 63–6, 133,
    143, 158, 187–9
Fishman, W.J., 38, 131
Flynn, T., 165–6, 168, 190
Ford, I., 72–5, 83, 86, 189
Frais, J., 35
Franks, L., 70
Freedman, S., 61, 83–9, 91, 189

Friend, H., 8, 28, 31, 35, 38, 186
Friendly Societies, Report of Chief
    Registrar (1876), 61
Friendly Society and Trade Union
    Register (1876), 61

Gales, A.J., 20
Galton, F.W., 16
Gartner, L., xvi, 65
Gasworkers' and General Labourers'
    Trade Union (GGLU), 71, 77–8, 84
Gaunt & Murson, 44
General and Municipal Boilermakers'
    Union (GMB), 190
General Federation of Trade Unions
    (GFTU), 85–6, 150, 164–8
George, H., 40
Girvan, R., 165, 168–9
Glasgow, 31, 84, 88, 91, 165, 174, 179
Goldstein, M., 79
Goldstein, S., 104
Goodman, M., 36
Grand National Consolidated Trade
    Union, 17
Grand National Union of Tailors (First
    Lodge), 16, 19
Great Synagogue, 135, 140
Green, S., 104
Greenwood and Batley, 28
Guilanoff, E., 143

Hardie, J.K., 88
Harmer, F.W., 26
Harrods, 101
Harvey Nichols, 102
Hebden Bridge, 27
Hebrew Socialist Union, 128–30
Hemyng, B., 14
Hepworth, J., 29, 30, 32–3, 70
Hillman, A., 190
Hipps Ltd., 171
Hitchcock Williams, 101, 103
Hobsbawm, E., 20, 75
Holloway Bros., 26
Hope Bros., 99, 102
House of Lords Select Committee on
    Homework, 120
House of Lords Select Committee on
    Sweating, 40, 50, 64, 69, 120, 134,
    136
Houses of Call, 5, 117
Huddersfield, 27

Hunter Burr, 31
Hyam, H., 3, 26
Hyndman, H., 63, 133

Independent Labour Party, 72, 83
Independent Tailors', Machiners' and
    Pressers' Trade Union, 139
Independent Tailors' Trade Union, 144
International Journeymen Tailors',
    Machiners' and Pressers' Trade
    Union, 139
International Mantle Makers' Trade
    Union, 144
International Tailors', Machiners' and
    Pressers' Trade Union, 139
International Women's Garment
    Workers' Trade Union (USA), 78

Jewish
    Board of Guardians (Leeds), 37
    Board of Guardians (London), 106
    Cabinet Makers' Trade Union, 145
    Capmakers' Trade Union, 145
    Free School, 37
    National Tailors' Trade Union, 154
    Syndicalist Tailors' Trade Union, 154
    Unemployed Committee, 134
    Workers' Union, 11
    Working Tailors' Trade Society
        (Leeds), 61–2
    Young Men's Association (Leeds), 39
Joseph, B., 88

Kaffir trade, 97, 99
Kantor, H., 180
Kaplan, P., 155–6, 188
Kingsley, Charles, 6
Knights of Liberty Group, 139
Kovno, 10, 36, 85
Krantz, P., 134
Kropotkin, Prince, 88, 127

Labour Party, 82, 84, 88, 150
Labour Representation Committee, 82,
    84
Lakeman, Insp., 132
Laybourn, K., 153
Leeds
    and District Tanners' Society, 61
    Independent Jewish Tailors',
        Machiners' and Pressers' Trade
        Union, 79
    Jewish Tailoresses' Trade Union, 86–7

Pattern Makers' Association, 61
    Tailoresses' Trade Union, 73–5, 80–1,
        152
    Trades Council, 62–3, 69, 76, 85, 87–8
    Wholesale Clothing Operatives' Trade
        Union, 2, 75–6, 79–80, 187
Lerner, S., 10, 173
Lew, Dayan Dr M., 187
Lewis, J., 47
Leylands, xviii, 35–6
Liberal Party, 132
Lieberman, A., 128–30
Lithuanian Tailors' Trade Union, 127
Little, D. & Co., 33
London
    (and Provincial) Clothiers' Cutters'
        Trade Union (L&PCCTU), 2, 84,
        119, 126, 151–2, 165
    Jewish Tailors' and Tailoresses' Trade
        Union, 2
    Ladies' Tailors' Trade Union (1908),
        see United Ladies' Tailors' Trade
        Union
    Society of Tailors and Tailoresses
        (LST&T), 2, 150–1, 154, 165
    Tailoresses' Union, 152
    Tailors' Council, 142
    Tailors', Machiners' and Pressers'
        Trade Union, 140
    Tailors' and Machinists' Society, 113
    Tailors' Machiners' Society, 132
    Tailors' Protection Association, 17–18
    Trades Council, 150
    Trouser Makers' Trade Union, 179
Lottery & Co., 109, 152
Loughlin, A., 181
Lubelski, D., 11, 35, 38–9, 40, 69
Lubelski, J., 39
Lyons, Lewis, 11, 14, 88, 109, 132–43,
    147, 152, 154, 158, 165, 179, 189
Lyons Ltd., 171

MacArthur, M., 120
MacDonald, J., 106, 116, 118, 135, 138–
    9, 149–52, 158, 190
MacDonald, J.R., 149
Machin, E., 176
Machzikei Haddath, 141
Maguire, T., 67–71, 73, 77, 189
Mallon, J.J., 120
Manchester, 21(n), 37, 91, 133, 146–8,
    150, 165–6, 188

Waterproof Garment Makers' Trade
    Union, 2, 171–2, 173, 176
Mann, Byers & Co., 31
Mann, T., 83, 136, 139, 152, 153, 189
Manningham Mills, 81
Marshall, A., 50
Marshall & Snelgrove, 102
Marston, W., 85
Master Tailors' Association (MTA)
    (Leeds, Jewish), 65–70, 89–90
    (London, Jewish), 118, 135–8, 145,
    180
    (London, English), 149
match-girls, 3, 46, 71, 133, 152
Mathison & Co., 116
Maycock, E., 176
Mayhew, H., 5–7, 14, 16, 108, 117, 119,
    132
Mearns, A., 40, 108
Mendelsohn, E., 18
Meyer, C., 114, 119
middlemen, 16
Middlesbrough, 74
Middleton, A.J., 151
Military Tailors' Trade Union, 144
Mills, A.H., 76
Mindel, M., 175, 177, 179–82, 190
Minsk, 10
Mond–Turner talks, 173
Mondism, 164
Montagu, S., 69, 132–3, 137–8
Morris, J., 121
Morris, W., 16, 63, 134, 142
Moses, E., 4, 26, 97, 99
Mosley, O., 177–9, 182
Mowbray, C., 135, 139, 145, 154
Myers, I., 65

Napoleon III, 117
National Insurance Act (1911), 80, 115,
    152, 154
National Minority Movement, 164, 172–
    3
National Union of Operative Boot and
    Shoe Riveters and Finishers, 64
National Union of Railwaymen, 1
National Union of Tailors and Garment
    Workers (NUTGW), xviii, 175–82,
    187, 190
Nazism, 164, 177, 190
New Delhi, 157
New Hebrew Congregation (Leeds), 39

New York, 87
Newcastle-on-Tyne, 84
Nicolls & Co., 117
Norwich, 26

Pale of Settlement, xvii, 8–10, 18, 39
Paterson, E., 19, 72
Pawsons & Leafs, 101
Paylor, T., 67, 71, 73, 77
Peter Robinson, 102
Place, F., 6
Poliakoff Ltd., 175
Poole, Henry, 97, 117
Potter, Beatrice, 70, 98, 105, 108–9, 111–
    13, 115

Rabbinowitz, E.W., 130
Ramsay, E., 132
Raskin, Insp., 41, 114
Rego Ltd., 173, 175
Reform Bill (1884), 64
Report of Board of Trade into Sweating
    System in Leeds (1888), 47
Rhodes & Co., (James), 29–30, 70, 77
Ries, M., 63
Rines, W., 150
Ripper, Jack the, 107–8
Rocker, R., 79, 131, 145, 147, 154–6,
    158, 174, 189
Rollin, A., 169, 178–82
Rothschild, Lord N., 69, 137–8
Rowlerson, G., 146–8, 168, 172, 174,
    176, 190
Royal Commission on Children's
    Employment (1864, 1865), 7, 13, 15,
    32, 109
Royal Commission on Labour (1892),
    44–5, 49, 119

Sailors' and Firemen's Trade Union, 78
Sala, G., 108
Savile Row, 3, 4, 97–8
Schneider & Son, 109, 152
Sclare, M., 11, 41–2, 60–1, 78, 84–5, 88–
    9, 133, 142, 169, 179, 190
Scott Adie, 102
Scottish Operative Tailors' and
    Tailoresses' Association (SOTTA),
    165–9, 171–2
Selfridge, G., 101
Selincourt, C., 102
sewing machines, 13, 54(n)
Shaw, Councillor, 88

Shinwell, E., 165, 185
Shorrocks, P., 17, 165
Sims, G., 40, 108
Singer Sewing Machine Co., 32, 105
Smith Award, 52, 90
Smith, L., 127–8
Social Democratic Federation (SDF), 3, 63, 133–5, 149, 189
socialism, 63, 67, 128, 130, 139
Socialist League (SL), 3, 16, 18, 38–9, 40, 63, 66, 69, 73, 75–6, 78, 83, 91, 114, 133–5, 139, 189
Soho, xviii, 3, 98, 115–16
South Africa, 32, 33, 97, 99
special order departments, 33–4
Spencer, A., 190
Stead, W.E., 40, 108
Steinberg, A., 104
Stepniak, 88, 127
strikes
    Leeds (1884), 64
    Leeds (1885), 65
    Leeds (1888), 66, 68–71
    Leeds (1889, tailoresses), 73–4
    Leeds (1911), 90–1
    London (1889), 135–9
    London (1906), 145–6
    London (1912), 153–6, 167
Stockport, 91
Stocker Award, 171
Stone, I., 11, 127–31
Stuart & MacDonald, 31–2
sub-divisional tailoring, 4, 6–8, 28, 34, 40, 50–2
Swan & Edgar, 101
Sweated Industries Exhibition, 120
Sweeney, J., 40, 50, 64–71, 77, 83, 189
syndicalism, 82, 90, 126, 153–4, 164

Taff Vale Judgement (1901), 145
Tailors' and Garment Workers' Trade Union (TGWU), 21(n), 84, 172–6
Tawney, R.H., 114
Taylor, G., 151
Thompson, E.P., xvi, 20
Thorne, W., 71
Tillet, B., 136
Torah, 8
Toynbee Hall, 142
Trade Boards Act (1909), 90–1, 112, 115, 119–121, 126, 142, 154
Trade Boards Act (1918), 121, 171, 174, 179
Trade Union Act (1876), 61
Trade Union Congress, 41, 81–2, 84–5, 88, 144, 150, 164, 173, 175–6
Trade Unions, see under respective titles
Truck Committee, Report of (1906), 11, 28

United Cloth Hat and Cap Makers of Great Britain, 145
United Clothing Workers' Union (UCWU), 173, 175, 178, 180
United Garment Workers' Trade Union, xvii, xviii, 1, 60, 151, 163, 170–2
United Garment Workers' Trade Union (UGWTU)(Jewish, 1902), 144
United Ladies' Tailors' and Mantle Makers' Trade Union (1892), 143
United Ladies' Tailors' Trade Union (ULTTU), 66, 144, 165, 170–1, 173–82
United Synagogue, 141

Vilna, 130

Wages Council, 190
Wales, Prince of, 117
Warsaw, 36, 38
Webb, Beatrice, see Potter
Webbs (Sidney and Beatrice), xviii, 20, 61, 71, 190
Wesker, S., 180
Wess, W. (Woolf), 135–9, 158, 189
Whately, T., 151
Whitechapel, xviii, 37, 108–9, 127
Whiteley, W., 99
Wholesale Clothiers' Federation, 175
Wholesale Co-operative, 100
Winchevsky, M., 38, 130
Windsmoor, 104
Wischnitzer, M., 8
Witney, H., 43
women (tailoresses), 5, 12–15, 19, 43–8, 71–5, 80–1, 86, 110–11, 114–16, 152–3, 180, 188
women's fashion, 100–2
Women's Protective and Provident League, 19, 72, 152

Yarmouth, 84
Young, J., 79–85, 91, 142, 190

Zeitlin, D., 133

Printed in the United States
by Baker & Taylor Publisher Services